Co-operation and Globalisation

Globalisation is associated with capitalist multinationals dedicated to the enrichment of wealthy, corporate shareholders. However, less well known is that English and Scottish Co-operative Wholesale Societies, owned by a growing number of local co-operative societies across the country, were early leaders in global commerce.

Owned by their working-class members, by 1900 there were over 1,000 societies and millions of individual members. Spreading profits widely through the 'divi' (dividend), which rewarded members shopping at the co-op store, and selling safe and wholesome food, the co-operative movement was a successful part of the emerging labour movement.

This success depended on the wholesales supplying societies with commodities from all over the world. Because local societies were free to source produce from whomever they chose, competitive pressures required the wholesale societies to develop the world's most formidable network of international supply chains, with branches, depots, plantations and factories in the USA, Canada, Denmark, Sweden, Spain, Greece, France, Germany, India, Ceylon, Australia, New Zealand, colonial West Africa and Argentina.

This book explains how the wholesales developed and managed these networks, giving them a competitive advantage in their dealings with the local societies. It will explore how and why this 'People's Global Colossus' declined in the later twentieth century, and how its focus in international commerce moved on to ethical sourcing, investment and Fairtrade.

Integral to these global networks were the UK movement's relations with foreign co-operative movements, especially through involvement in the International Co-operative Alliance, and promotion of co-operatives in the Empire by successive British governments as a tool for economic development. The 'People's Colossus' was thus a political as well as a commercial player in the increasingly complex world of the late nineteenth and twentieth centuries.

Anthony Webster is Professor in History at Northumbria University, Newcastle upon Tyne, UK.

Routledge International Studies in Business History

Series editors:
Jeffrey Fear and Christina Lubinski

For more information about this series, please visit: www.routledge.com/
Routledge-International-Studies-in-Business-History/book-series/SE0471

Co-operation and Globalisation

The British Co-operative Wholesales, the Co-operative Group and the World Since 1863

Anthony Webster

Routledge
Taylor & Francis Group

LONDON AND NEW YORK

First published 2019 by Routledge

2 Park Square, Milton Park, Abingdon, Oxon, OX14 4RN
605 Third Avenue, New York, NY 10017

Routledge is an imprint of the Taylor & Francis Group, an informa business

First issued in paperback 2020

Library of Congress Cataloging-in-Publication Data
Names: Webster, Anthony, author.
Title: Co-operation and globalisation : the British co-operative
  wholesales, the co-operative group and the world since 1863 /
  Anthony Webster.
Description: New York : Routledge, 2019. | Series: Routledge
  international studies in business history | Includes bibliographical
  references and index.
Identifiers: LCCN 2018059783 | ISBN 9781138501355 (hardback) |
  ISBN 9781315144290 (ebook)
Subjects: LCSH: Co-operative Wholesale Society (Great Britain) |
  Cooperation—Great Britain—History. | Retail trade—Great
  Britain—History | Wholesale trade—Great Britain—History
Classification: LCC HF5421.5.G7 W425 2019 | DDC 334/.
  60941—dc23
LC record available at https://lccn.loc.gov/2018059783

ISBN: 978-1-138-50135-5 (hbk)
ISBN: 978-0-367-78668-7 (pbk)

Typeset in Sabon
by Apex CoVantage, LLC

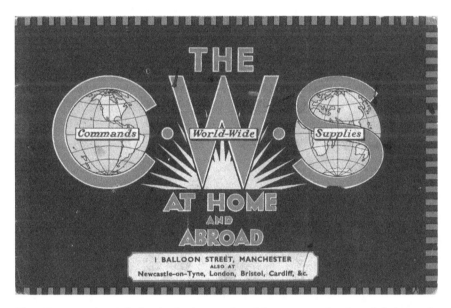

The Co-operative Wholesale Society—advertising poster for its global supply networks in the 1930s

Dedicated to my wife, Lesley

Contents

Acknowledgements

This book is the result of five years of intensive work, and I would like to thank the staff of the Co-operative College and the National Co-operative Archive for their support during this period, especially the wonderful Gillian Lonergan for her expert guidance on numerous topics. I would also like to thank Brad Hill and Michael Fletcher of the Co-operative Group for their advice on the more recent international initiatives of the Co-operative Group. I must also acknowledge the advice of my old friend Stuart Bradbury on sections of the manuscript. His thoughts were, as always, welcome, constructive and useful. I would also like to thank my many generous and kind colleagues at Northumbria University. My last five years have been the happiest of my working life, and that is due almost entirely to the pleasure of working with such wonderful colleagues. Lastly—but certainly not least—I must thank Lesley, my lovely and supportive wife, without whose love and friendship I would have achieved very little.

Tony Webster
November 2018

1 Mr Bates Goes to Washington

Industrialisation, Consumerism, Overseas Trade and British Co-operation 1800–1890— An Overview

I

On 20 August 1892, the English Co-operative Wholesale Society (CWS) Director, William E. Bates, disembarked in New York from the S.S. *Etruria*, arrived that day from Liverpool. He was beginning a two-and-a-half-month tour of the US as a representative of the CWS, exploring the mercantile links that it had developed across North America, and he was empowered to make new deals with new trading partners. It was to be an intense and exhausting ten or so weeks, involving daily rail travel as well as countless meetings with people he had never met before. But as is perhaps less and less the case with modern business trips, there were also opportunities for sight-seeing and recreation. On his first night, Bates was whisked to the New York resort of Coney Island, where he freely engaged in the amusements it offered. He noted in his diary that there was a roughness about the place that "would not do for the goody, goody sort of people".[1] But business quickly moved centre stage. The next few days were spent mainly in the New York Produce Exchange (which also housed the CWS' New York branch), with Bates meeting a long procession of New York dealers, merchants and brokers, many of whom provided letters of introduction to merchants and manufacturers across the continent. The whirlwind tour began on 29 August, with Bates and his companions reaching Buffalo on the 31st of the month, where he met local leather merchants with a view to securing supplies for the boot and shoe factories owned by the CWS in the East Midlands. On 1 September, Bates met with the Chicago producers of tinned meat, Armour, and a week later held talks with Pillsbury's, the grain miller in Minneapolis. En route to meet a range of fruit growers and salmon packers in Washington State and California, Bates travelled through Montana, where he saw native Americans on horseback: "The women rode like men. They were dressed like the Indians brought over by Buffalo Bill".[2] Bates' tour took him through Salt Lake City, Denver, Omaha, Kansas, St Louis and Louisville, with deals done along the way to supply CWS with leather, a wide variety of foods and even a consignment of pick axe handles! Perhaps the high point of the tour was in Washington, where, after a visit to the Capitol and the sights, Bates was introduced to the Republican President of the USA, Benjamin Harrison. Such were the circles in which senior CWS figures moved. Bates' tour continued through Baltimore; Portland, Maine; and Montreal before he returned to New York. His last meeting was with the mayor of New York, before he departed for Liverpool on 4 November.

Bates' diary is a remarkable document, capturing as it does a colourful mixture of the personal, the mundane and the extent of the CWS' integration into the US business world after fewer than 20 years of operations from its New York branch. But what it signals most emphatically is just how major a player the organisation had become on the global stage, just 30 years after it first commenced operations from a small office and premises in Manchester. Bates' handshake with the US president indicated that CWS (and through it the co-operative movement in England, and its corresponding organisations in Scotland, including the Scottish Co-operative Wholesale Society) occupied a position in the world that commanded the attention of national leaders, as well as the phalanxes of merchants, manufacturers, farmers, bankers and brokers who were integral to the operation of both major national economies and the emerging global system of international commerce and finance.

This book offers the first detailed analysis of the global supply chains and trading system that the two British co-operative wholesales constructed, and that enabled them to become, for a time, arguably the most sophisticated international commercial operator in the world. It addresses important questions about the wholesales as both commercial operations and political actors on the domestic and world stages. In many ways, it is a companion to an earlier volume that the author wrote in collaboration with John F. Wilson and Rachael Vorberg-Rugh, *Building Co-operation*, and it picks up on some key themes for which there were too limited space to address comprehensively.[3] In particular, it will examine in detail how and why the wholesales extended their overseas activities so rapidly and so widely. The New York branches mentioned in the opening of this chapter were established in 1875, just 12 years after the English CWS was established, and new branches in Copenhagen (1881) and Hamburg (1884) followed swiftly. The reasons why this reaching out across the seas occurred will be explored in later chapters. A major theme of the book will be the strategies that guided the management of the wholesales' expanding global connections and assets. Today, the strategies and methods by which retail and other businesses organise themselves to ensure that commodities for sale are produced or procured to the requirements of consumers and delivered on time at a price that consumers are willing to pay is known as supply chain management (SCM). It will be argued that while it would be anachronistic to describe the international commodity procurement strategies of the wholesales as SCM in the strictly modern sense of the concept, they were nonetheless more sophisticated than suggested in some of the literature on the practices of companies in the pre-SCM period.

To help illustrate the point, it is worth running through the main features of modern SCM as conceived by academics and managers and considering them briefly in respect of the practices of the wholesale societies. These include: increased control by retail organisations over secondary distribution (that is, the transfer of goods from warehouses to shops); greater control by retailers over the production and delivery of manufactured stock; enhanced control of information about the supply chain to eliminate inefficiencies and to minimise inventory (the amount of stock kept on hand to ensure that demand can be met); and more effective response to demand and customer requirements, or ECR (Efficient Consumer Response).[4] Central to the maturation of SCM as a discipline from the 1980s onwards was the greater assertion of control over the supply chain by retailers: in effect, a shift of power away from manufacturers and other 'links in the chain', such as wholesalers, towards retail actors.[5] Implicit in this was not only far closer collaboration and information-sharing between increasingly dominant retailers and their suppliers but also the effective takeover by retailers of key functions of those suppliers, including branding and even marketing.[6] The assumption is that not only were manufacturers the masters of supply chains before the 1980s but that retailers were also essentially 'passive' in their operation, working on hope as much as anything.[7] Studies of food retail companies, even quite large ones, have tended to confirm this perception of a lack of structure or scientific organisational management. In the UK, fresh food supplies to retailers before the late 1900s have been described as 'disorderly'.[8] Tesco, the supermarket retail giant, is a case in point. In the 1970s, manufacturers and suppliers held the whip hand when it came to delivering to Tesco stores, while ordering was left in the hands of individual store managers, with little or no central control. It was only when the existing arrangements proved inadequate to successfully supply the stores during *Operation Checkout*, launched in 1977 to massively expand business, that reforms were implemented that led to the successful and sophisticated SCM systems of the end of the twentieth century.[9] Of course, modern SCM also makes extensive use of very modern computer technologies that allow automatic electronic ordering and the optimisation/minimisation of inventory and storage through 'Just in Time' (JIT) ordering and supplying—technologies that were simply unavailable 40 or so years ago. In this sense, SCM is very much a product of the modern age.

But it will become clear that, modern technological capabilities apart, even during the last decades of the nineteenth century the British consumer co-operative movement and its wholesale wings cannot be characterised as passive, haphazard, disorganised or at the mercy of manufacturers and suppliers. Indeed, building the capability to manage its supplies in a coherent way was prioritised in the developing structure of the consumer movement from a very early stage in its development—in 1863 with the formation of the English Co-operative Wholesale Society, and the establishment of its Scottish equivalent five years later. Both wholesales were secondary co-operatives—that is, co-operatives whose members consisted of the hundreds of local co-operative societies that were springing into existence across Britain from the mid-1840s onwards. By 1900, there were 1,400 such local societies across the country, most of them members of one of the wholesales, furnishing the latter, through membership subscriptions, with a formidable capital resource with which to finance their operations. The creation of the wholesales was in direct response to fears among local societies that private shopkeepers were pressuring wholesalers to either refuse to sell to co-operative societies or to treat them as second-class customers in terms of price and quality. Thus, for the societies, the question of supply chains became a very real and pressing issue in the 1850s. The very creation of the wholesale societies indicated that from a very early period, the exercise of some measure of control over supply chains was at the heart of the British consumer co-operative movement. It will become clear that pressures both external and internal to the movement compelled the wholesales not only to become producers of commodities for sale to the societies but also to reach across the world to procure the widening range of global produce increasingly desired and required by working-class British households from the mid-nineteenth century onwards. Controlling supply chains was 'hard-wired' into the movement from its earliest days by necessity, circumstance and organisation. While the rest of this book will explore in detail the ways in which the wholesales developed strategies to maximise overseas supplies—and how the networks they created ultimately unravelled after the Second World War—this chapter will first examine both the rise of consumer co-operation in Britain and the national and global context in which the movement emerged and flourished.

II

The establishment of the Rochdale Society of Equitable Pioneers in 1844 is popularly seen as the beginning of the modern British consumer co-operative movement. A group of weavers, cotton operatives and others— many with a background in political activism either in the co-operative movement or Chartism—formed a co-operative store to sell food to its members in response to the poverty and inadequate access to cheap and wholesome food that characterised many British industrial towns in the 'Hungry Forties'. The long walk to and from Manchester to stock the tiny candle-lit Toad Lane store with basic provisions (principally flour) a few days before Christmas has become the stuff of legend within the British co-operative movement. It throws into dramatic relief the subsequent growth in membership, wealth and commercial activity of the Pioneers Society and the rapid spread of co-operative societies on the Rochdale model across the UK in the following decades. But it is important to recognise that Rochdale represented a stage in the development of co-operative organisation that built upon a longer history of co-operative experiment in Britain, albeit the first to create the most sustainable model to date. To grasp why co-operation emerged as such an attractive and powerful movement in nineteenth-century Britain, it is important to review the unprecedented social and economic changes wrought by industrialisation.

From the latter half of the eighteenth century, Britain experienced change on a scale and at a speed never witnessed before. New technologies in agriculture prompted the widespread enclosure of land, and with it a reduction in demand for agricultural labour as well as the loss of common land available to the very poorest. Thus began a shift in population from the countryside to towns and cities, where new employment opportunities were emerging in the factories of the industrial revolution. Inevitably, this was an uneven, disruptive and frequently chaotic process. The demand for labour in new industries such as cotton in the north of England was often sporadic, as the early industrial economy was subject to periodic slumps, widespread lay-offs and bankruptcies. During the first half of the nineteenth century, it was not uncommon for urban workers to find themselves unemployed and destitute during economic downturns. The notorious 1834 Poor Law Amendment Act introduced a punitive regime for those without employment or income, with the dreaded workhouse the final port of call for the very desperate. Urban living conditions were also hazardous. Poorly built housing, bad sanitation, pollution and overcrowding made many towns and cities notorious for ill health and disease. Cholera, caused by infected water supplies, killed thousands in several epidemics that swept through Britain in the first half of the nineteenth century. It was not until major local government investment in public sanitation later in the century that such problems abated. In the countryside, reduced demand for labour and a hardening of attitudes by the landed elite also produced hardship for the very poor. Increasingly, landowners came to view their property as capital assets to be worked as efficiently as possible for the market. In the process, traditional social relations between social groups began to break down. The eminent historian E.P. Thompson described the 'Moral Economy' of pre-industrial rural life, in which the lowest ranks of society accepted the existing order in exchange for paternalistic regard by the landed elite. This meant that there were socially acceptable limits when it came to the pricing of essentials such as bread.[10] But Thompson shows that with the increased monetisation of transactions in the eighteenth century, these traditional customs gave way to a new regime in which prices and social relations were increasingly driven by the market. Bread prices, customarily held within commonly understood bounds, began to be raised solely based on the balance of supply and demand—to popular outrage. The result was bread riots, while other infringements of perceived social norms elicited equally violent and even more frightening resistance. Luddism and the spate of violent attacks on factories and new technologies in Nottingham and Yorkshire caused major concerns for the authorities in 1811–12, while agricultural workers took to burning hay ricks and attacking the property of the landed gentry during the 'Swing Riots' of the late 1820s.[11] Responses to the 'new moral order' of agricultural and industrial capitalism varied in accordance with local issues and circumstances.[12]

But crucially, they were not always violent. Some groups, faced by the challenges and problems created by capitalism, resorted to other strategies—especially by organising to secure necessities of life denied by the prevailing social and economic order. The late eighteenth and early nineteenth centuries saw the flourishing of numerous flour and bread societies, in which people unable to secure these essentials at a reasonable price combined and pooled capital to produce their own. Perhaps the most famous of these was the Hull Anti-Mill, established in 1795, which survived for almost one hundred years. It was but one of many such initiatives, a large proportion of which proved highly durable, lasting for several decades.[13] Moreover, it is clear that many of these societies emerged in areas of the country already beset by unrest and conflict about rising food prices.[14] Bread and flour societies were not the only collective self-help organisations to emerge in response to the difficulties presented by early industrialisation. Friendly societies also sprang into existence to deal with a range of challenges, including access to sickness benefits, an income in old age and other forms of mutual support. Factors that contributed to the emergence of solidarity among those who established these various mutual organisations included common employment, especially among miners, handloom weavers and the early cotton operatives, as well as shipwrights and dockworkers.[15] Research has shown that the stresses of migration from rural areas into the towns and cities also stimulated new arrivals to club together to create mutual self-help organisations of various kinds, especially as migration involved the severance of family and other ties in the areas from which migrants relocated. Mutual organisation among migrants was therefore an attempt to address the social and psychological consequences of the loss of community, family and identity—and it is important to realise that in many instances, mutualism was as much an attempt to address psychological as physical or economic need.[16] The early co-operatives were also part of this widespread response to the social and economic dislocations of industrialisation.

Of course, the practical problems of early industrial life were always a main driver of co-operative and mutual organisation among the poor and those facing the problems of early industrial urban life. Food supply to urban communities in a period when transport was still relatively undeveloped and there were few regulations to govern quality presented many hazards, especially for the very poor. Even in a city such a Manchester, which was comparatively well served for food supplies in the early nineteenth century, the poorest were frequently confronted by high prices, shortages and rotten or nearly inedible victuals.[17] The rapidity of urban growth contributed to the uncertainty and consumer disadvantage. There was a time lag between the rise of the city's population and the emergence of new grocers and shopkeepers to meet the demand for food. In a city like Sheffield, for example, the provision of a market by the authorities was in response to a growing political clamour for something to be done about the exploitative prices charged by food suppliers.[18] There is evidence that this phenomenon was widespread in Britain's rapidly growing industrial towns during the nineteenth century.[19] What this suggests is that the economic and social imperative driving the rise of mutualism was implicit in the processes of industrialisation and urbanisation, as growth of demand outstripped supply for the necessities of life. Unscrupulous grocers could charge extortionate prices, and by providing credit could effectively coerce loyalty from customers who became heavily in their debt. In some instances, the exploiters were those who provided industrial employment for the new workers. The 'Truck System' involved employers making it a condition of employment that workers only buy from shops run by the employer, in some extreme instances insisting workers be paid in tickets exchangeable only in the firm's shop. While such arrangements tended to prevail principally in remote locations and were made illegal in 1831, there is evidence that the practice continued on a small scale illicitly thereafter, especially where the workforce were ruthlessly intimidated.[20] Notwithstanding the legal suppression of Truck, the early nineteenth-century state did little to alleviate the food problems of the poor. The dominance of national politics by the landed elite was epitomised by the Corn Laws of 1815, which were designed to bolster food prices to the advantage of the landowner and to the disadvantage of the consumer. Even when the Anti-Corn Law League campaigned to liberalise food imports in the 1840s, the openly stated motive of many employers was that cheaper food would enable them to drive down wages. Local government followed the prevailing political economic mantra of low taxes, low spending and balanced budgets. In practice this meant minimal regulation in food standards. Poor knowledge of sanitation and methods of preservation made food poisoning a daily hazard for all, but especially for the poorest consumers. Moreover, food adulteration was rife. Watering milk, adding alum to bread to make it whiter and the addition of all kinds of material to bulk out food made the daily shop a precarious business. Nor was this merely a matter of taste or public morality. For poor people, already weakened by insufficient food, insanitary and overcrowded living conditions and excessively long working hours, healthy and nourishing food was a matter of life and death. Legislation to regulate food would not be effective until late in the century, and as seen in the Poor Law of 1834, the state's view of the poor was persecutory and unsympathetic.

Of course, experiments in food co-operatives, and indeed other types of co-operatives to meet other needs such as employment, were part of this mutual response. But what perhaps sets co-operation apart from these early mutual experiments was how it captured the imagination of a section of the intellectual elite who were dismayed by the harshness and apparent amorality of the emerging industrial capitalist order. Among these, several key individuals and groups emerged who sought not only to promote and support co-operatives of various kinds but also to develop co-operation as a cogent alternative ideology and system to industrial capitalism. The industrialist Robert Owen was perhaps the earliest and most prominent co-operator, and he remains an icon for the modern co-operative movement. Born in 1771 in Newtown, Wales, Owen rose from a modest background to become an accomplished industrial manager, first in Manchester and later in Scotland. Manager of the New Lanark Mill in Scotland from 1800, Owen championed the idea of treating his workers humanely, providing decent working conditions, schools and good housing for them—a set of aspirations that were highly unusual for industrialists of the time. But Owen's ideas developed further. Although he supported social reforms through parliament, Owen concluded by the 1820s that a better option for many working-class people might be to escape the harshness of industrial capitalism through the establishment of self-sustaining agricultural co-operative communities, in which the necessities of life would be produced co-operatively on land communally owned. This would provide the basis of a new social and moral order, built on social and economic equality, democratic decision-making and values of fellowship and mutual support. Owen described these envisaged self-supporting co-operative communes within, and yet separate from, mainstream capitalist society as the basis of a new socialist society. It was an idea that Owen struggled and ultimately failed to turn into reality. The barriers to establishing such communities were formidable. How to secure the funds to purchase land and equipment and to construct buildings when those supposed to construct these communities were among the poorest in society? How to develop the skills needed to make the commune not just economically self-sustaining but also able to deliver a higher standard of living than available in mainstream society, among people who had received not even the most basic education? And how to inculcate the personal qualities and values needed to ensure a co-operative mindset, based on collective effort and trust?[21]

While in theory the accumulation of capital to buy land and establish a commune would be achieved by the creation of co-operative enterprises, which would allocate part of their profits to founding communes, this was an aspiration that was rarely fulfilled. In practice, Owen sunk a large portion of his personal fortune in the 1820s into short-lived experimental co-operative communes in Orbiston, Scotland, and 'New Harmony' in Indiana in the USA. But while Owenism as co-operation proved a practical failure, it inspired other intellectuals to take up the co-operative cause. In the late 1820s, Dr William King, a university-educated physician, emerged as both a major supporter of co-operative experiments in his locality (Brighton) and, more crucially, as founder and editor of *The Co-operator*, one of the earliest journals proselytising co-operation. By the 1840s, co-operation, as an apparent economic and social alternative, had attracted a cohort of British Christian intellectuals who were dismayed by the harshness and apparent amorality of early industrial capitalism. Men such as Reverend F.D. Maurice, Professor of Theology at Kings College London; the barrister J.M. Ludlow; the poet Reverend Charles Kingsley; and the famed author of *Tom Brown's Schooldays*, Thomas Hughes, became not only intellectual devotees and promoters of co-operation but also keen activists seeking to establish co-operatives among working people and staunch defenders of existing co-operatives. Among these Christian Socialists was Edward Vansittart Neale, who became probably the most important legal adviser to the co-operative movement in the 1860s, assisting with successful campaigns to place co-operatives on a more secure legal footing. This resulted in the Industrial and Provident Societies Act of 1852, which strengthened the legal position of co-operative societies; and the Act of the same name of 1862, which enabled the creation of secondary co-operatives and thereby the creation of the Co-operative Wholesale Society in the following year.[22]

By the 1840s, although this intellectual strain of co-operation could point to only a modest contribution to the rise of the movement, indirectly its impact was important and would become more so as the century progressed. Among the small group of weavers and other working men who established the Rochdale Pioneers in 1844, at least four had invested in Owenite co-operative communities earlier in the century, while one of its leading members, Charles Howarth, had been involved in an earlier experiment in Owenite co-operation in Rochdale in the early 1830s.[23] While the Pioneers were highly practical and pragmatic entrepreneurs rather than co-operative theorists, they had been influenced by the intellectual strand of the movement and would seek to collaborate with it further as the movement grew from strength to strength.

III

The Rochdale Society of Equitable Pioneers have become probably the best known and most mythologised symbol of British co-operation. The society and the Pioneers themselves were elevated to a unique status in the late 1850s, most notably by the famous co-operator intellectual and historian G.F. Holyoake, in serial and then book form.[24] Subsequently, the site of their first store in Toad Lane was re-opened as a museum in 1931, and two celebratory films were produced by the movement in 1944 and 2012. Much of the mythology claims exceptionalism for the society as the first to develop a sustainable organisational template for consumer co-operation and to establish a code of organisational principles; this would be easily imitated by others in order to spread the model firstly across the UK and later the world. A powerful image has been constructed of 28 'original' co-operators, unique in their foresight, commitment and energy, as working-class heroes and symbols of the movement. But the debate about the wider significance of consumer co-operation in the growth and development of the British labour movement led to a rather different view emerging of the Pioneers and the consumer movement generally. There has been a tendency to see the success of consumer co-operation and the 'Rochdale model' as evidence of a turning away from the political radicalism of the early nineteenth century following the failure of Chartism in the 1840s to more practical, if prosaic, schemes to improve the lot of the working class. In this view, consumer co-operation, with its emphasis upon improving living standards through providing better quality and cheaper goods, was essentially a reconciliation with the capitalist system, whereas Owenism had been a challenge to it.[25] The search for 'respectability' formed the core of the new ethos, and the aim, in addition to material improvement, was to win rights and acceptance by demonstrating that at least the better off and more educated sections of the working class were fit for the right to vote. In other words, co-operators tended to be seen increasingly by some historians as part of an elite section of the working class, part of a 'Labour Aristocracy' of skilled workers with little affinity to the lower paid and unskilled.[26] This contributed to an assumption that 'Rochdale Man', as Rose dubbed those involved in developing consumer co-operatives, was therefore unrepresentative of the wider working class.

But more recent historians have challenged this characterisation. Walton's survey of the Rochdale Pioneers suggests that at least some were poor textile workers living in straitened circumstances.[27] Kirk also refutes the notion that Rochdale style consumer co-operatives attracted only a working-class elite.[28] However, perhaps there are arguably more significant questions than the social composition of the Pioneers and the wider co-operative movement. Firstly, why did consumption emerge as a central focus of a working-class movement in the 1840s and after? Secondly, what was the provenance of the Rochdale principles, and why were they taken up so enthusiastically in the second half of the nineteenth century? Recent research has shown how access to good, cheap food became a major political issue in the 1840s. Chartism, a movement to extend the franchise to the working class, was also a champion of bringing cheap food to the masses. Like some earlier political movements that campaigned during the agitation, leading to the Great Reform Act of 1832, Chartists promoted boycotts and discrimination against retailers who were unsympathetic to the cause, a practice known as 'Exclusive Dealing'. From this, Chartism also encouraged workers to form their own consumer co-operatives to provide for their own needs.[29] Indeed, the 'Hungry Forties' saw issues around food supply, retail and trade move to the fore of British politics. The Anti-Corn Law League, as well as Chartism, made access to cheap food a central part of its political manifesto, albeit with fundamentally different ends.[30] In this context, the emergence of consumer co-operatives in this period is not so surprising, or perhaps as unique to Rochdale as is sometimes imagined. Four such societies sprang up in Sunderland in 1840 and one in Durham, all with close Chartist connections, though they were short lived.[31] These wider circumstances help explain why it is unsurprising that a town such as Rochdale, with a strong Chartist tradition and the site of a bitter textile strike in the early 1840s, should see a bold experiment in co-operation at this time. Walton's examination of the backgrounds of the Rochdale Pioneers, surrounded and buried by layers of mythologising from Holyoake to Cole and from the wider movement generally, offers, albeit from relatively few and piecemeal sources, some important clues as to their motives and strategies. Among their ranks were Chartists who must have been aware of the movement's support for co-operatives; Owenite activists who had been involved in earlier co-operative experiments, including in Rochdale itself; and people connected with men of capital and influence able to lend respectability and expertise to the enterprise. Nonconformist religious affiliations also played a role, especially the influence of the Clover Street chapel.[32] What emerges perhaps most strongly, however, is a strong sense of pragmatism, of seeking to establish an organisation that was robust enough to last and attractive enough to build membership and expand.

This latter point is important in explaining the emergence of what became known as the Rochdale principles: open membership; democratic decision-making on the basis of one member, one vote regardless of size of share-ownership; political neutrality; fixed interest on capital invested in the society; commitment to non-adulteration and high quality produce for sale; the payment of dividend to members on the basis of the amount of business they did with the society; the promotion of education; and the emphasis upon cash trading and prohibition of credit. The co-operative movement's depiction of the creation of these principles can be misleading, as they are sometimes presented as a coherent and original programme devised by the Pioneers from the outset, with a prophetic eye on what was most likely to promote the spread and growth of a national movement. But there is little evidence that the principles were established at the commencement of the Pioneers; indeed, different accounts of the Pioneers have suggested slightly different lists of the principles.[33] A more likely explanation is that what became known as the principles were ideas borrowed from other co-operatives (probably dividend on purchase); extrapolated from longstanding Chartist and Owenite beliefs (member democracy and a commitment to education); and practical strategies developed over time to enhance sales and curb bad debt (non-adulteration; cash-only trading). The central point is that the Pioneers almost certainly needed to be guided by pragmatism as much as by principle, and that the 'principles' were neither the exclusive product of pre-meditation nor original. Rather, they were the product of a steep learning curve as the Pioneers struggled daily to turn what was initially a rather limited operation (the original store was open only a few nights each week and sold only a limited range of provisions) into a thriving and growing concern. Of course, deeply ingrained beliefs and learned experience played an important part in the development of the business. But what is often missed is the centrality of experiential learning, learning by doing, which must have been crucial in launching, sustaining and growing a retail business in the fraught circumstances of late 1840s Rochdale. This is no mere passing observation. Much of the literature on the Pioneers rightly focuses upon their social backgrounds and political beliefs. But equally important, though less considered, was their development as entrepreneurs and business managers. A core group of the Pioneers grew, for ten years or so after the foundation of the society, into formidable business leaders and managers; these individuals not only led and expanded their co-operative society in terms of membership and turnover but also successfully proselytised their emergent co-operative model, in the process assisting directly in the creation of new co-operative societies across the north of England and beyond. Moreover, they extended their knowledge and experience into new areas; between 1851 and 1858, it even ran its own wholesale wing to support other societies.[34] Their leaders were central to the creation of the Co-operative Wholesale Society in 1863.

This trajectory of personal, professional and entrepreneurial development among the Pioneers would be repeated in the following decades across the movement within newly emergent societies, and certainly within the English and Scottish Co-operative Wholesale Societies. One consequence would be a recurrent tension between the fundamental beliefs and principles of co-operation and the demands of running successful businesses in a highly competitive capitalist environment. It led, perhaps inevitably, to a suspicion among many co-operative and left-wing political activists that the leaderships of the wholesales and most societies were businessmen first and co-operators, radicals or socialists as a very poor second. It helped consolidate the view among trades unionists that co-operative societies were just another employer with a chequered history of treating their workers. It also contributed to the view of those, like Beatrice Webb, who regarded the consumer co-operative movement as essentially limited in its ability to reach beyond the better off section of the working class, that the co-operative movement alone was inadequate for the task of reforming society along socialist lines.[35] Arguably, the 'Labour Aristocracy' interpretation of British consumer co-operation also reflected this perception of co-operative business leaders as essentially conservative and limited in aspiration. But it is the contention here that the demands of running democratic business organisations such as a local consumer co-operative or a national co-operative wholesale demanded a unique combination of skills and attributes: an ability to manage often complex commercial transactions and structures while being able to communicate the reasons for often controversial decisions to a mass membership, and to persuade their acceptance. Far from being the unimaginative and narrowly profit-focused figures suggested in many contemporary and later historical commentaries, leaders of British consumer co-operation were frequently dynamic and imaginative people, able to address complex business challenges and to take a frequently sceptical mass movement with them. Of course, reconciling co-operative ideals with the demands of the market would frequently prove to be extremely difficult, if not impossible—and this remains the case today. But if one is to understand the startling success of British consumer co-operation—especially as an actor in the global market—one must recognise that this unique blend of entrepreneurial dynamism, passionate political advocacy for tough decisions and strong belief in the principles of co-operation were at the heart of British consumer co-operative leadership in the nineteenth and twentieth centuries. The depiction of the leaders of British co-operative societies and wholesales as timid, unimaginative, self-interested, anti-co-operative or cynical is, in most cases, a caricature that does not stand up to scrutiny.

The growth of consumer co-operatives across the UK was truly prodigious in the second half of the nineteenth century, both in terms of new societies springing up and the creation of new and innovative wider co-operative umbrella organisations. The Pioneers helped promote the establishment of societies in nearby towns, but knowledge of the idea spread further, and co-operatives grew especially quickly in parts of Yorkshire and the North-East, and in some parts of the south and the Midlands. By 1860, some 200 societies existed across the country.[36] Growth continued steadily, and by 1900 there were some 1,400 societies with a combined membership well over one million.[37] But the geographical spread of societies was not even. Certain occupational groups seemed to offer especially fertile ground for society development, notably where workers dominated a locality and strong community bonds had been developed. Miners in North-East England and cotton workers in the North-West were two such examples.[38] Other factors also played a role. The extent to which initiatives to establish co-operatives met with resistance from private retailers and wholesalers was one factor; another was the extent to which local needs were being met by existing provision. As a result, there were swathes of the country in which co-operation made rather less progress—London and large swathes of the south of England became known as co-operative 'deserts', though this perhaps exaggerates the case, as even here co-operative societies were formed.[39] Scotland also saw a similar geographical variation in co-operative development.

IV

The socio-economic context of the later nineteenth century profoundly shaped the ethos, strategies and culture of these emergent co-operatives. The processes of industrialisation and urbanisation continued and accelerated, and while the economy still experienced periods of difficulty and recession, the latter half of the nineteenth century saw a pronounced rise in living standards for the middle class and the more prosperous sections of the industrial working class.[40] It is estimated that average income per head rose from £20 to £50 between 1850 and 1914, figures that, notwithstanding the inequalities they hide, is generally agreed to have boosted the living standards of most of the working population.[41] Improving living standards were boosted by falling prices of foodstuffs, especially after the late 1860s, when new advances in transport technologies, including the spread of railways and increased steam shipping, reduced transport costs. Food and primary producers outside Europe responded by increasing output and exports to the fast-developing European economies. Added to this was the opening of the wheat belt of the American mid-west and the expansion of food exports. As one of the most open economies following the move towards free trade in the 1840s and 1850s, Britain was well placed to take advantage of this flood of cheaper food imports from outside Europe. As well as opening new opportunities for retailers and wholesalers to expand their business in imported foodstuffs, falling food prices raised disposable income and demand—also a fillip for British retail. Social changes also opened new retail opportunities, though it also increased competition. In the last 30 years of the century, the pace of urbanisation rapidly accelerated, bringing new mouths to feed into cities and towns already struggling to house and feed their inhabitants. In 1871, notwithstanding the rapid pace of industrialisation to date, two-thirds of the 31 million population of the British Isles still lived in rural areas or small towns of less than 10,000 people. By 1911, 40 per cent of a population of 45 million lived in towns or cities of more than 100,000 people.[42] Figures for specific cities over a slightly longer period reinforce this point. The population of Manchester grew from 252,000 in 1841 to 645,000 in 1902. Liverpool increased from 299,000 to 704,000; Birmingham grew from 202,000 to 781,000; and London exploded from 2.2 million to 6.5 million as its suburbs spread out, facilitated by the developing underground rail network.[43] Little wonder then that the period saw a dramatic flourishing of retailing, especially in food; and that co-operative societies sprang up and grew rapidly in response to higher incomes and larger urban markets.

This urban retail revolution reshaped the geography of cities, as new market buildings, department stores and shops challenged street hawkers and created new spaces in which people could consume, in conditions that were cleaner and more attractive than previously experienced.[44] One of the earliest studies of retail change in this period by Jefferys tends to depict the later nineteenth century as a period of very rapid change and innovation, with the rise of multiple chains of shops, large department stores, co-operative societies, modern advertising techniques (in part a response to growing rates of literacy) and the emergence of stronger national and international supply chains.[45] More recent studies of British retail have amended Jefferys' view in two ways. Firstly, the development of modern retail is seen as a much more gradual process, with many of the supposedly 'modern' techniques of marketing being pioneered in the eighteenth or early nineteenth century.[46] Secondly, a swathe of studies demonstrates that older forms of retail, including itinerant hawkers and pedlars and market traders managed to survive and co-exist with the new shops, department stores and co-operative societies. The reason for this was that, notwithstanding the general rise in living standards, high levels of inequality meant that for the poorest the new outlets were too expensive or too distant. Thus, the older forms of trade were able to persist by servicing the poorest households.[47] In addition, there was a great deal of local variation in the pattern of retailing, which reflected the considerable diversity in culture, class and income that made up Britain's towns and cities.[48] Michael Winstanley's seminal study of British shopkeeping captures this complexity and variation across the UK, as well as the priorities, beliefs and concerns of a wide range of retailers.[49] Co-operative societies emerged in this complex environment of competing retail forms, local variation and accelerating change. Unsurprisingly, this also intensified the already fierce competition between private shopkeepers and the co-operative societies, leading ultimately to outright political struggle.

From their earliest days, co-operative societies were seen as a major threat by many shopkeepers. The payment of dividend to members was regarded by opponents as a form of unfair trading, the offer of an artificial incentive for customers to use the co-op store instead of its competitors. Initially, opposition was quite localised, but it blossomed into a national movement as co-operative societies became more numerous and successful. In spring 1876, the *Grocer's Journal* advocated the establishment of a "Retail Traders League", largely in response to complaints from London traders that they were losing trade to the Civil Service Co-operative.[50] A few weeks later the *Grocer's Journal* repeated its call to create a "grocers trade union" and condemned consumer co-operatives as "futile".[51] Private traders tried to fight back in a variety of ways. Threatening wholesalers with boycotts if they continued to supply co-operative societies, or at least offered them favourable terms, was a favourite tactic, but one that ultimately pushed the co-operative societies towards establishing their own Co-operative Wholesale Society. Sometimes local traders pressured employers of co-operative activists to threaten the latter with dismissal or other sanctions. Thus, in 1886, local traders threatened to redirect their trade to a rival railway company if the Maryport and Carlisle Railway Company did not act to discourage their workers from being active in the local co-operative society. Unfortunately for the traders, the co-operative society was the Maryport and Carlisle's largest freight customer, and this resulted in no action being taken.[52] But in the same month, the Midland Railway Company did intimidate those of their workers involved in the leadership of the Birmingham Industrial Society by threatening them with dismissal if they persisted.[53] A similar attempt to 'persuade' a railway company to penalise its co-operator employees was made in Scotland in April 1888. Private traders in Paisley and Kilmarnock threatened to shift their business from the Glasgow and South Western Railway to the Caledonian Railway Company unless the former dismissed employees involved in a local co-operative society. But with the support of the Scottish Co-operative Wholesale Society (SCWS), the Glasgow and South Western faced the threat down.[54] Rather cruder methods were employed in the following January in Salisbury, when a meeting to try to set up a co-operative society was broken up by a rowdy group of youths and shopkeepers.[55] Indeed, the late 1880s saw opposition to the co-operative movement grow into an organised and formidable force. In 1888, a Traders Defence Association was set up in the west of Scotland and quickly spread across the country.[56] By the 1890s, they were able to take much tougher action. After a prolonged press attack on co-operation across the UK, in 1896 the principal meat suppliers for Glasgow, the Master Fleshers, refused to trade with co-operative societies. The SCWS acted in the courts, but it was 1899 before a large section of the meat wholesalers backed down, allowing the co-operative movement to claim victory.[57] The anti-co-operative movement spread to England, and attempted boycotts of co-operative societies were made in various towns and cities, including Newcastle, Plymouth, Bolton and, most successfully, St Helens in 1902.[58] The boycotters even established their own newspaper, the *Tradesman & Shopkeeper*. Efforts were made to persuade parliament to tax co-operative dividends to members as profits (which eventually succeeded during the First World War).[59] Then in 1910–11, a long-running feud between the co-operative movement and Lever Brothers, the soap manufacturing giant, erupted when Lever took 38 co-operative societies to court for refusing to stock Lever Brothers soaps. As with so many of the earlier attempts to curb co-operative business, the case failed.[60] While the co-operative movement successfully defended itself through a combination of mobilising co-operative members and bringing to bear the wealth and expertise of the wholesales, the competitive and political threat of private enterprise shaped the structures of British consumer co-operation in various ways. As will become clear in the next chapter, it also strongly influenced the strategies of both local co-operative societies and the co-operative wholesales.

Firstly, the creation of the English CWS and the SCWS was a direct response to the political and commercial threat posed by intense competition and hostility of the private traders. Throughout the 1850s, co-operative societies were only too aware of their potential vulnerability to hostile retail rivals and unsympathetic wholesale merchants. An alternative co-operative wholesale was long recognised as an important alternative source of essential provisions in the event of local societies facing major opposition from their rivals. This was why the Rochdale Pioneers experimented with their own wholesale service for other societies briefly in the 1850s. They abandoned it principally because it deflected resources and time away from the challenges of running a successful and expanding local society. But the need for a national co-operative wholesale remained, and from the time of the closure of the Rochdale wholesale department in 1858, moves were made to create a wholesale for England based on the principle of a federated co-operative society, the members of which would be co-operative societies rather than individual people. As such organisations were not legal, a double pronged approach was required to make a new Co-operative Wholesale Society a reality: one to drum up support among co-operators and societies for such an initiative, and one to persuade parliament to change the law. Both were undertaken successfully. In August 1860, a famous meeting of representatives from various societies in the North-West of England met at Lowbands farm ('Jumbo Farm') near Middleton, itself a co-operative farm established as part of the Chartist Land Scheme; the idea of a co-operative wholesale was mooted and supported in principle. While further meetings were held to develop the idea and organisational machinery of the wholesale society, sympathetic parliamentarians (including the MP for Shrewsbury R.A Slaney, a longstanding co-operative supporter, and the Liberal champion of free trade, Richard Cobden) secured passage of the Industrial and Provident Societies Act of 1862, which allowed limited liability for co-operatives, and made legal the investment in co-operatives by other co-operatives— thereby permitting the formation of a federation of co-operatives. This success not only reflected the progress consumer co-operation had made in the 19 years since the formation of the Pioneers Society but also demonstrated that co-operation's middle-class support base had grown, capturing the approval of prominent Liberals such as Cobden.[61] The Act paved the way for the establishment of the 'North of England Co-operative Wholesale Agency & Depot Society Ltd' (name to be replaced by Co-operative Wholesale Society within a few years), which was legally established in August 1863; within two months, 48 societies had enrolled as members. Premises, in the form of a small warehouse in Cooper St Manchester, were secured, and trading began on 14 March 1864.[62]

Secondly, the creation of a wholesale set in train other major national co-operative initiatives. In 1867, the Co-operative Insurance Company was set up to provide active co-operators with life insurance, again as an alternative to little-trusted private providers.[63] Then in the following year, Scottish co-operators followed their English counterparts and established the Scottish Co-operative Wholesale Society (SCWS).[64] Following discussions at national co-operative congresses in the late 1860s, the Co-operative Union (CU) was established in 1871, and this effectively became the national political mouthpiece of the movement, its central arena for debate and its principal promoter of co-operative education.[65] In 1871, the movement secured a new national newspaper, *The Co-operative News*, which replaced *The Co-operator*, a co-operative journal set up by Henry Pitman at the beginning of the 1860s, and named after William King's sortie into journalism some 30 years earlier.[66] The net result was that by the early 1870s, co-operation had become a truly national movement, speaking for itself in the world of politics as well as the press. Notwithstanding the movement's official rejection of involvement in politics, the challenges of private enterprise and the need to maintain vigilance over government policy in retailing and other related fields led to the Co-operation Union setting up its own Parliamentary Committee, with a brief to ensure that co-operative interests were not ignored at a national level. As will be seen in the next chapter, the CWS would grow quickly to become an international as well as a national actor, with its own bank, shipping line, factories, farms and a global procurement system. Then, in 1884, the Co-operative Permanent Building Society was established (known today as the Nationwide Building Society), which promoted home ownership among co-operators across the country, using the consumer co-operative society network to verify the credit worthiness of society members who were applying for mortgages.[67] Co-operation had become a truly national force by the 1880s, and with the creation of the International Co-operative Alliance in the 1890s, its voice would soon be heard on the global stage as well. But what is most striking of all these developments was not just the creation of the CWS and SCWS in the 1860s, but their meteoric rise as major players on first the domestic and later the international commercial scene. In respect of the latter, the challenges of managing an international commercial network in addition to directing a growing Empire of domestic activities, will be explored. Why—and how—this rapid global growth occurred, and how it was managed in its early years, will be some of the central themes of the next chapter.

Notes

1. The Diary of W.E. Bates, 1892 Misc SC BAT, National Co-operative Archive (NCA), Manchester, 1.
2. Ibid., 23.

3. J.F. Wilson, A. Webster & R. Vorberg-Rugh, *Building Co-operation: A Business History of the Co-operative Group, 1863–2013* (Oxford, Oxford University Press 2013).

4. J. Fernie & L. Sparks, "Retail Logistics: Changes and Challenges" in J. Fernie & L. Sparks (eds.), *Logistics and Retail Management: Insights into Current Practice and Trends from Leading Experts* (London, Kogan Page 2004) 1–25; 6–9.

5. W.S. Randall, B.J. Gibson, C.C. Defee & B.D. Williams, "Retail Supply Chain Management: Key Priorities and Practices" *The International Journal of Logistics* 22:3 (2011) 390–402; 390; J. Fernie, L. Sparks & A. McKinnon, "Retail Logistics in the UK: Past, Present & Future" *International Journal of Retail and Distribution Management* 38:1/12 (2010) 894–914; 895.

6. Fernie, Sparks & McKinnon, "Retail Logistics in the UK" 900.

7. L. Sparks, "Supply Chain Management and Retailing" *Supply Chain Forum: An International Journal* 11:4 (2010) 4–12; 4.

8. M. Hingley, A. Lindgreen & B. Casswell, "Supplier–Retailer Relationships in the UK Fresh Produce Supply Chain" *Journal of International Food & Agribusiness Marketing* 18:1/2 (2006) 49–86; 53.

9. D. Smith & L. Sparks, "Logistics in TESCO: Past, Present & Future" in Fernie & Sparks (eds.), *Logistics and Retail Management* 101–120; 102–104.

10. E.P. Thompson, "The Moral Economy of the English Crowd in the Eighteenth Century" *Past & Present* 50:1 (1971) 76–136.

11. A. Randall, *Before the Luddites: Custom, Community and Machinery in the English Woollen Industry, 1776–1809* (Cambridge, Cambridge University Press 1991); *Riotous Assemblies: Popular Protest in Hanoverian England* (Oxford, Oxford University Press 2006).

12. K. Navickas, *Protest and the Politics of Space and Place, 1789–1848* (Manchester, Manchester University Press 2015).

13. J. Bamfield, "Consumer-Owned Flour and Bread Societies in the Eighteenth and Early Nineteenth Centuries" *Business History* 40:4 (1998) 16–36.

14. Ibid., 20–21.

15. Ibid., 17; G.D.H. Cole, *A Century of Co-operation* (Manchester, Co-operative Union 1944) 14.

16. K.D.M. Snell, "Belonging and Community: Understandings of 'Home' and 'Friends' among the English Poor 1750–1850" *Economic History Review* 65:1 (2012) 1–25; M. Gorsky, "The Growth and Distribution of English Friendly Societies in the Early Nineteenth Centuries" *Economic History Review* 51:3 (1998) 489–511.

17. R. Scola, *Feeding the City: The Food Supply of Manchester 1770–1870* (Manchester, Manchester University Press 1992).

18. J. Blackman, "The Food Supply of an Industrial Town: A Study of Sheffield's Public Markets" *Business History* 5:2 (1963) 83–97; 94.

19. J. Blackman, "The Development of the Retail Grocery Trade in the Nineteenth Century" *Business History* 9:2 (1967) 110–117.

20. J. Birchall, *Co-op: The People's Business* (Manchester, Manchester University Press 1994) 11–13.

21. Probably still the most useful account of Owen's co-operative experiment is R.G. Garnett, *Co-operation and the Owenite Socialist Communities in Britain 1825–45* (Manchester, Manchester University Press 1972).

22. Wilson, Webster & Vorberg-Rugh, *Building Co-operation* 47–51.

23. J.K. Walton, "Revisiting the Rochdale Pioneers" *Labour History Review* 80:3 (2015) 215–247.

24. G.J. Holyoake, *Self Help by the People, History of Co-operation in Rochdale* (London, George Allen & Unwin 1857).

25. S. Pollard, "Nineteenth Century Co-operation: From Community Building to Shopkeeping" in A. Briggs & J. Saville (eds.), *Essays in Labour History, 1886–1923* (London, Macmillan 1960) 74–112.
26. See J.O. Foster, *Class Struggle and the Industrial Revolution* (London, Weidenfeld & Nicolson 1974); M.E. Rose, "'Rochdale Man' and the Staleybridge Riot" in A.P. Donajgrodski (ed.), *Social Control in Nineteenth Century Britain* (London, Croom Helm 1977) 185–206.
27. Walton, "Revisiting the Rochdale Pioneers".
28. N. Kirk, *The Growth of Working Class Reformism in Mid Victorian England* (Manchester, Manchester University Press 1998) 46–48.
29. P. Gurney, "Exclusive Dealing in the Chartist Movement" *Labour History Review* 74:1 (2009) 90–110.
30. P. Gurney, "'Rejoicing in Potatoes': The Politics of Consumption in England during the 'Hungry Forties'" *Past & Present* 203 (2009) 99–136.
31. Gurney, "Exclusive Dealing" 103.
32. Walton, "Revisiting the Rochdale Pioneers" 241.
33. A point made in A. Bonner, *British Co-operation* (Manchester, Co-operative Union 1960) 48; M. Hilson, "Rochdale and Beyond: Consumer Co-operation in Britain before 1945" in M. Hilson, S. Neunsinger & G. Patmore (eds.), *A Global History of Consumer Co-operation since 1850: Movements and Businesses* (Leiden, Brill 2017) 59–77; 62.
34. Wilson, Webster & Vorberg-Rugh, *Building Co-operation* 48.
35. B. Potter, *The Co-operative Movement in Great Britain* (London, Swan Sonnenschein 1904) 236–241.
36. *The Co-operator* December 1860, 96.
37. Hilson, "Rochdale and Beyond" 66.
38. M. Purvis, "The Development of Co-operative Retailing in England and Wales, 1851–1901: A Geographical Study" *Journal of Historical Geography* 16:3 (1990) 314–331.
39. M. Purvis, "Crossing Urban Deserts: Consumers, Competitors and the Protracted Birth of Metropolitan Co-operative Retailing" *International Review of Retail Distribution and Consumer Research* 9:3 (1999) 225–243.
40. F. Crouzet, *The Victorian Economy* (London, Methuen 1982) 57.
41. P. Mathias, *The First Industrial Nation: The Economic History of Britain 1700–1914* (London, Routledge 1990) 343.
42. J. Harris, *Private Lives, Public Spirit: Britain 1870–1914* (London, Penguin 1994) 41–42.
43. Crouzet, *The Victorian Economy* 96–97.
44. F. Trentmann, *Empire of Things: How We became a World of Consumers from the Fifteenth Century to the Twenty-First* (London, Allen Lane 2016) 206–207.
45. J.B. Jefferys, *Retail Trading in Britain 1850–1950* (Cambridge, Cambridge University Press 1954) 1–39.
46. Blackman, "The Food Supply of an Industrial Town"; "The Development of the Retail Grocery Trade in the Nineteenth Century"; J. Stobart & A. Hann, "Retailing Revolution in the Eighteenth Century? Evidence from North West England" *Business History* 46:2 (2004) 171–194.
47. G.R. Rubin, "From Packmen, Tallymen and 'Perambulating Scotchmen' to Credit Drapers' Associations, c1840–1914" *Business History* 28:2 (1986) 206–225; D. Hodson, "'The Municipal Store': Adaptation and Development in the Retail Markets of Nineteenth Century Urban Lancashire" *Business History* 40:4 (1998) 94–114; R. Scola, "Food Markets and Shops in Manchester 1770–1870" *Journal of Historical Geography* 1:2 (1975) 153–167; Scola, *Feeding the City*.

48. A. Mutch, "Public Houses as Multiple Retailing: Peter Walker and Son, 1846–1914" *Business History* 48:1 (2006) 1–19; J.H. Porter, "The Development of a Provincial Department Store 1870–1939" *Business History* 13:1 (1971) 64–71.
49. M.J. Winstanley, *The Shopkeeper's World 1880–1914* (Manchester, Manchester University Press 1983).
50. *Co-operative News* 10 June 1876, 322.
51. *Co-operative News* 5 August 1876, 418.
52. *Co-operative News* 8 May 1886, 444–445.
53. Minutes of the Grocery and Provisions Committee of the CWS, 13 May 1886, 78–79.
54. J. Kinloch & J. Butt, *History of the Scottish Co-operative Wholesale Society Ltd* (Glasgow, CWS 1981) 246.
55. *Co-operative News* 5 February 1887, 137.
56. Kinloch & Butt, *History* 246.
57. Ibid., 246–263.
58. Winstanley, *The Shopkeeper's World* 87–88.
59. Wilson, Webster & Vorberg-Rugh, *Building Co-operation* 111.
60. Ibid., 119–120.
61. P. Gurney, "The Middle Class Embrace: Language, Representation, and the Context over Co-operative Forms in Britain, c1860–1914" *Victorian Studies* 37:2 (1994) 253–286; 265.
62. Wilson, Webster & Vorberg-Rugh, *Building Co-operation* 49–52.
63. Bonner, *British Co-operation* 77.
64. Ibid., 75–77.
65. Ibid., 81–83.
66. Ibid., 83–84.
67. L. Samy, "Extending Home Ownership before the First World War: The Case of the Co-operative Permanent Building Society, 1884–1913" *Economic History Review* 65:1 (2012) 168–193.

2 Butter, Dried Fruit and the Big Apple

The Rise of the CWS/SCWS as a Global Business 1863–1890

I

At first glance, the growth of the CWS in the first 30 years of its existence was very impressive. In 1865, its first full year of trading, it sold £120,754 of stock, boasted a share capital of £7,182 and represented some 24,005 individual members of affiliated co-operative societies. By 1890, sales had reached £7,429,073, share capital was £434,017 (reflecting the huge expansion of retail societies affiliating to CWS) and the total individual membership of affiliated societies was 721,316.[1] It had, in short, become arguably the central institution at the heart of a truly national business movement. The advance of the SCWS was also impressive. In 1870, SCWS had just 70 societies affiliated to it, a share capital of £2,668 and sales of £105,250. By 1890, 261 societies were members, share capital was £84,454 and sales had risen to £2,475,338.[2] But perhaps even more impressive was the dramatic growth of the CWS and SCWS as major producers and players in a wide range of productive and related commercial activities. CWS opened its first factory at Crumpsall, Manchester in 1873 to manufacture sweets and biscuits. In the same year, it began to produce shoes and boots in a factory in Leicester; it expanded productive capacity in 1880 by moving to larger premises in Leicester and by opening another factory at Heckmondwicke in Yorkshire, as Leicester boot and shoe sales to co-operative societies boomed from 368,964 pairs (£91,985) in 1883 to 747,563 (£172,266) in 1889.[3] In 1874, CWS established a soap works in Durham, subsequently moving production to a larger plant at Irlam, Manchester, conveniently situated on the new Manchester Ship Canal, as Durham sales grew from £14,751 in 1883 to £24,643 in 1889.[4] In the late 1880s, CWS moved into textile production, opening a woollen mill in Batley, Yorkshire. Less successful were CWS ventures in coal mining. Led initially by the co-operative principle of supporting independent producer co-operatives, in the 1870s CWS procured coal for its co-operative society customers from a few enterprising co-operatively owned and run coal mines. But when these failed, CWS became drawn into buying them out to try to turn around their fortunes. They were unsuccessful, and when it became apparent in 1881 that CWS had had to write off £32,000 in debts, there was uproar and a souring of consumer co-operative attitudes to producer co-operatives that lasted well into the twentieth century.[5] But these were untypical of CWS success as a producer, and from the 1890s, further expansion of production was undertaken, including into tobacco production, crockery and eventually agriculture. In Scotland, the SCWS' move into production was more tentative, following some early unsuccessful relations with producer co-operatives in the 1870s. But by the 1880s, SCWS was involved in shirt-making, tailoring, boot and shoe manufacture, furniture and cabinet making and printing. By the end of the 1880s, the SCWS had a fast-developing industrial complex at Shield-hall, near Glasgow.[6]

Expansion of the CWS was not limited to production. In 1872, CWS set up its own banking department to manage the money of member societies, provide loans, invest CWS funds and to generally extend CWS activity into the field of financial services. Business grew rapidly, especially in the 1880s. Turnover rose from c£15 million in 1884 to nearly £23 million in 1889.[7] By June 1890, some 256 co-operative societies banked with the CWS, and between June 1878 and September 1890, some £438,000 was loaned by it to 158 societies, with loans of varying amounts and for different purposes, from tiding over small societies in their early years of trade, to substantial loans to build new stores and buildings.[8] CWS even became a shipowner and operator. It purchased its first ship, S.S. *Plover*, in 1874, and launched its first custom-built vessel, S.S. *Pioneer*, in 1879. Other acquisitions followed. By the end of the 1880s, CWS was running its own shipping lines between Goole in Yorkshire and Calais and Hamburg, and Garston and Rouen. It exported coal for various mine-owning companies, such as Pope & Pearson, and imported a variety of produce (sugar, butter, vegetables, meat) for sale to co-operative societies.[9] Linked to this was the CWS' role as a major investor in the Manchester Ship Canal, opened in 1894. S.S. *Pioneer* was in fact the first ship to arrive in Manchester via the canal from overseas, and the first to unload a cargo there. Little wonder that the canal became a major site for later CWS industrial development.[10]

But the focus of this book is of course the enormous expansion of the CWS' overseas procurement (and later production) operations, which also grew remarkably in this period. Initially buying its imports from brokers and merchants in major cities such as Liverpool and London, CWS worked much in the same way as other wholesale operations. But, significantly, in the 1870s CWS departed from this model, choosing instead to open procurement branches in key overseas locations. Depots were established in, among other places, New York (1876), Copenhagen (1881), Hamburg (1884), Aarhus (1891), Montreal (1894), Gothenburg (1895), Denia in Spain (1896) and Sydney (1897)—and shortly before the First World War, Freetown and other locations in West Africa. Overseas productive facilities followed: a slaughtery and bacon factory in Herning, Denmark, tea estates in Ceylon and India and a tallow factory in Sydney. In addition, CWS employees and directors traversed Europe and the USA, purchasing vegetables, grain, dried fruit and other produce directly from manufacturers, farmers and merchants. By the inter-war period, these were supplemented with more sophisticated financial arrangements and joint enterprises. These included the New Zealand Produce Association (NZPA), a London-based company jointly owned and run by CWS and New Zealand-based producers, which dominated imports of New Zealand produce into the UK. The CWS banking department became instrumental in financing a huge expansion in Australian wheat farming in the 1920s, as well as controversially helping to fund Soviet export production and financial recovery in the 1920s. Part and parcel of this was CWS' relations with the co-operative movements of other countries, exemplified through its efforts to secure closer collaboration with them through the International Co-operative Alliance (ICA); financial help in the form of loans was also offered to European wholesales after the First World War, in both new states like Poland and Rumania and established ones such as Belgium, which were struggling to recover from the devastation of war. At the same time, the CWS had developed very close relations with the co-operative creameries of Denmark, which was in many ways a model of transnational collaboration between consumer co-operatives in one country and producer co-operatives in another. What this amounted to was the creation of a quite unique global system of supply chains, which, far from being the product of haphazard or opportunistic deals, contained within it strong features of strategic planning and direction. In this respect, CWS was in many ways a unique example of early attempts to manage international supply chains in a coherent way. This chapter will explore the reasons why CWS emerged as a global player so quickly after its establishment, how it constructed the basic framework of its international network in the period to 1890 and the early strategies it developed for managing it in this early, and often experimental, period of development.

II

A key reason for the rapid growth of CWS and SCWS as major players in both production and international trade lay in the relations between the two organisations and the individual co-operative societies that made up their memberships. As the societies created the wholesales to protect themselves from unscrupulous merchants and private wholesalers, one might expect them to display a fierce loyalty to CWS and SCWS in terms of directing their business towards the latter. But this was not so. It is important to understand that while membership of the wholesales conferred considerable incentives on local co-operative societies in the form of dividends on goods purchased as well as democratic rights in wholesale policies, when it came to sourcing CWS or SCWS goods, the relationship was essentially a commercial one. Co-operative societies purchased supplies from CWS or SCWS, but they were under no obligation to do so. Both wholesales put moral pressure on their respective members to trade with them, but securing loyalty proved much more difficult than one might expect, and as will be seen, this was an important driving force in the development of British co-operative wholesale strategies. Why, then, were so many local co-operative societies apparently reluctant to pledge total commercial loyalty to their wholesale?

The reasons for this were related to the wider social and commercial milieu in which co-operative societies had to operate. By the later nineteenth century, when most consumer co-operative societies were being formed, Britain was a society and economy that was quite advanced along the path of industrialisation. Its burgeoning towns and cities were already rich in the range of industries and businesses they hosted. As a result, British business and industrial development was characterised by close and complex communities of businesses and firms, dependent upon each other as suppliers, markets and sources of essential services and skilled labour. Local clusters of business operated as networks, outsourcing essential services from each other, rather than developing them in house.[11] This accounted for the relatively slow development in Britain of the investor/stock market/public limited company, with its corporate business structures, professional managers and access to large amounts of financial capital—lauded by such business historians as Alfred Chandler as the optimum business model for the new period of advanced industrial capitalism emerging in the late nineteenth and early twentieth centuries.[12] British consumer co-operatives became integrated into these localised networks. In their early years, the co-operative wholesales were simply unable to supply local co-operative societies with all their needs, so some dependence on local suppliers, wholesalers and manufacturers was unavoidable. Moreover, although the advance of the British rail network did reduce transport costs in the long term, local suppliers had a significant cost advantage over the national co-operative wholesales, which frequently had to transport supplies to local societies over large distances. Faced with tough competition from private traders, co-operative societies had to be mindful of costs. Society members wanted goods as cheap as possible and margins that would allow them reasonable dividends on their purchases. Also, in the face of the hostility of private retail competitors described towards the end of the last chapter, it was in the interest of many co-operative societies to win the custom and favour of key local wholesalers, lest they succumb to the entreaties of private retailers to discriminate against the 'co-ops'. But in addition to these quite hard-headed political and commercial reasons for adhering to local suppliers, there were cultural and social factors that embedded co-operative societies firmly within their localities. Co-operative societies were not merely commercial and economic organisations in the experience of local members but also hubs of social and leisure-based interaction.[13] Societies ran reading clubs, tea dances and day trips; hosted visiting lecturers and speakers; and some even ran small libraries or reading rooms. This created a powerful sense of belonging not just to the society but to the locality more generally. Stressing localism and community identity through social activities was a powerful tool in spreading co-operation, especially in the cotton towns of Lancashire.[14] In addition, though co-operative societies tended to be politically neutral, many individual co-operators did not feel so constrained, becoming involved in local politics, initially through the Liberal Party following the extension of the franchise under the Reform Acts of 1867 and 1884, and later through trades unionism, as working-class organisation in the workplace gathered momentum with the rise from the late 1880s of 'New Unions' representing less skilled workers.[15] The ability to mobilise locally was also a powerful weapon for societies confronted by hostile traders' boycotts. No wonder then that local loyalties figured prominently in shaping the procurement strategies of many co-operative societies. A correspondent to *Co-operative News* observed in 1875 that each co-operative store in North-East England was a "little centre of power in its district".[16] But if they were unwilling to pledge total loyalty to the co-operative wholesale why then did societies join the latter and pay subscriptions to them? What did they hope to gain?

Co-operative society motives for joining the co-operative wholesales varied between societies and over time. In the first few years of their existences, the wholesales simply lacked the operational scale and breadth of commodity acquisition to meet the needs of co-operative societies. But interestingly, even after they had grown, co-operative society loyalty as customers was often lukewarm. Many co-operative societies seem to have regarded their wholesale as a kind of 'insurance policy': an alternative supplier to local wholesalers or traders should the latter become hostile or greedy in their dealings with the local co-operative society. Some societies, either because of geographical isolation or ideological commitment to the co-operative movement, were more assiduous in trying to direct business towards CWS or SCWS, but often the demands of society members for low prices and high dividends meant that commercial considerations frequently trumped co-operative loyalty. The enduring reason for affiliation to the SCWS and CWS was that it widened the range of choice enjoyed by societies when it came to procuring supplies. Competition between local suppliers and the co-operative wholesales ensured that local societies were frequently able to optimise their buying strategies, ensuring that they secured the best quality for the lowest prices, thereby maintaining healthy margins and dividends to keep members loyal. There is compelling evidence that some societies strategically divided their purchases between local suppliers and their respective CWS. This was especially the case in the North-East of England during the 1860s and 1870s, as societies spread their procurement across a wide range of suppliers, optimising profitability and also ensuring that they became important and accepted components of local business networks and communities.[17] It is a pattern that can be found elsewhere; in securing supplies, similar policies were employed by the Great Grimsby Society and the Bridge End Equitable Society in the 1880s.[18] In this way, many co-operative societies sought to keep a foot planted firmly in both camps.

Perhaps unsurprisingly, the partial loyalty of many co-operative societies to their wholesales proved to be a serious bone of contention between the CWS and SCWS and their members. The view of CWS/SCWS was that their member societies owed customer loyalty to the wholesale as a matter of co-operative principle, and for the greater prosperity of the movement in the long term. From the 1880s there were bitter arguments between the Board of the CWS and local societies in a variety of fora. In 1876, an official of the Gloucester Society stressed to the *Co-operative News* that society committees owed their principal loyalty to their members, and that while a measure of loyalty was certainly due to the CWS, they had the right and indeed duty to buy from alternative sources if better terms and quality could be found there.[19] When that policy was attacked, another Gloucester Society official spelt out Gloucester's overall procurement strategy in more detail. He might have been speaking for a large swathe of co-operative societies:

> Of all goods that are sold, where it is practicable, samples are obtained from some of the leading firms in the country, always including the Wholesale Society, and the committee compare them with each other and test them, none of the committee being aware by whom the samples are supplied, the choice being by ballot; and when the Wholesale goods are equal to those of other houses, the Wholesale society invariably gets the order. We do not expect the Wholesale Society's goods to be better. I trust that the day is not far distant when they will be able to supply us with as good an article as any firm in the kingdom, and then I am satisfied that they will be more largely supported by the Gloucester Committee, but the time is not yet.[20]

In 1887, a Plymouth society representative told a conference in Exeter that his society faced so much tough private competition that it had to choose cheaper sources over the CWS for hard and practical commercial reasons.[21] Sometimes CWS travellers met with a difficult reception when they visited societies because of problems of quality. Societies in Leeds and Bury had a reputation for hostility to the CWS in the 1870s.[22] In the 1880s, the Langley Mill and Aldercar Society were stern in their reception of CWS overtures to increase the society's purchases. They rejected CWS coffee in 1882, buying instead from private suppliers, and four years later such was their contempt for CWS quality that they voted against CWS plans to move into cocoa production.[23] Similar problems of society disloyalty were also reported north of the border in the 1860s, particularly in respect of the Port of Glasgow society and the Kilmarnock Society.[24] The ill will that existed between some societies and the wholesales was captured in 1878 by a representative of the Newbottle society:

> The fact is, a great many of our officers and managers have no more practical sympathy with the movement than a cat has for a mouse, or a Muscovite has for an Ottoman; and so long as we have some of our stores to a great extent under the control of such men, there will always be this cry of 'better elsewhere'.[25]

For its part, the CWS furiously tried to assert the principle of society member loyalty to the wholesales, and it adopted various stratagems to promote this. In the late 1880s, it held major conferences around the country on the importance of society loyalty to the wholesale. The Chairman of CWS, J.T.W. Mitchell, attacked representatives from co-operative societies at a conference in Nottinghamshire in October 1890 for taking almost £200,000 of their trade outside the co-operative movement.[26] In the following year, he openly denounced two named societies for their weak record of giving business to CWS.[27] The CWS leadership was strongly supported in this view by *Co-operative News*, which consistently offered support for loyalty to CWS in its editorials. It regularly published lists of the value of society purchases from CWS to embarrass disloyal societies, one of which proved to be the Rochdale Pioneers, which in 1879 bought only 16 per cent of its purchases by value from CWS.[28] As late as 1892, the picture was stark. An article in the *CWS Annual* for that year showed that across the country, societies purchased only 37 per cent of their supplies by value from CWS, with considerable national variation. The Home Counties tended to be most loyal, while Wales and the West Country were least; with Lancashire, consumer co-operation's heartland, almost exactly duplicating the national picture.[29]

Significantly, from the earliest years there was a serious disagreement within the co-operative movement over what the role of the wholesales was supposed to be. The leaderships of the wholesales themselves had no doubt as to what they should be: organisations that aspired to become overwhelmingly the main suppliers to societies, if not the sole ones. In pursuit of this aim, they expected co-operative societies to be loyal customers, not just because of the value of the dividend on purchases from CWS for these societies but also because of wider principles of co-operative solidarity. For their part, the co-operative societies tended to view the wholesales as merely one of a variety of potential sources of supplies, a useful source of leverage against retailer and wholesaler hostility and one to which a measure of conditional loyalty was due—but only if they could match alternative suppliers in quality and price, and if costs of carriage from sometimes distant wholesale depots were acceptable. Even then, there were countervailing factors linked with local politics and business networks that meant local suppliers needed to be kept on side. While CWS or SCWS dividends on society purchases were an incentive for societies to direct at least some trade to the wholesales, they were ultimately more exercised by the demands of their own members for high quality produce, low prices and dividends and the intense competition from private retailers in the towns and cities. Societies were only too aware that disgruntled members and other consumers could always shop elsewhere. Blind customer loyalty to the wholesales was thus seen as a luxury that most societies could ill afford. British consumer co-operation was a federation of societies and wholesales—but in many respects a rather dysfunctional one in terms of its structural coherence.

In practical terms, the problem of society disloyalty placed considerable pressure on the wholesales to maximise their competitive potential. Constitutionally, they were restricted to selling only to their co-operative society members (adherence to which, as will be seen, was occasionally interpreted flexibly), while the societies were free to source supplies from wherever they chose. What this meant was that the co-operative wholesales were under huge pressure to win the custom of their members by proving that they offered the best deals. Thus, from the earliest days, CWS and SCWS had to focus all of their resources on being better than private wholesalers and suppliers in meeting the supply requirements of the co-operative movement. Attempting to manage supply chains was key to this drive to competitiveness to ensure that CWS/SCWS could offer unparalleled quality at highly attractive prices. This was why CWS expanded rapidly into producing many of its own goods and in developing highly sophisticated national and international supply chain networks. Ultimately, it was this domestic competitive environment that drove CWS into globalising its operations. They were assisted in this by the rapid growth of society membership from the 1860s, which provided a steady flow of capital to finance the development of the wholesales' own factories, mills, warehouses, overseas branches, farms, tea plantations and ships as well as a chain of depots across the country to serve individual co-operative societies. The freedom of co-operative societies to source their supplies from wherever they wished set a tough competitive challenge for the wholesales, but the willingness of so many co-operative societies to become members of the wholesales equipped the latter with the resources to meet that challenge. How, then, in the first 30 years of their existence, did the wholesales organise themselves to assert and defend their position in the market, and how did that translate into the expansion of their global networks?

III

Any examination of the rapid growth of the wholesales and their expansion into domestic production and large-scale overseas trade in the period up to 1890 must begin with a review of their emergent business structures and cultures. It is important to recognise that the wholesales developed ways of doing business that were unlike most of British commerce at the time. Many British businesses in the late nineteenth century were owned and run by families and were, as a consequence, inherently hierarchical, with a sharp division between owners (who were also frequently managers) and employees. Even among the relatively few public limited companies that existed in Britain during this period, shareholders varied in their wealth and power within the company, with many taking a minor or passive role in the oversight of the business. The co-operative wholesales were radically different. Their quarterly general meetings were a coming together of elected representatives from member co-operative societies, most of whom were themselves experienced and involved in the running of their local societies. This subjected those who ran the wholesales to a high degree of knowledgeable scrutiny in an atmosphere of open and democratic debate. CWS and SCWS directors expected and experienced rigorous challenges to policy and criticism of performance from the outset. Fortunately, those who rose to positions of prominence in both wholesales were people whose mettle had been tested and skills honed by experience in local co-operative societies and elsewhere.

In Scotland, such a key figure was William Maxwell (1841–1922), who rose to prominence in the latter part of the nineteenth century. A coachbuilder by trade, he was an active trade unionist and joined the St Cuthbert's Co-operative Society in Edinburgh in the 1870s, becoming its secretary in 1878. From there he joined the Board of SCWS in 1880 and was instrumental in the creation of the Shieldhall industrial complex. He became President of SCWS in 1908, serving also as President of ICA until he retired from all his posts in 1921. His was a story of latent entrepreneurial talent being realised through service to the co-operative movement.[30] In the CWS, Abraham Greenwood (1824–1911), like Maxwell, learned his business skills working for a local society, in his case the Rochdale Pioneers, which he joined in 1846. After rapidly rising to the management committee, Greenwood led the establishment of the Rochdale Corn Mill Society and played a key role in the Pioneers' experiment in wholesaling in the 1850s. These experiences equipped him with the breadth of knowledge and flexibility to lead the CWS, and he emerged as its first president. In that position, he was a powerful and active advocate for societies to join CWS. In 1874, he stood down from the presidency to lead another new venture for CWS—the CWS banking department. In his capacity of CWS bank manager, Greenwood not only oversaw the growth of the banking business but also developed its relationship with societies, particularly through handling their accounts and providing loans for new buildings and plants. In this capacity, he did much to promote a stronger commercial relationship between CWS and local societies.[31] Greenwood's successor to the CWS presidency, John T.W. Mitchell (1828–95), also offered a formidable range of experiences. Born in 1828, his beginnings were humble; he grew up as a devout Christian and teetotaller, and at the age of 10 he started as a cotton mill worker in Rochdale. Through attending classes at the local Providence Independent chapel, he was taken under the wing of a local flannel manufacturer, who in 1848 gave Mitchell a job in his warehouse; he rose to the position of manager before leaving in 1867 to become a flannel dealer in his own right. He combined his experience in this career with membership of the Rochdale Pioneers from 1853, and from 1856, he was a member of its management committee. In that capacity, he utilised his growing experience of the textile trade to assist in the creation and running of the Rochdale Co-operative Manufacturing Society. As with Greenwood, here was a man whose practical employment experience would prove invaluable to the development of CWS, not least through his skills as an effective manager of people.[32] In fact, Mitchell was not elected to the Board of CWS until 1869, an elevation certainly assisted by his resignation as warehouse manager the year before. His honed managerial skills enabled him to emerge rapidly as Greenwood's successor, and he was elected to the presidency in 1874, a position he held till his death in 1895. He was elected just at the moment when CWS was on the brink of rapid expansion into manufacture, banking, shipping and overseas trade, and Mitchell's time became synonymous with the aggressive expansion of CWS to become a national commercial giant.[33] Mitchell was in many ways a model entrepreneur, a self-made man, but one whose commitment was to the elevation of working people generally rather than to himself. This was reflected in a quite disciplined personal lifestyle, which revolved around his local church and the Rochdale home in which he lived with his mother and in which he died in 1895, leaving only a few hundred pounds in personal wealth. He was a consummate politician, ferocious in debate and able to assert himself in large meetings and small committees. He was also a commanding presence in the Co-operative Union (CU), and while he was unable to prevent divisions between CWS and the CU over time, he was instrumental in the development of a reasonable working relationship between the two organisations. Ultimately, Mitchell was a unique combination, a highly competent manager, a charismatic and powerful political presence, and yet someone who was also a co-operative visionary, with a real commitment to the flourishing of co-operation as a social as well as an economic movement. Some contemporaries, such as Beatrice Webb, were slow to recognise Mitchell's deep-seated idealism, but at least one historian has shown that Mitchell was more than simply a business pragmatist.[34]

While the commercial expertise and political skill of their working-class leaders was crucial to growth of the wholesales, so also was the managerial and governance structures that emerged on both sides of the border. Central to the working democracy of both wholesales were the quarterly general meetings, at which SCWS/CWS leaders were accountable to representatives from member societies for the running of the wholesales. In England, three branches were established—the Headquarters in Manchester and major branches in Newcastle and London—to curb suspicions that the Manchester people dominated proceedings. Quarterly meetings of local CWS societies were held in Newcastle and London to roughly coincide with the Manchester meeting, thereby ensuring that there were in effect three separate quarterly meetings at which CWS leaders could be interrogated. Meetings were often heated and debate quite complex, which helped ensure that the leaderships of SCWS/CWS had to maintain a strong grip and understanding of commercial affairs, and be prepared to argue their case in public. Both wholesales were run by an elected General Committee of 12, which became known as the Board of Directors, and which became their central executive bodies. Directors took an active role in the organisation, taking key strategic and some operational decisions, and visiting in rota both domestic and overseas factories, branches and depots. The CWS Board met weekly, and very quickly, as its operations expanded, the Board meeting itself became inadequate for handling the growing volume of business. To meet this challenge, a system of sub-committees was established to deal with specific areas of business. By the end of the 1870s, two sub-committees particularly played a vital role. The Finance Committee oversaw the general financial affairs of CWS and more specifically the work of the CWS Bank. The other key sub-committee was the Grocery and Provisions Committee. The prosaic title belied its crucial role within CWS, especially in the field of overseas commerce. It took responsibility for procuring the supplies of commodities to be sold to co-operative societies. It maintained contact with co-operative societies to ensure that CWS goods for sale met local approval, and that the efforts of competing suppliers could be monitored and responded to. By 1880, as CWS expanded its activities in shipping and in manufacturing, two further sub-committees were established: the Drapery Committee and the Shipping Committee. In addition, the Newcastle and London branches set up their own sub-committees on these lines, and though these were subordinate to their Manchester counterparts, the intelligence they could provide about societies in their locality ensured that their influence was real, a fact underpinned by regular joint meetings between the HQ and branch sub-committees. So effective was this committee-based approach that the SCWS, which had largely been able to manage with monthly Board meetings in its early years, consciously copied CWS and set up its own sub-committees in 1881 for Finance, Grocery and Drapery, to be followed in 1885 by a Building and Production Committee.[35] As will be seen, this coincided with moves to co-ordinate SCWS and CWS activities in certain areas of overseas commerce.

The work of the committees shaped the operations of the wholesales in fundamental ways and certainly helped streamline decision-making and develop important skill sets among both directors and leading employees. Each committee consisted of three or four directors, and over time there was redeployment of directors between committees to deepen directorial understanding of the growing and complex SCWS/CWS Empires. On these committees, they worked closely with senior full-time employees with practical and professional experience in a range of fields, from accounting to buying and marketing. As a result, the committees were not only able to offer a high degree of expertise but also cement some very close working relationships between employees and elected directors, striking a balance between commercial expertise and political know-how. The wholesales also became renowned from the outset for recruiting highly skilled full-time employees—frequently backed by substantial administrative support. The principle was established early on. Within weeks of the establishment of CWS (then called the North of England Co-operative & Wholesale Industrial Society Ltd) in November 1863, the organisation unsuccessfully tried to recruit the senior buyer of the Rochdale Pioneers. They only succeeded in ratcheting up the man's remuneration by the Pioneers, who were desperate to keep him.[36] Instead, the CWS embarked upon an exhaustive recruitment process, interviewing 200 people before they eventually appointed a Mr Simpson on £200 per annum.[37] This set a pattern for recruiting talented and experienced professionals to key permanent positions as CWS employees, especially in key fields such as buying and liaising with co-operative societies. Junior staff were recruited, trained and brought through as experienced employees with real prospects of career advancement.

The career of John Andrew emphasises not only the importance of well-equipped permanent employees for the rapid growth generally of CWS but also its centrality in the organisation's global expansion. It also offers important insights into how CWS efficiently linked its own procurement strategies with the demands of societies and co-operative consumers. Andrew, a Rochdale man, spent several years in his youth in Germany before returning to Rochdale to work first in a mill and later for the Rochdale Pioneers, rising to become manager of its Bamford branch.[38] He joined CWS in July 1876 as a salesman whose role it was to visit and sell to co-operative societies—almost a 'poacher turned gamekeeper'. The importance of the role, and of his impressive expertise, were underlined by his starting salary of £140.[39] He spent the next five years travelling around the societies of Northern England, trying to persuade hard-headed co-operative society committees to purchase a wide range of supplies from CWS. He thus became closely acquainted with the tastes and desires of co-operative society members and consumers and regularly reported these to the CWS grocery and provisions commit-tee. In this way, CWS salesmen were vital in equipping the organisation to compete effectively with private wholesalers and manufacturers. They enabled CWS to provide what is known in modern supply chain manage-ment as Efficient Consumer Response (ECR). It was Andrew's long expe-rience of co-operative consumer tastes, both as a society manager and as a salesman, which enabled him to achieve even greater elevation in 1881, when he was appointed as manager of a new branch of CWS in Copen-hagen that bought Danish butter, eggs and bacon for sale to co-operative societies in the UK. With his expert knowledge of British co-operative con-sumers, he was ideally placed to ensure that the quality of the produce he purchased would be attractive to them. His knowledge of the German language, though not of itself of much direct use in Denmark, seems to have enabled him to master Danish, and it shall be seen that under his leadership, the British presence in Scandinavia would grow from strength to strength. There were many others who progressed to senior positions in the CWS' overseas service through a path similar to that followed by Andrew. John Gledhill was a salesman for CWS in the early 1870s, rising to become an important adviser to the Grocery and Provisions Commit-tee. This experience was crucial to his appointment in November 1875 to head the newly established New York branch.[40] Clearly, then, the evolv-ing governance and management structures of the wholesales, and their personnel, proved assets in the development of overseas connections and the procurement of foreign produce. How did these networks develop in the initial phase of co-operative wholesale development between the 1860s and 1890?

IV

The first venture overseas for supplies by CWS was not international and was very close to home. The strong demand among co-operators for butter and cheese resulted in CWS going directly to the Irish butter market to procure supplies. The reasons for this originated in difficulties confronting the wholesales and co-operative societies in securing supplies solely through brokers and other middlemen. Many brokers charged high rates of commission, and to secure lower prices the wholesales needed to buy in bulk—but it was notoriously difficult to judge exactly how much the co-operative societies' market could absorb. As a result, a recurring problem was that CWS and SCWS on occasion found themselves with excessive stocks on hand that then had to be offloaded by selling at discount prices to the non-co-operative society market, an action that ran contrary to co-operative principles and tended to result in severe losses.[41] By purchasing directly from the producer, such losses could be avoided or ameliorated in several ways. Firstly, by having representatives where commodities were locally produced, stock could be purchased at the optimum time in terms of price and quality. Secondly, the fact that SCWS and CWS were buying at least some of their requirements directly from the producers put pressure on middlemen not to try to overcharge or offload poor stock to the co-operative wholesales. The implication was that a failure to give satisfaction would result in CWS and SCWS increasing their direct purchases from producers. Thirdly, local representation where commodities were produced strengthened the knowledge and expertise of the wholesales in crucial commodities, enabling them to develop more effective long-term strategies for procurement.

The first manifestation of this strategy was in Ireland, where a series of butter-buying branches were set up from the late 1860s, including Limerick (1868), Armagh and Waterford (1873), Tralee (1874) and Cork (1877). These were manned by CWS buyers who would negotiate purchases from local butter markets. The arrangements for this were complex and required a full understanding the local butter trade and extensive local contacts. The opening of the Cork branch reveals not only the complexity of engaging directly with the Irish market but also the fact that there was opposition and some hostility to CWS, which was regarded as an unwelcome competitor and player. Before the branch was opened, two of CWS' most experienced officials, Mr Kay and Mr Stott, undertook exhaustive research into feasibility and the problems buyers were likely to encounter. One such difficulty was the fact that many butter merchants and producers insisted that buyers purchase all of their butter, including that of poorer quality. While CWS was concerned that there was a danger that CWS would overstock itself with butter it could not sell, it calculated that because there was an active local resale market for all qualities of butter between merchants, it would be able to avoid excess stocks of poor quality butter by selling on to other merchants who specialised in the inferior product.[42] But what these arrangements also revealed was that for CWS to be truly effective, it had to master the full complexities of local markets, networks and commercial practice. It was a lesson CWS learned well and adapted to conditions elsewhere.

The early growth of the wholesales in the 1860s and 1870s of course coincided with expansion of the North American economies, as the US recovered rapidly from its civil war and westward expansion gathered pace, opening the great plains to the global economy as railway construction into the interior gathered pace. American produce, especially cheese, lard and hams, attracted CWS involvement from an early stage. By 1874, CWS was purchasing hams and cheese through a Mr Ware, a private agent acting on its behalf in New York. Purchases were growing so quickly that Kay the buyer suggested the time was fast coming when it might pay CWS to have one of its own staff permanently located in New York to buy for it.[43] Just two months later, the rapid sale of American cheese cleaned out CWS stocks and no further shipments were due until June, indicating just how buoyant the American trade was at this time.[44] Indeed, when the shipments did arrive, they had already been sold to societies in advance.[45] But the need for reliable intelligence about the trade with the USA was underlined just three weeks later, when a sudden rush of imports of American cheese into Liverpool suddenly suppressed prices, hitting the profitability of the trade.[46] The upshot was the establishment of the CWS New York branch in September 1876; Gledhill, the new depot manager, wasted little time in delivering hams, bacon, cheese and lard to the CWS. Though SCWS were put out by the fact that CWS had not consulted them before setting up the New York branch, they quickly utilised its services and ordered commodities through it.[47] From the outset, Gledhill set about taking full advantage of having a branch *in situ*. In particular, he made every effort to build networks and relationships with local merchants, brokers and producers. Under him, the CWS branch was the first organisation to rent space for its headquarters in the prestigious New York Produce Exchange, designed by the renowned architect George B. Post and fully completed in 1884. Even before the building was opened, Gledhill had been elected in June 1882 as a manager of the New York Produce Exchange, a post that involved helping to supervise and organise the work of the body. His work as a manager took him to other major commercial centres in the USA, such as Chicago, enabling him to extend his network of personal commercial contacts across the continent. It was a testament to the impact that Gledhill had already made that he was elected by 1,328 votes out of a possible 1,612.[48] He had already placed the services of CWS at the disposal of some key New York players by providing information services for them. In March 1882, he agreed for a fee to regularly cable Liverpool prices of cheese to the Butter, Egg and Cheese Exchange in New York, to help merchants in their decision-making.[49] What this meant practically was that Gledhill and the CWS branch were ideally placed to secure intelligence of the best prices and the best possible deals, and that the branch was in a position of influence and power that disposed it favourably to a wide range of merchants and brokers. This was not a haphazard arrangement, but a carefully calibrated strategy to optimise the buying power of CWS in the American market. The New York branch worked closely not just with CWS, but also SCWS in order to maximise the size of purchases it could make on behalf of both societies, enabling it to secure extremely favourable deals. For example, in 1884, under the auspices of the New York branch, a joint CWS/SCWS deputation visited the meat packers Armours in Chicago, and the negotiations enabled the New York branch to import Armour tinned meats with CWS labels.[50] It was a policy that would be urged on the New York branch by CWS buyers throughout the decade, especially in promotion of *Pioneer* brand, a label that neatly combined the CWS' Rochdale roots with its exploits on the American frontier.[51] The same deputation struck a deal with flour millers in the USA that would allow Gledhill and the New York branch to buy flour directly from them, reducing dependence on CWS buying flour through expensive agents in the UK.[52] Interestingly, one of these firms, Washbourne Crosby, asked CWS to be discreet about its purchases of flour from them, lest this cause friction with some of its other customers in Britain. Clearly the hostility of private enterprise to co-operation even made itself felt across the Atlantic.[53] Certainly the opening years of the New York branch down to the mid-1880s were counted a success. Between April 1877 and September 1883, CWS Manchester sold goods supplied by the New York branch worth £521,990, generating a profit of £27,892. The figures for the same period for the Newcastle and London Branches were £321,767 (profit £3,222) and £112,823 (profit £4,535) respectively.[54]

But perhaps the most startling evidence of the success of the New York branch was the fact that private, non-co-operative organisations asked CWS if its New York branch could also supply them. Gledhill made tentative suggestions in September 1876 that he be permitted to purchase stocks in excess of CWS' immediate requirements, as this would enable him to secure the best prices. Of course, that then raised the question of how such surplus commodities could be disposed of—by implication, this would mean selling on to a third party. Significantly, the CWS Board gave its permission for Gledhill to go ahead.[55] By March 1882, Gledhill was supplying the lard firm Kilverts with pig fat procured in Chicago, for which the firm offered to pay CWS £450 per annum in commission.[56] CWS held out for £500 pa, and Kilverts agreed but insisted that Gledhill join the Chicago exchange to ensure access to the best quality fats.[57] Gledhill duly complied.[58] By November 1883, Gledhill was furnishing the CWS with intelligence on Chicago meat prices for publication.[59] CWS employees in Liverpool even handled Kilverts' imported lard.[60] Then, in July 1885, CWS arranged to supply Fowlers, a Liverpool firm, and Dixon & Co, a Manchester company, with American cheese.[61] Similar deals followed that involved the New York branch supplying sugar to British firms, most notably McFie's of Liverpool.[62] In 1888, a contract with the firm of Goodwin Bros was signed to supply resin.[63] When the policy of purchasing for private firms on commission was questioned within the co-operative movement, it was decided that it was too lucrative and useful to discontinue.[64] The New York branch was thus a resounding success, but even it had to work hard to meet the demands of the British co-operative consumer. Gledhill regularly had to return to Britain and tour local co-operative societies in England, Wales and Scotland to monitor changing tastes and sometimes to accept quite challenging criticism. Sometimes customers were bitterly disappointed, and the Newcastle Branch of CWS was on occasion very vocal in its criticisms of the quality of bacon and ham imported from the New York branch.[65] Indeed, by late 1882, the Newcastle branch incurred the disapproval of the Manchester leadership when it became clear that it was sourcing almost four times more American bacon through private firms than it was through the New York branch.[66] In January 1884, the Newcastle Branch complained formally to Manchester about the poor quality of New York supplies of bacon.[67] So serious was the rift between the Newcastle Branch and New York that the SCWS/CWS deputation that visited the USA in 1884 specifically investigated conditions at both the plants producing the meat and storage facilities in New York, and insisted that the New York branch investigate the reasons why Newcastle had been sent so much poor quality meat.[68] What the episode demonstrated, however, was that even a successful and sophisticated procurement operation such as that conducted by CWS New York would be very quickly brought to heel if it ever failed to deliver the highest quality. A well-developed system of procurement still had to meet the highest expectations of consumers.

Just as the New York depot developed key strategies for procuring the best quality at the most competitive prices through securing positions of commercial authority and influence, building transcontinental networks and branching out into commission work to facilitate bulk buying, so other new branches established in this period developed similar and distinctive procurement strategies. A depot was opened in Rouen in 1879 to develop trade with northern France. But the CWS Copenhagen branch opened in 1881 proved to be especially successful. The choice of the Danish capital by CWS partly reflected the revolution that had taken place in Danish agriculture since the country's defeat by Prussia in the war of 1864 and the loss of Schleswig-Holstein, although recent research shows that even earlier in the century there was a flourishing trade between Britain and Denmark conducted principally through Hamburg, a city with well-established links with Britain that enjoyed the port and service facilities of a well-developed commercial hub.[69] Defeat in war rendered this earlier dependence on Hamburg unpalatable to the Danes and promoted the development of trade from Copenhagen and other Danish ports. The legacy of problems left by the war was compounded from the late 1860s by the influx of cheap grain from North America, and like farmers across the continent, the Danes were compelled to seek new survival strategies. In Denmark, this involved radical innovation in the nature, technologies and institutional arrangements for agricultural production. Danish farmers moved increasingly into dairying and progressively overcame barriers of capital, skill and knowledge by working together through co-operatively owned creameries that could purchase member farmers' milk and process it into butter. The success of dairy co-operatives in Denmark is highlighted by the fact that by 1903, 81 per cent of all owners of milch cows were members of co-operative creameries.[70] The rapid growth of dairy co-operatives reflected the fact that Danish farmers owned substantial cattle herds and could therefore could take full advantage of the reduction in feed grains facilitated by overseas imports and afford to invest capital in creameries with their neighbours. They could also afford for their children to be educated at the 'Folk High Schools', which equipped them with the mathematical and other skills to take fullest advantage of major innovations in organisation and technology.[71] A striking feature of this agricultural revolution was the way in which new technology was successfully employed, including the application of the automatic cream separator from the late 1870s, and how this was combined with successful organisational innovation through the co-operative creameries, which disseminated knowledge of new cattle-rearing practices among farmers to increase yield and improve quality.[72] Another major innovation was the successful development of winter dairying, enabling butter of the highest quality to be produced all year round, in contrast to the seasonal pattern of production that continued in other major butter producing countries such as Ireland.[73] Improvements in production were accompanied by a significant rise in the standard of Danish butter, the esteem in which it was held, and the price it could command in the British market.[74] By the late 1880s, the Danish state also played a role in ensuring that Danish butter was monitored and its brand (Lurbrand) protected from imitation.[75] From 1888, a Danish Agricultural Commissioner was appointed in London by the Danish government with the specific task of protecting the reputation of Danish butter and checking that nothing else was being passed off as the genuine Danish product.[76] A major consequence of this was that Denmark rapidly emerged in the late nineteenth century as the primary supplier to the British market. Ireland suffered particularly from this shift. In 1860, Ireland commanded 46.6 per cent of the British market, a proportion that fell to just 11.9 per cent by 1910.[77] By contrast, Danish butter's share of imports into the British market grew from 13.5 per cent for the period 1880 to 1884 to 40 per cent between 1910 and 1913.[78] The Newcastle Branch of CWS became a large and growing market for 'foreign' butter (predominantly Danish). In the last quarter of 1877–8, some 2,962 cwt of butter was purchased by Newcastle, and this had risen to 3,369 cwt in the same quarter in 1878–9.[79] Little wonder, then, that the CWS began to see the advantage of a branch at the heart of this agricultural revolution. In the years up to February 1881, when CWS decided to establish its branch in Copenhagen, CWS imported 32,000 casks of butter from Denmark and Sweden worth £200,000.[80] Most of this was purchased through a Mr Kramer, a Copenhagen broker.[81]

Once the new branch was established, John Andrew wasted little time in making an impression in the Danish capital. In October 1881, within months of the opening of the new branch, Andrew began by-passing by the brokers and merchants in Copenhagen with whom Kramer had dealt, instead directly approaching Danish farmers to arrange butter purchases. Kramer was furious and warned that there would be a reaction from the Copenhagen men.[82] In fact, Andrew had been planning this since June and had been seeking a clerk with strong Danish language skills to facilitate it.[83] That Kramer was unaware of these plans is evident from his reaction, and this perhaps indicates why a branch run by a CWS man was preferable to relying upon local agents. Sure enough, a meeting of the Copenhagen merchants was called, which warned Andrew that they would boycott sales to CWS if he persisted in making direct approaches to farmers.[84] But Andrew faced them down, gambling on the fact that the CWS was such a huge potential market that mercantile solidarity would be trumped by opportunity. He was correct, and the threatened boycott soon faded. In any case, it was never Andrew's intention to source Danish butter solely from the farmers; using intermediaries would enable CWS to respond quickly to market changes such as sudden demand or changes in taste. But sourcing at least some butter from the farmers implied the direct threat that if merchants or brokers tried individually or collectively to impose unfavourable conditions on CWS, it could and would by-pass them and go straight to the producer. It was a useful strategy to keep the merchants and brokers honest: to effectively manage the terms of the Danish butter supply chain. In the first week of 1882, of 270 casks of butter sent from Copenhagen, 46 had come directly from the farm.[85] Andrew took advantage of CWS' status as a direct buyer by rejecting butter offered by brokers that was of lower quality.[86] The relationship with Denmark's co-operative farmers enjoyed the benefits of ideological affinity, and this helped pave the way for a more direct relationship, including the advance of money by CWS to Danish farmers to ensure supplies.[87] The Danish Farmers' Journal advertised the CWS branch in Copenhagen from November 1883.[88] Farmers were also treated to entertainment at Andrew's home, part of a strategy of building close personal and social links to underpin commercial relations.[89] Andrew's position in Danish commercial circles was further consolidated when CWS became a member of the Royal Agricultural Association of Denmark in December 1882.[90] The relationship was cemented by personal meetings with the President of the Association and numerous farmer members, who asked Andrew to provide information about the butter trade in the UK.[91] Another very useful customer and ally courted by Andrew was one Herr Donnersdorf, a farmer who supplied butter to the CWS Copenhagen Branch and who was also an MP and President of the Danish CWS.[92] Andrew was approached to develop commerce between CWS and its Danish counterpart, an initiative that resulted in a large consignment of rice from CWS to the Danish CWS in December 1885.[93] Just as Gledhill had built links with powerful friends and allies to smooth the way for CWS trade in the USA, Andrew followed a very similar strategy in Denmark, with the added advantage of being able to take advantage of common ideological beliefs as well as mutual self-interest.

In August 1884, Andrew boasted that 30 per cent of his butter purchases across Scandinavia was directly from farmers.[94] By summer 1885, some 101 farmers across Scandinavia were directly supplying CWS Copenhagen with butter.[95] However, the aim was never for farmers to displace brokers and merchants completely, only to ensure that they would be compelled to offer the best terms to CWS. This is clear from the fact that between June 1886 and June 1887, of 97,527 casks (£548,966 by value) of butter procured from Sweden and Denmark, about 16.8 per cent by volume came directly from farmers, or 16.6 per cent by value.[96] But especially impressive was the startling growth of the trade of the Copenhagen branch. In the year ended June 1883—just two years after the branch had been established—CWS shipments were worth £261,796, compared with £211,976 shipped from New York.[97] In October 1883, Andrew was permitted to raise his credit limit with local banks from £6,000 to £8,000 to facilitate the rapid growth in business.[98] By August 1887, this had been raised to £14,000 per week.[99] As shown, the value of shipments was to double within the next four years. In 1885, when CWS was shipping about £9,000 to £10,000 of butter each week, it was clear that CWS had become the biggest single butter trader in Scandinavia.[100] Little wonder that by February 1884, Andrew's annual salary had risen to £450.[101] Just a year later it was raised again to £500.[102] Such was his integration into local society that he bought a house in the capital and took Danish citizenship.[103] He was also made a Burgher of Copenhagen, enabling him to trade with exactly the same legal rights as other merchants in the capital.[104]

But, like Gledhill, Andrew was not immune to criticism. In September 1889, it was his turn to face the ire of the Newcastle CWS branch, which registered numerous complaints with Manchester about the quality of butter he had recently sent to Newcastle. So serious were these that Manchester wanted the Newcastle branch to send a deputation to Copenhagen to address the issue.[105] Newcastle demurred, asking that Andrew come to them.[106] By the end of the month, Manchester's concerns had escalated to consider a special deputation of its own to Denmark to investigate the "unsatisfactory manner in which the butter trade is done".[107] Andrew appeared before the various bodies of the CWS branches, and whatever concerns had been entertained were obviously successfully addressed, as Andrew's report on the progress of business in Denmark was deemed satisfactory in April 1890.[108] But the affair illustrated that the demands and scrutiny of the CWS militated against any lapses in efficiency or quality even by the most successful overseas operators.

The increasing importance of CWS trade with northern Europe was signalled by the decision in 1883 to open a branch in Hamburg.[109] This was a connection that largely stemmed from another important CWS sortie into international commerce; the development of its own shipping line. Concern about the cost of shipping freight emerged as an issue for CWS in the early 1870s, as its overseas commerce began to expand. As early as September 1874, Cockshaw, one of CWS' most experienced buyers, negotiated reductions of freight costs with various shipping firms.[110] But just as sourcing services and goods from the non-co-operative sector was problematic in other areas, CWS leaders soon came to the view that ownership of its own shipping line would strengthen CWS' ability to negotiate favourable freight rates. The first such ship acquired was S.S. *Plover* in 1874.[111] This was in many ways an experiment, but by 1878, growing CWS trade with the continent persuaded the leadership that a more serious venture would be advantageous. In July 1878, CWS accepted a tender to build a vessel for £11,250.[112] By the following November, the S.S. *Pioneer* had been named and was under construction.[113] CWS promoted its new venture widely throughout the movement, even displaying a model of it at an exhibition at Hebden Bridge in 1879.[114] It was launched in February 1879.[115] The December quarterly meeting in Manchester noted that while S.S. *Plover* was undergoing repairs, a vessel would be chartered to fulfil CWS contracts to deliver coal to continental consumers on behalf of British mining companies who chartered space on CWS vessels.[116] Already a pattern of commerce had been established. To make CWS voyages economic, CWS would export on behalf of British producers, especially coal mining companies, while return journeys would focus principally—but not exclusively—on importing produce for the CWS. The aim was never that CWS goods would be confined to CWS ships—and much business was still channelled through private shipping firms. The aim was to send a clear signal that CWS would not be exploited through exclusive dependency on the private firms. From the outset, CWS recognised that shipping firms often collaborated with each other through shipping conferences, setting freight rates and even allocating custom between them. This made CWS potentially vulnerable to anti-co-operative agitation and organisation aimed at the shipping companies. A CWS presence in shipping effectively prevented this. Two major shipping routes were developed by CWS initially: Goole to Calais and Garston to Rouen.[117] The latter emerged in late 1879 and was operated weekly, initially by S.S. *Pioneer* and a second vessel specially chartered for the purpose.[118] On its first six voyages, it registered a profit of £43–14s-9d, using on average about 350 of its capacity of 500 tons.[119] But the uncertainties of international trade, high costs and ferocious competition impacted upon profitability, with losses in excess of £300 being incurred on the *Pioneer* and chartered steamers by September 1880.[120] The Goole–Calais line, which was running by March 1881, was operated by chartered vessels, the costs of which persuaded the CWS leadership that ownership of ships would produce higher profits.[121] It acted on this, purchasing the hitherto chartered S.S. *Cambrian* in May 1881 for £7,470.[122] Other lessons were being learned. In April 1881, it secured a temporary agreement with the French *Treport Line* to reduce freight rate competition.[123] Then, at the end of the month, a lucrative deal was done with Pope & Pearson for a year under which CWS vessels would export coal to Calais.[124] Notwithstanding these strategies, coal shortages due to a miners' strike in Lancashire and bad weather resulted in losses of £500 on the Garston–Rouen and Goole–Calais lines.[125] To alleviate the situation, it even chartered out the *Pioneer* to a private company for several voyages to Jersey.[126] Sensitive to the negative response ongoing shipping losses would elicit from the membership, the CWS leadership found itself having to defend its actions and promise better results in future. When in September 1881, losses were still substantial (£212 on the Garston–Rouen line and £184 on Goole–Calais), the CWS Board argued that matters would improve now that the *Cambrian* was CWS-owned and the freight deal with *Treport* was being honoured.[127] Fortunately, *Cambrian* delivered, and a profit of £155 on Goole–Calais was made in the quarter to December 1881, and even though Garston–Rouen still showed a loss, it had been reduced to £109.[128] By March, further steps had been taken, with management of the Garston–Rouen line being taken from the Liverpool agents to whom CWS had previously subcontracted and run in-house instead, producing a profit of £73 on the line (Goole–Calais made a profit of £118).[129] In spite of this improvement in fortunes, the CWS shipping trade would be dogged by periodic losses as a result of weather, accidents at sea and the difficulties that beset international commerce during this period. Further ships were built specially for CWS or chartered, such as S.S. *Progress* in April 1884 for £300 a month.[130] Among others, S.S. *Equity* was built and launched in 1888.[131] The shipping committee kept a constant watch on how its freight rates compared with those of competitors.[132] In March 1886, Mr Cameron, who had long been involved in the CWS' shipping arrangements, was made full manager of the shipping department on a salary of £350 per annum, reflecting the newfound importance of shipping in the CWS business portfolio.[133] Perhaps inevitably, CWS became embroiled in the wider politics of the shipping industry. In February 1887, it joined other Goole shipowners in petitioning parliament to prevent the Hull Dock Company being allowed to sell or lease its businesses to railway companies, who were beginning to try to expand their transport Empires into shipping.[134] But perhaps one of the most ominous developments related to CWS shipping, and indeed to CWS overseas trade generally, was the initiative launched in the early 1880s to build the Manchester Ship Canal. First mooted in 1881, CWS seems to have become seriously interested in October 1883, when Mitchell attended a meeting about the project in the Free Trade Hall.[135] By the following June, CWS was urging societies to support a petition to parliament in favour of the scheme.[136] In November 1884, the CWS Board requested at the quarterly meetings that a donation of £500 be approved to meet the expenses of a petition to parliament in favour of the Ship Canal.[137] Then, in August 1885, following a meeting between the CWS Board and Daniel Adamson, the leading promoter of the canal, CWS decided to ask permission from the membership to invest 1,000 £10 shares in the canal.[138] Such was CWS enthusiasm for the project that, in June 1887, it secured membership support for CWS investment to be doubled to £20,000.[139] By the end of the decade, as the Ship Canal promised to become reality, CWS began to vie with other companies for land adjoining the canal and the prospect of relocating factories and plants there to take advantage of the new access to the sea.[140] Thus did CWS become a major player in the development and exploitation of the Manchester Ship Canal.

It was during 1882 that CWS shipping began to trade between Goole and Hamburg. In November 1882, CWS was contracted to deliver between 15,000 and 20,000 tons of coal there for Pope & Pearson.[141] In the same month, two CWS officials were sent to Hamburg to seek out an agent who could procure commodities for CWS for the return journey of S.S. *Lottie Kershaw*, which had been chartered by CWS for the new Goole–Hamburg route.[142] In the following month, a Mr W. Loden became the CWS agent in Hamburg.[143] Being paid on commission, he dealt with the Hamburg end of business for importing coal from Britain and also procured commodities for the CWS to ship back as return cargo.[144] So successful did the trade with Hamburg become that within a year CWS decided to follow the Copenhagen example and establish its own branch in the city.[145] In December 1883, William Dilworth was appointed as manager of the Hamburg branch on £350 per annum.[146] Dilworth had followed in Andrew's footsteps, replacing him as CWS traveller when Andrew took over the Copenhagen branch. Like Andrew, Dilworth had served time as a society manager, in Rawtenstall in Dilworth's case. The branch began functioning in April 1884, when Dilworth was empowered to draw up to £5,000 per week for purchases on behalf of CWS.[147] By the end of the year, CWS was supplying a Hamburg businessman, Mr Westphal, with coal imported from Goole.[148] But securing return cargoes proved more difficult. Initially high prices made Hamburg butter uncompetitive.[149] However, in November 1884, Dilworth detected that Hamburg brokers were advising butter merchants against trading with CWS.[150] In January 1885, he was excluded from a meeting of butter buyers in the city on the grounds that CWS was not a Hamburg firm and that he was a foreigner.[151]

But at this point, CWS demonstrated that it was, to use a twenty-first-century idiom, a 'learning organisation'. In February 1885, Dilworth went to visit Andrew in Copenhagen to learn first-hand how his more experienced colleague dealt with middlemen and, more crucially, how he had built direct commercial relations with Danish farmers.[152] The visit was pivotal. In March 1885, Dilworth reported that he had learned much from Andrew and that not only was he now poised to make deals with German farmers in Holstein but that he was also on the brink of a major deal with a Berlin dairy company.[153] By July, Dilworth was attending the annual meeting of a Farmers Club in Braelstorf.[154] Less than two weeks later, he confirmed weekly deliveries of 30–40 casks of butter direct from farmers in Schleswig.[155] The results were significant and impressive.

Between September 1886 and June 1887, the Hamburg branch purchased 31,170 casks of butter (value £134,676), of which 5,489 casks (£23,200) were sourced directly from farmers, or 17.6 per cent by volume.[156] The similarity between the percentages of farmer-sourced butter between Copenhagen and Hamburg are striking and reinforce the fact that CWS had successfully transplanted commercial techniques and strategies from one city to the other. By March 1889, the prospects for growth in the trade with Hamburg had increased, and Dilworth was empowered to draw £11,000 per week to finance purchases—more than double the £5,000 he had been allowed on commencement, just five years earlier.[157] At the end of the decade, Hamburg, like Copenhagen, promised to become a major gateway to an extended CWS presence on the continent.

However, it would be a mistake to see the CWS presence in Europe, or indeed further afield, as entirely channelled through the major branches in Denmark, Germany, France or the USA. Within Europe, especially as CWS shipping began to regularly trade with the continent, CWS officials and sometimes directors embarked upon speculative missions to take advantage of new opportunities, such as local surpluses of goods, or to address shortages at home. Thus, in November 1878, a CWS buyer was sent to buy butter in response to shortage and high prices in Britain.[158] In 1880, the services of an agent, a Mr Audet, were engaged in Paris to secure produce to send back to the CWS via the Garston–Rouen line.[159] In October 1881, a CWS buyer secured a deal to source yeast in Holland.[160] Throughout the period, there were many such speculative adventures by CWS buyers, motivated by the principle that trade conducted as close to the producer would generally produce better results than working through brokers. Dissatisfaction with brokers—from whom the CWS procured most dried fruit up to the mid-1880s—proved to be the basis of a major CWS initiative to secure dried fruit overseas, especially from Greece.[161] Two CWS buyers, Messrs Tweedale and Lobb, were asked to explore the possibility of buying direct from producers and merchants in Greece, and they sought advice from the Greek Consul in Manchester in June 1885.[162] Just over a year later, Tweedale was sent to Greece to see if fruit could be purchased on favourable terms.[163] He set off on 30 July and spent two months travelling across Europe, and he furnished a detailed report of his exploits that were later printed and circulated across the movement.[164] What becomes clear from the report was that this was not only a business trip to Greece, but in fact an exploratory mission to establish commercial contacts right across the continent. Tweedale bought potatoes in Antwerp, apples in Bonn, flour in Vienna, Budapest and Serbia, maize in Rumania and Odessa in the Ukraine, before proceeding to Constantinople to get on with the main business of buying dried fruit. The Board were delighted with Tweedale's work and ordered that he embark upon a second trip in 1887, this time accompanied by a CWS director. When this was being organised, the Grocery Committee reflected upon Tweedale's success. He had purchased dried fruit (mainly currants) worth £40,635, on which a net profit of £2,046 had been subsequently realised. The Grocery Committee unreservedly recommended the second trip, citing the larger sales of better-quality fruit procured and the cost savings on brokerage by buying directly in Greece. It even asked whether a placing permanent buyer in Greece might be advisable in the long term.[165] As a result, annual trips to Greece by a director and a buyer became a regular event, and from some of the early printed reports, the pattern of a tour across Europe to supplement the dried fruit orders with additional deals seems to have become the norm. Tweedale was accompanied by Mr Lord, CWS director, on his next expedition at the end of July 1887. This time, the return as well as the outward journey saw a 'Cook's Tour' of commercial dealing. Arriving in Belgium on 30 July, the CWS representatives found that little business could be done in green fruit because of a poor crop; but important agreements on the conduct of trade were made at a visit to the Rhine Sugar Factory at Cologne. Oranges were inspected in Corfu before the main business of buying fruit commenced in Greece. They purchased fruit through several agents, including the firm of Lochnner, Marcopli & Co., Denis Marcuplo and even a Mr Coundouros, tobacco merchant, from whom 70 cases of figs were purchased. The CWS representatives used quotes by different firms and traders to secure the best deals, and the dried fruit deals were deemed a great success. On the way back, flour was purchased again in Hungary, sugar in Prague, Magdeburg and Paris and finally apples in Ghent.[166] The trip in the following year followed a similar pattern. What is described by the reports—and is evident from other sorties onto the continent—is a cross-continental network of commercial relationships that was delivering to the co-operative wholesales a wide range of products at competitive prices. Moreover, the development of these links was not accidental or based upon blind speculation. Rather it was a systematic and painstaking construction of commercial links that followed a clear strategy directed from Manchester. If this was not supply chain management as commonly understood in late twentieth or early twenty-first-century terms, neither was it the blind, speculative and undirected activity described in much of the business literature as typical of 'pre-SCM' practice.

In addition, international links were being sought by foreign interests in several important ways. Almost from its inception, knowledge of the English CWS spread overseas among people who had emigrated but who still had links with co-operators in the UK. As early as 1865, CWS was approached by the agent of three co-operative stores in Newcastle, New South Wales to see if the wholesales could supply them with goods.[167] Then, in November 1865, a newly formed co-operative society in Cape Town, South Africa asked for CWS to supply it.[168] At this stage, both requests had to be refused, as CWS simply lacked the resources to trade internationally. But requests continued. By the late 1870s, as CWS had grown, so had its ability to consider overseas requests more seriously. In October 1879, CWS promised to consider seriously a request from a group of Brisbane farmers for the wholesale to act as agents in the UK to sell their sugar and molasses.[169] Two years later a Sydney firm, Tate Bros, approached CWS to act as their agents in selling butter, honey and tallow, and CWS agreed to buy goods that societies would be prepared to purchase, though they did not promise any long-term relationship.[170] In September, CWS agreed to receive consignments of butter from the firm, but stressed that all was at the sender's risk.[171] In 1882, they had to turn down an offer from Mr Plummer of Sydney who wanted to send CWS frozen meat, a refusal they repeated to a New Zealand entrepreneur nearly two years later.[172] But in August of the same year, CWS did agree to supply goods to the Toronto Society, which indicated that it wished to become a member of CWS.[173] From February 1884, the New York Branch began to supply the Toronto Society with coal.[174] In December 1887, the New Plymouth Society of New Zealand applied to join CWS and was accepted.[175] As CWS' international reputation grew, so also did the volume of foreign applications for membership and offers of trading relationships with overseas producers and suppliers. There was a 'pull' factor at work in the globalisation of CWS as well as 'push' factors.

Thus, by 1890, CWS had grown from being essentially a domestic operation to becoming a major international importer of produce and an emerging exporter to foreign societies. It had been a process driven by the huge competitive pressure on the organisation resulting from the preference among member societies to 'shop around' for their supplies, and by the rapid growth of CWS membership, which furnished the organisation with sufficient capital to develop its international commerce. In the process, CWS had developed considerable expertise in managing its international commerce, and it demonstrated an impressive ability to learn from experience and to imbue up and coming managers and directors with that knowledge. Not all of CWS' initiatives had worked, and some of its most successful ones had been spontaneous responses to new opportunities, rather than planned actions. But certain principles and learned practices underpinned much of its overseas expansion: a recognition of the advantages of dealing with local producers and the leverage this gave CWS with local merchants; the importance of securing well-networked positions of authority and strong allies; the benefits of working with a range of suppliers and not tying the organisation to just one; and the value of applying successful strategies in new international contexts. All this amounted to an international strategy for procurement that was much more than the rather haphazard and disorganised approach suggested of the pre-SCM period in much of the business supply chain literature. As will become clear in the next chapter, a foundation had been laid upon which deeper international relationships and supply chains could be built—and it will become clear that vertical integration into production overseas was an important part of this trend. Commodities that have not featured in this chapter—notably tea—will be seen to be important new fields of co-operative wholesale globalisation. It will also become clear that from the 1890s, not only did the geographical reach of the co-operative wholesales extend into new parts of the world and British Empire, but also that the British co-operative movement and its continental counterparts were beginning to develop a truly global perspective and voice and, with them, aspirations for the establishment of a worldwide co-operative economic system.

Notes

1. Wilson, Webster & Vorberg-Rugh, *Building Co-operation* 68.
2. Kinloch & Butt, *History of the Scottish Co-operative Wholesale Society Ltd* 377.
3. Printed Report of CWS presented to quarterly meetings in November and December 1889, Co-operative Wholesale Society Board Minutes (CWSBM). Figures from quarterly reports of the CWS, contained in CWSBMs.
4. Figures from quarterly reports of the CWS, CWSBM.
5. Minutes of General Quarterly Meeting, Manchester 18 June 1881, CWSBM.
6. Kinloch & Butt, *History of the Scottish Co-operative Wholesale Society Ltd* 105–113.
7. Figures from quarterly reports of the CWS, contained in CWSBM.
8. Wilson, Webster & Vorberg-Rugh, *Building Co-operation* 94.
9. Ibid., 93.
10. P. Redfern, *The New History of the CWS* (London, Dent 1938) 3.
11. See J.F. Wilson & A. Popp (eds.), *Industrial Clusters and Regional Business Networks in England c1750–1970* (Aldershot, Ashgate 2003) 1–18 (introduction); F. Carnevali, "'Crooks, Thieves and Receivers': Transaction Costs in Nineteenth Century Industrial Birmingham" *Economic History Review* 57:3 (2004) 533–550.
12. A. Chandler, *Scale and Scope: The Dynamics of Industrial Capitalism* (Cambridge, MA, Harvard University Press 1990).
13. P. Gurney, *Co-operative Culture and the Politics of Consumption in England, c1870–1930* (Manchester, Manchester University Press 1996) 199–201.
14. J.K. Walton, "The Making of a Mass Movement: The Growth of Co-operative Membership in Lancashire 1870–1914" in B. Lancaster & P. Maguire (eds.), *Towards the Co-operative Commonwealth: Essays in the History of Co-operation* (Manchester, Co-operative College and History Workshop Trust 1996) 17–29; 27.
15. Cole, *A Century of Co-operation* 194–195; S. Creighton, "Battersea: The 'Municipal Mecca'" in Lancaster & Maguire (eds.), *Towards the Co-operative Commonwealth* 35–38.
16. letter from J. McKendrick, *Co-operative News* 6 February 1875, 67.
17. M. Purvis, "Stocking the Store: Co-operative Retailers in North-East England and Systems of Wholesale Supply, circa 1860–77" *Business History* 40:4 (1998) 55–78.
18. Wilson, Webster & Vorberg-Rugh, *Building Co-operation* 61.
19. Letter from Dealing with the Wholesale Society, *Co-operative News* 11 March 1876, 123.
20. Letter from Mr Sargent of the Gloucester Society, *Co-operative News* 18 March 1876, 141.

21. Report on Co-operative conference in Exeter on 2 April 1887, *Co-operative News* 16 April 1887, 370.
22. CWS GPCM 8 May & 1 September 1878, National Co-operative Archive (NCA).
23. Minutes of Langley Mill and Aldercar Co-operative Society 23 March 1882 and 11 November 1886, MID/1/2/3/1/1/3 (NCA).
24. Kinloch & Butt, *History of the Scottish Co-operative Wholesale Society Ltd* 86–88.
25. G. Scott, letter, *Co-operative News* 29 June 1878, 429.
26. Report on Conference at Long Easton, *Co-operative News* 1 November 1890, 1102.
27. *Co-operative News* 18 July 1891, 728.
28. "The Wholesale and the Retail Societies" *Co-operative News* 15 March 1879, 171.
29. "Co-operative Societies and the Wholesale" *CWS Annual 1892* 489–521.
30. M. Alman & J.M. Bellamy, "Maxwell, Sir William" in J.M. Bellamy & J. Saville (eds.), *Dictionary of Labour Biography*, vol. 1 (London, Palgrave Macmillan 1972) 234–235; Bonner, *British Co-operation* 502.
31. Wilson, Webster & Vorberg-Rugh, *Building Co-operation* 68–70.
32. J.M. Bellamy & J. Saville, "Mitchell, John Thomas Whitehead" in J.M. Bellamy & J. Saville (eds.), *Dictionary of Labour Biography*, vol. 1 (London, Palgrave Macmillan 1972) 241–242.
33. M. Cole, *Makers of the Labour Movement* (London, Longmans 1948) 131–144.
34. See S. Yeo, *Who Was J.T.W. Mitchell?* (Manchester, Co-operative Press 1995). See especially 33–34 re: Beatrice Web's view of Mitchell.
35. Kinloch & Butt, *History of the Scottish Co-operative Wholesale Society Ltd* 207.
36. CWSBM 7 & 21 November 1863.
37. CWSBM 16 & 28 January 1863.
38. Biography of Andrew on His Death, *Co-operative News* 9 September 1899, 994.
39. GPCM 1 July 1876, 2/0/1, 53.
40. GPCM for 1874–1875 3 November 1875, 175–176.
41. GPCM 30 May 1877, 2/0/1, 155.
42. GPCM 8 December 1876, 2/0/1, 96–98.
43. GPCM for 1874–1875, 25 March 1874, 1–2.
44. GPCM for 1874–1875, 12 May 1874, 21–23.
45. GPCM for 1874–1875, 24 June 1874, 36–37.
46. GPCM for 1874–1875, 15 July 1874, 42–44.
47. Kinloch & Butt, *A History of the Scottish Co-operative Wholesale Society Ltd* 83–84.
48. GPCM 21 June 1882, 2/0/1, 353.
49. GPCM 29 March 1882, 2/0/1, 303 and 5 April 1882, 308.
50. GPCM, 10 December 1994, 2/0/5 124; Kinloch & Butt, *A History of the Scottish Co-operative Wholesale Society Ltd* 210.
51. GPCM 13 January 1887, 2/0/6, 325.
52. Special Joint Committee Meeting, CWSBM 26 July 1884.
53. GPCM 19 November 1884, 2/0/5, 102.
54. CWSBM 25 January 1884.
55. GPCM 27 September 1876, 2/0/1, 78–79.
56. GPCM 5 April 1882, 2/0/1 311; CWSBM 31 March 1882.
57. CWSBM 7 April 1882.
58. CWSBM 5 May 1882.

59. CWSBM 16 November 1883.
60. CWSBM 21 December 1883.
61. GPCM 1 July 1885, 2/0/5, 264–265 and 30 July 1885, 287–288.
62. GPCM 2 December 1886, 2/0/6, 280.
63. CWSBM 31 August 1888.
64. CWSBM Joint Committee Meeting 19 December 1888.
65. CWSBM 15 March 1879; CWS Printed Report for Quarterly Meeting December 1879.
66. CWSBM 22 December 1882.
67. CWSM 25 January 1884.
68. CWSM 26 July 1884.
69. M. Lampe & P. Sharpe, "How the Danes Discovered Britain: The International Integration of the Danish Dairy Industry before 1880" *European Review of Economic History* 19 (2015) 432–453.
70. I. Henriksen, "Avoiding Lock in: Co-operative Creameries in Denmark 1882–1903" *European Review of Economic History* 3 (1999) 57–78; 57.
71. Ibid., 59–60.
72. I. Henriksen, M. Lampe & P. Sharp, "The Role of Technology and Institutions for Growth: Danish Creameries in the Late Nineteenth Century" *European Review of Economic History* 15 (2011) 475–493.
73. I. Henriksen & K.H. O'Rourke, "Incentives, Technology and the Shift to Year Long Dairying in Nineteenth Century Denmark" *Economic History Review* 58:3 (2005) 520–524.
74. D.M. Higgins & M. Mordhorst, "Reputation and Export Performance: Danish Butter Exports and the British Market, c1880–1914" *Business History* 50:2 (2008) 185–294.
75. Ibid., 197.
76. Ibid., 195.
77. I. Henriksen, E. Mclaughlin & P. Sharp, "Contracts and Cooperation: The Relative Failure of the Irish Dairy Industry in the Late Nineteenth Century Reconsidered" *European Review of Economic History* 19 (2015) 412–431; 412.
78. Higgins & Mordhorst, "Reputation and Export Performance" 188.
79. Printed Report of Manchester Quarterly Meeting, March 1879, CWSBM 15 March 1879.
80. CWSBM 5 March 1881; Printed Report of Quarterly Meeting in Manchester 5 March 1881.
81. CWSBM 3 June 1882.
82. GPCM 11 October 1881, 2/0/3, 227.
83. GPCM 15 June 1881, 2/0/3, 169.
84. GPCM 10 October 1881, 2/0/3, 230.
85. GPCM 11 January 1882, 2/0/3, 269.
86. GPCM 18 October 1882, 2/0/4, 52.
87. GPCM 4 October 1883, 2/0/4, 288.
88. GPCM 22 November 1883, 2/0/4, 316.
89. GPCM 31 January 1884, 2/0/4, 369.
90. CWSBM 22 December 1882.
91. GPCM 12 April 1882, 2/0/4, 312–313; GPCM 28 December 1882, 2/0/4, 87.
92. GPCM 4 March 1885, 2/0/5, 182.
93. GPCM 16 December 1885, 2/0/5, 404.
94. CWSBM 29 August 1884.
95. GPCM 19 August 1885, 2/0/5, 303.
96. GPCM 7 September 1887, 2/0/7, 69.
97. GPCM 4 October 1883, 2/0/4, 289.

98. CWSBM 5 October 1883.
99. CWSBM 12 August 1887.
100. GPCM 11 March 1885, 2/0/5, 186.
101. CWSBM 18 February 1884.
102. CWSBM 27 February 1885.
103. CWSBM 10 October 1884 and 17 October 1884.
104. GPCM 26 February 1885, 2/0/5, 176.
105. CWSBM 6 September 1889.
106. CWSBM 20 September 1889.
107. CWSBM 27 September 1889.
108. CWSBM 18 April 1890.
109. Minutes of Joint Committee, CWSBM 25 June 1883.
110. GPCM for 1874–75, 9 September 1874, 60–61.
111. Wilson, Webster & Vorberg-Rugh, *Building Co-operation* 94.
112. CWSBM 12 July 1878.
113. CWSBM 30 November 1878.
114. CWSBM 25 January 1879.
115. Printed Report of CWS Quarterly Meetings March 1879.
116. Manchester Quarterly Meeting Printed Report December 1878, CWSBM 20 December 1878.
117. Wilson, Webster & Vorberg-Rugh, *Building Co-operation* 93.
118. CWSBM 18 October 1879.
119. Printed Report of CWS Manchester Quarterly Meeting December 1879, CWSBM 6 December 1879.
120. Printed Report of CWS Manchester Quarterly Meeting September 1880, CWSBM 4 September 1880.
121. Printed Report of CWS Manchester Quarterly Meeting March 1881, CWSBM 5 March 1881.
122. CWSBM 27 May 1881 and 29 July 1881.
123. CWSBM 16 April 1881.
124. CWSBM 30 April 1881.
125. Printed Report of CWS Manchester Quarterly Meeting June 1881, CWSBM 18 June 1881.
126. CWSBM 29 July 1881.
127. Printed Report of CWS Manchester Quarterly Meeting September 1881, CWSBM 3 September 1881.
128. Printed Report of CWS Manchester Quarterly Meeting December 1881, CWSBM 3 December 1881.
129. Printed Report of CWS Manchester Quarterly Meeting March 1882, CWSBM 4 March 1882.
130. CWSBM 11 April 1884.
131. CWSBM 8 June 1888.
132. CWSBM 21 November 1884.
133. CWSBM 5 March 1886.
134. CWSBM 11 February 1887.
135. CWSBM 26 October 1883.
136. CWSBM 27 June 1884.
137. CWSBM 14 November 1884.
138. CWSBM 21 August 1885.
139. CWSBM 18 June 1887.
140. CWSBM 27 September 1889.
141. CWSBM 17 November 1882.
142. CWSBM 24 November 1882.
143. CWSBM 22 December 1882.

144. CWSBM 29 December 1882.
145. CWSBM 8 November 1883.
146. CWSBM 13 December 1883.
147. CWSBM 4 April 1884.
148. CWSBM 5 December 1884.
149. GPCM 16 October 1884, 2/0/5, 89.
150. GPCM 19 November 1884, 2/0/5, 104.
151. GPCM 14 January 1885, 2/0/5, 148.
152. GPCM 11 February 1885, 2/0/5, 169.
153. GPCM 25 March 1885, 2/0/5, 197.
154. GPCM 30 July 1885, 2/0/5 286.
155. GPCM 12 August 1885, 2/0/5, 296.
156. GPCM 12 October 1887, 2/0/7, 101.
157. CWSBM 8 March 1889.
158. GPCM 6 November 1878, 2/0/1, 365.
159. GPCM 24 June 1880, 2/0/2, 350.
160. GPCM 11 October 1881, 2/0/3, 226.
161. GPCM 16 July 1884, 2/0/5, 9.
162. GPCM 8 June 1885, 2/0/5, 248.
163. CWSBM 4 June 1886.
164. Tweedale's Report, October 1886, Printed in 'Overseas Deputations 1886–1900' NCA.
165. GPCM 27 April 1887, 2/0/6, 436–437.
166. Report on Lord and Tweedale's Trip to Greece and Turkey, 29 July to 23 September 1887, Printed in 'Overseas Deputations 1886–1890'.
167. CWSBM 19 August 1865.
168. CWSBM 4 November 1885; *The Co-operator* 1 February 1866, 206.
169. CWSBM 18 October 1879.
170. GPCM 1 June 1881, 2/0/3, 165.
171. GPCM 28 September 1881, 2/0/3, 222.
172. GPCM 10 July 1882, 2/0/3, 366; GPCM 21 February 1884, 2/0/4, 388.
173. GPCM 30 August 1882, 2/0/4, 26.
174. CWSBM 15 February 1884.
175. GPCM 1 December 1887, 2/0/7, 156.

3 Indian Cuppas, West African Soap and Irish Failures

The Maturing of a Global Supply Network? The CWS' International Trade, British Co-operation and the British State 1890–1918

I

By 1890, then, the co-operative wholesales, principally CWS, had established the basis of a global supply chain network to feed the British co-operative movement with essential commodities in what was becoming an increasingly competitive domestic retail market. It had already amassed a wealth of experience in establishing and running overseas branches, developing new forms of commercial relationship that brought the CWS into direct contact with producers and fostering local networks with people and institutions well placed to promote and protect the interests of the British co-operative international wholesale trade. Far from being haphazard and unplanned, the construction of these overseas connections had resulted from careful research, skilful planning and an ability to adapt flexibly to unexpected opportunities and rapidly changing contexts. Moreover, CWS—the leader in this process of internationalisation—had demonstrated that it could reflect on and learn from its experiences, applying knowledge and strategies applied in one part of the world to other contexts. In addition, the wholesales went to great lengths to ensure that the goods procured from overseas met the requirements of their intended markets: the individual co-operative society consumers and members who would buy the goods in the co-operative stores. CWS ensured that those who led overseas branches would be men experienced in selling to co-operative societies first hand, and they frequently had experience of working for local co-operative societies. CWS also received regular feedback from co-operative societies and their buyers on the quality of goods supplied from abroad; leading overseas branch managers such as Gledhill, Andrew and Dilworth were expected to visit the UK generally, tour societies and be rigorously debriefed by the Board in Manchester, the general committees in Newcastle and London and the SCWS. In this way, CWS ensured that decisions far afield were firmly aligned with domestic consumer demand.

The 1890s ushered in a new period of consolidation, further geographical expansion and, in some cases, vertical integration that took CWS directly into production overseas. It involved greater international supply chain involvement in some commodities, such as tea, and expansion in certain well-established foreign footholds into new commodities, notably bacon production in Denmark. As always, the wider context is all important in understanding these developments. The growth of British co-operation accelerated during this period. Membership of co-operative societies in Britain almost doubled from 1.7 million in 1890 to over 3 million by 1914, a figure rendered all the more impressive by the fact that many societies during this period only allowed one person from a family to become a member.[1] Co-operative society trade grew from the custom of non-members as well as members. By 1914, co-operative societies commanded about 8 per cent of the total retail trade of the UK, and about 20 per cent of the trade in groceries and food.[2] As a result, CWS sales boomed, from just under £7 million per annum in 1890, to £14.7 million in 1900, and onwards and upwards to £25 million in 1910 and £41.5 million in 1915. Even allowing for inflation, this was spectacular growth.[3] But the pressure of competition also intensified during this period, and it took on political as well as commercial form.

Firstly, major changes were afoot in the wider retail sector. From 1890, a group of multiple retail chain stores began to emerge. Eastman's the butchers, Home & Colonial and Lipton's (which specialised in tea) and Maypole (dairy produce) expanded their branches, reaching the hundreds by 1914. Future giants such as Marks & Spencers and Boots also began to make their presence felt on the high street.[4] The competition these multiples offered to the co-operative movement was made more conspicuous and felt more sharply by the modern advertising and marketing strategies they adopted. Secondly, the issue of reluctance on the part of some societies to demonstrate customer loyalty to the wholesales remained a pressing factor in CWS/SCWS calculations, and this also continued to drive efforts to maximise wholesale efficiency and competitiveness. Thirdly, smaller shopkeepers and some manufacturers—who were also under pressure from the growth of the multiples as well as the co-operative movement—were also increasingly active in protecting their interests. As well as forming their own trade associations, many independent shopkeepers stepped up the aggressive anti-co-operative campaigns that had appeared sporadically in the 1870s and 1880s. The boycott of sales to co-operative societies by the Master Fleshers of Glasgow in 1899 was mentioned in the last chapter.[5] The boycott of the St Helens Society in 1902 represented the high point in this anti-co-operative agitation, though the co-operative movement proved itself adept at defending itself. But increasingly, fractious relations took on both a legal and a political dimension. For example, in 1905 a government committee investigated whether co-operative dividends should be taxable as profits, which up till this point had not been the case. While the committee found in favour of not taxing dividends, private enterprise had lobbied hard to reverse this, alerting the co-operative movement to the likelihood of a stronger political attempt to outflank the movement in the future.[6]

This chapter will outline some of the new and emergent strategies to deal with this much tougher environment. The second section will show how existing overseas branches were developed and strengthened, especially through expansion into new commodities and by 'downward' vertical integration into production. In the third section, it will be shown that the period was not one of unremitting success, that retreat as well as expansion was part of the process of maturation and that some initiatives were an abysmal failure, even though guided by experience and careful future planning. The fourth section will consider the geographical expansion of wholesale operations and what drove it on. It will be seen that movement into new regions was often accompanied by the kind of vertical integration outlined in the second section. The final part of the chapter is concerned with how political developments affected CWS global interests, especially as consumer and other forms of co-operation emerged in other countries. There were efforts to build commercial and political links between national co-operative movements, which culminated in the formation of the International Co-operative Alliance (ICA) in 1893. In addition, the relationship between the British state and the co-operative movement grew in importance in reference to international relations and policy in two important ways. Firstly, the overseas activities of CWS made it an important political actor in the debate emerging after 1900 about whether Britain should continue its policy of international free trade or opt for Tariff Reform, as advocated by the Conservative politician Joseph Chamberlain and the Tariff Reform League from 1903. It will be seen that CWS emerged as a potent ally of the free trade lobby that won the day—at least until the First World War. Secondly, certain forms of co-operation, including credit and agricultural producer co-operatives, began to be seen by the British state as useful innovations to promote colonial development, and the extent to which the British wholesales had an input into that movement will be an important question. Finally, as part of the section on the British state, the chapter will examine how the First World War impacted upon the wholesales' international networks and interests, and how national domestic problems of war began to shape co-operative post-war plans.

II

If the period to 1890 had been one of establishing overseas depots to enable CWS to trade competitively for the produce of North America and parts of Northern Europe, the quarter of a century that followed saw these commercial bridgeheads built and expanded upon to meet the growing demand of British co-operative members for food. In northern Europe, Denmark, Sweden and Finland, CWS set about expanding its operations to procure butter and bacon, and also began to source other produce. In October 1891, John Andrew's assistant, Mr Madsen, was put in charge as buyer at a new depot at Aarhus, on a salary of £300 per annum.[7] Madsen was given permission to draw £5,000 from the bank to fund his purchases, and it was indicative of the success of the new depot that this was doubled to £10,000 per week within two years of opening.[8] Encouraged by this success, in late September 1894 Mr Pearson, a senior buyer, was sent to Scandinavia to explore the possibility of other new depots.[9] The result was CWS' first depot in Sweden, at Gothenburg, opened in collaboration with SCWS in August 1895.[10] Another assistant and acolyte of Andrew's, Kongstad Petersen, was promoted to head the new depot.[11] In the early days he worked closely with Andrew, and as had proved so successful in Copenhagen, Petersen quickly set about approaching local farmers to supply butter.[12] But the new depot encountered a rather less supportive state apparatus than had been found in Denmark. In November 1895, the Swedish authorities refused to allow CWS to trade in Sweden under its own name; it took lobbying of the Swedish ambassador in London, a contentious court case in February 1896 and a further period of uncertainty before CWS was permitted to trade in the names of the President and the Secretary of CWS.[13] There were also disputes over taxation, which resulted in lengthy legal disputes.[14] But such was the demand for Scandinavian butter that trade expanded. Further new depots in Denmark were established at Odense (raised from a minor outpost to a full depot in November 1899) and Esbjerg in July 1905.[15] Both proved to be roaring successes in the butter trade. Initially Odense had a weekly credit arrangement at the bank for £8,000, but such was the demand for its butter purchases in the UK that this was doubled by December 1902.[16] At Esbjerg, weekly bank drawing limits were raised from £6,000 in August 1905 to £23,385 in June 1914.[17] Copenhagen's limit had been raised to £29,000 in June 1914 from £18,000 in March 1891.[18] By July 1902, it was boasted that in its 21 years of existence, the Copenhagen branch had shipped £16 million of commodities to the UK.[19] By the eve of the First World War, CWS and SCWS commanded a formidable chain of butter buying depots across Scandinavia that delivered a significant proportion of the butter needs of the British population. By 1906, Denmark represented the largest source of foreign butter into the UK, with 83,788 of the 216,917 tons imported in that year.[20] As early as 1899, Denmark was the largest foreign supplier for CWS in terms of value, with almost £1 million of Danish produce (mainly butter) imported in the half year to 23 December 1899 alone.[21] One Danish newspaper, on the death in August 1899 of John Andrew, the first CWS manager in Denmark, said that about one-fifth of Danish exports to the UK had been channelled through the Copenhagen CWS branch.[22] But, notwithstanding the heavily co-operativised nature of the

Danish butter industry, it will be seen relations between it and CWS gave rise to considerable friction, especially over price.

Danish bacon also became an important CWS commodity. In 1895, information was passed to the London branch of CWS that a ring of London bacon factors had sought to persuade Danish farmers and merchants to stop supplying CWS. They requested that Benjamin Jones, one of their leading figures, be permitted to accompany the next CWS deputation to Denmark, to try to ensure the security of bacon supplies.[23] The London ring seems to have continued its threat to the CWS Danish trade. CWS was considering establishing its own bacon curing facility in Ireland as early as May 1897.[24] In June 1899, a CWS deputation to Denmark had agreed to rearrange its bacon purchases through a London agent, who charged 0.5 per cent commission, instead of through its own Aarhus depot.[25] But CWS clearly bridled in the face of this concerted attempt by London merchants to undermine their freedom to trade, and the remedy was soon identified as direct entry by CWS into producing its own bacon, as a way of breaking the apparent collusion of Danish producers and London merchants. In October 1899, a deputation to Denmark reported the availability in Herning of land for a slaughtery that could be rented by CWS as a first step towards producing its own bacon.[26] Such was the urgency of the situation that, within a month, CWS had taken out a five-year lease for the property at an annual rent of £240.[27] Following construction, the factory was opened in the summer of 1901.[28] This came not a moment too soon. The London branch of CWS had encountered severe difficulties in securing bacon from suppliers earlier in the summer, and in June was greatly relieved to hear not only of the imminent opening of the Herning facility but also of plans for a CWS bacon factory in Tralee, southern Ireland.[29] Following its construction, the Tralee bacon factory opened for business in September 1901.[30] The London branch continued to complain of the high prices it had to pay for bacon due to the 'ring' of bacon factors in the capital, even after Herning was up and running.[31] Once again, a key factor driving CWS towards downward vertical integration of its supply chain to producers was the fierce hostility of certain sectors of private enterprise in the domestic market. Notwithstanding problems of losses on Herning in 1902 and 1905, and problems of embezzlement in 1906, CWS remained firm in its commitment to the factory—such was its concern about resisting the perceived threat from bacon wholesalers, especially in light of a concerted assault of private trading interests on co-operation and recent memories of the boycott of the Glasgow Master Fleshers in 1896.[32] Ultimately, the patience paid off so well that by 1912 the Herning building was extended at a cost of £857.[33] The CWS' efforts to defend its interests in this commodity were also assisted by the advance of co-operative bacon production in Denmark, which seems to have harboured a strong ideological affinity with fellow co-operators in the UK. In June 1899, Mr Madsen, a senior CWS official, attended a meeting of the Committee of Associated Bacon Slaughteries of Denmark.[34] In 1908, it was reported that the Holbeck Co-operative Slaughtery was the single largest supplier of bacon to CWS, a relationship that prompted a deputation to it to try to secure better terms of trade.[35] By 1912, 63 per cent of Danish pigs were produced by the country's 38 co-operative slaughteries, which had come to dominate Danish bacon production since the opening of the first co-operative slaughtery in 1887.[36]

CWS bacon production demonstrated the same efforts at international co-ordination that had characterised the development of its butter interests in northern Europe. Attempts were made to boost profits in both Tralee and Herning by developing a common policy for the disposal of offal.[37] More widely, CWS and SCWS consolidated their position in Scandinavia (especially Denmark) by deepening their commercial relations with the Danish co-operative movement, and within the local commercial world more generally. For example, CWS exported bran, a by-product of its flour mill at Dunston near Newcastle, for animal feed. In 1901–2, 200 tons of bran were supplied by CWS to Danish co-operative dairies to help with winter feed.[38] Halpin followed Andrew as a *grosserer*, a member of the *grosserer-societet*—The Merchants Society, a commercial body that brought the CWS manager into intimate contact with Denmark's relatively small mercantile community, and that also controlled the nation's stock exchange.[39] A year later, Mr Kirchoff, manager of the CWS Odense branch, joined Halpin as a grosserer.[40] The ongoing relationship with the Danish CWS remained an important source of influence for CWS, and care was taken not to undermine this relationship. Thus, when in November 1901 the Haag Co-operative Society asked CWS to supply it, they were refused and redirected to their own Danish CWS for supplies.[41] In fact, CWS were suppliers for the Danish CWS, an arrangement that underpinned the warm fraternal political relations between the two bodies.[42] Notwithstanding these well-embedded CWS political and commercial roots in Denmark, there were areas of friction. Even with their unparalleled reputation for quality, Danish butter producers still felt fierce criticism from CWS and its member societies when quality failed to satisfy. None other than the Rochdale Pioneers complained in October 1901 about the quality of Danish butter they had received through CWS.[43] But a much more difficult problem was the increasing price that Danish butter began to command in the market. By the mid-1890s, this was beginning to cause some concern, and John Andrew was asked to report on how Danish butter prices were set.[44] A committee of merchants and farmers met to set prices, and CWS had a representative on this committee, but it struggled to hold down prices as demand for Danish butter on the international market grew rapidly. Matters became especially difficult after mid-1912, when the committee was split into two separate committees (one each for farmers and merchants), in which the farmers tended to have the dominant position.[45] For this reason, from the early 1890s, CWS began to look to boost Ireland's position as a butter supplier to the British market, a strategy that, as will be seen, ultimately had to be abandoned.

Similar steps were also taken to deepen the command of CWS and SCWS in North America as a source of foodstuffs. An important manifestation of this was the growth in CWS wheat purchases from the 1890s, a move that reflected the organisation's expansion into flour milling. Co-operative mills had operated in Britain since the 1850s, and by the 1880s there were 30 to 40 of these across the country.[46] Initially, this made CWS hesitate to incite the hostility of the wider movement by developing its own capacity, but falling wheat prices, technological advances in flour production and increased CWS flour imports from the continent persuaded CWS leaders that the organisation could not afford to leave flour milling to emergent new private capitalist organisations.[47] The period 1890 to 1914 saw a dramatic expansion of milling capacity, beginning with the opening of the CWS Dunston mill in 1891, the Silvertown mill (London) in 1900, the acquisition of the Rochdale, Star (Oldham) and Sun (Manchester) mills in 1906 and completed by the opening of Avonmouth (Bristol) mill in 1910.[48] There were parallel developments north of the border. In 1894, SCWS opened its Chancelot mill in Leith, followed by its second mill in Leith, Junction mill, in 1897; the Regent mills in Partick were acquired in 1907.[49] During the 1890s, orders for wheat through the New York depot became more frequent. SCWS identified this as important for their new mill in November 1894.[50] By March 1900, the Boston firm of Messrs Blood & Hale proposed that orders for SCWS and CWS be consolidated, as orders to them from the various CWS branches and the CWS were coming in so frequently.[51] So substantial were the New York branch's purchases, and so well connected with the trade was it, that a Dutch co-operative society, *Nederlandschen Cooperatieven Bond*, asked for the CWS depot to purchase wheat for them.[52] But perhaps the clearest signal of CWS' intentions to expand its purchases was its decision to establish another depot at Montreal in 1894.[53] Initially progress was slow, as CWS flour milling capacity was too limited for the potentialities of the wheat trade to be realised. In August 1905, the Montreal depot had to refuse an offer to buy 200,000 bushels of wheat from Regina Wheat Growers because of lack of capacity to deal with such a large order both in Canada and UK.[54] It hesitated when a similar offer was made by the Farmers Grain and Supply Company of Spokane, Washington, which handled 2 million bushels of wheat during that year.[55] But this situation was about to change radically—not only as a result of the acquisition of the Star, Sun and Rochdale mills but also because of a bold initiative from SCWS. In December 1905, SCWS announced it intended to establish a wheat buying depot at Winnipeg.[56]

Uncertain that it could take advantage of the depot, CWS initially hesitated when SCWS invited their involvement, indicating that it wanted to see how its negotiations to acquire the Sun, Star and Rochdale mills would proceed.[57] It was not until August 1906, by which time CWS was confident of acquisition of its new mills, that CWS agreed to become full partners in the depot.[58] It proved to be a wise decision. By 1913, Winnipeg had eclipsed Montreal in terms of the scale of business undertaken. Its turnover in that year was £363,953, compared with less than £15,000 at Montreal, and it generated a profit of £2,039.[59] By the outbreak of the First World War, the wholesales were major players in the wheat trade and flour milling, and they began to buy wheat from other sources, notably South America and Australia.

The extension of depots and operations in Scandinavia and North America also saw the growth of relatively new lines of trade. Tinned salmon and fruit from the Pacific Coast became increasingly important, so much so that by 1909, on the advice of a deputation sent to North America, the Board of Directors instructed that CWS consolidate its dealings with several major companies best equipped to meet CWS demands, particularly salmon from the British Columbia Packing Company and fruit from the California Packers Association. So substantial was the latter that the Board wanted direct trade between California and Manchester rather than through the New York depot.[60] Wieland, manager of the Montreal depot, was instructed to build links with cheese producers in his locality to develop this line of commerce. In Scandinavia, new lines of commerce also emerged. In 1899, CWS deputations went to Sweden and Norway to buy timber for CWS furniture and cabinet works.[61] Then, in 1912, a deputation made a deal with the firm of Tingstad's in Gothenburg, for £5,500 worth of wood for boxes, amounting to 25 per cent of CWS needs for its boxes for that year.[62] In this way, Scandinavia and North America, already the leading sectors of CWS overseas expansion before 1890, were developed and consolidated in the last decades before the First World War.

III

However, the period between 1890 and 1914 saw retreat as well as advance in the wholesales' international commercial strategies and activities. The period saw CWS/SCWS first expand and then withdraw from key areas of commercial activity, with important implications for the global reach and strategies of the wholesales. The first was in a sphere that was very close to home and would not have been regarded as 'international' at the time, but might well be regarded as 'imperial' today: the expansion of CWS into butter production in Ireland. Either way, it will be seen that the initiative was certainly closely linked with CWS' international commercial strategy. The second was in shipping, a field of activity that by the

1890s had almost come to symbolise CWS' aim to become a global oper-ator. The Irish episode showed that CWS was as capable of commercial misjudgement as any private organisation, while both demonstrated that it had the capacity to adjust strategy to meet changing circumstances.

As seen, CWS had been buying butter in Ireland since the 1860s, but in the mid-1890s it decided to move into butter production on a large scale by acquiring or building creameries in south-west Ireland. From the out-set, this was a deeply controversial move within the co-operative move-ment. Since 1889, the aristocratic champion of agricultural co-operation, Horace Plunkett, and Robert A. Anderson, a former land agent, had cam-paigned to promote the growth of co-operative creameries in Ireland on the Danish model, in which the farmers who supplied the milk would own the creamery and share the profits.[63] Initially, the CWS, already a major presence in Ireland though its butter-buying depots, were support-ive of the idea of Irish co-operative creameries, and in fact led the way. In 1889, the first Irish co-operative creamery was established at Drum-collogher, County Limerick, largely due to the efforts of the CWS agent W.L. Stokes. CWS took up ten £1 shares in the society, as it did with the Castlemahon Creamery, another CWS-sponsored co-operative society.[64] Plunkett and his supporters, inspired by this initiative, launched their own co-operative creamery campaign, establishing their first at Butte-vant, County Cork in April 1890; and by 1895, the umbrella organisa-tion founded in 1894 by Plunkett, the Irish Agricultural Organisation Society (IAOS), boasted 33 dairy co-operative societies, all in south-west Ireland.[65] But relations between IAOS and CWS began to break down when, in 1895, CWS bought its first creamery and made it clear that it planned to buy or build many more.

The reasons for this decision by CWS reflected two urgent concerns it had about the butter trade and Ireland's position in it. Firstly, the deep problems of poverty in the Irish countryside raised doubts in the minds of CWS leaders about the capacity of even a successful farmers' co-operative movement to improve productivity and raise living standards as speedily as it had in Denmark. Indeed, it was the near failure of the co-operative dairy society at Castlemahon that began the process of CWS acquiring creameries, when it stepped in to take it over in January 1895.[66] Secondly, doubts about the pace at which Irish farmers' co-operation could mod-ernise Irish butter production, improve quality and increase output were intensified by a growing awareness of CWS dependence on Danish but-ter supplies, the price of which was rising steadily. A thriving Irish butter industry would provide an ideal alternative to Danish supplies, keeping prices down by expanding production and strengthening the position of co-operative consumers in the UK. It came to believe that the shortage of capital faced by many poor Irish farmers was a major obstacle to the rapid transformation of butter production, and that the British wholesales alone possessed the resources to force the pace of change. Its perspective, of course, was one that reflected the interests of the co-operative consumer, and almost from the outset it triggered bitter opposition from Plunkett and IAOS, for whom agricultural co-operation was essentially about producer interests and rural development.[67]

For Plunkett, CWS creameries that purchased milk from local farmers to generate butter and profits for English co-operative consumers were no better than capitalist creameries buying milk for private profit. Plunkett feared that an extensive intervention in production by CWS would stifle the movement to create co-operative creameries. As a result, the next ten years were dogged by bitter rivalry and recriminations between IAOS and CWS. Sometimes it erupted locally, as CWS lobbied local farmers about the benefits of having a local CWS creamery to which they could sell milk. In Blarney in June 1897, a CWS meeting for local farmers was disrupted by supporters of IAOS who, having tried unsuccessfully to set up their own meeting, attended the CWS meeting and made proceedings most unpleasant.[68] By October of the same year, CWS was seeking legal advice about dealing with IAOS disruption of its efforts to win over farmers.[69] When the SCWS started to open its own creameries with a major creamery at Enniskillen in 1898, it also faced fierce opposition from IAOS.[70] Of course, the IAOS network of co-operative creameries was expanding at the same time. Between 1895 and 1905, the numbers of co-operative creameries in Ireland rose from 56 to 275.[71] Almost inevitably, this led to local clashes when CWS tried to establish creameries near co-operative ones. In October 1898, IAOS complained that a CWS creamery planned for Tankerton Crossroads threatened to undermine the nearby Lissarda Co-operative Dairy Society.[72] A similar clash occurred between IAOS and SCWS over a planned SCWS auxiliary creamery at Glenfarne in September 1901.[73] In summer 1899, the IAOS' weekly paper, *The Irish Homestead*, accused CWS of exploiting farmers by underpaying for milk from Irish farmers, an accusation that was picked up by some member societies of CWS.[74] Furious, W.L. Stokes challenged IAOS to allow a comparison by a public auditor of the books of six CWS creameries with six affiliated with IAOS, to demonstrate that there was no exploitation.[75] IAOS declined.[76] There were efforts to solve difference by negotiation, notably at a conference in Liverpool on 10 January 1900.[77] CWS took a long time to consider the report emerging from the conference, but no agreement could be reached.[78] A second conference in Dublin in May 1900, however, did set up a joint sub-committee to explore the possibility of greater co-operation between IAOS and CWS in the future.[79] A major sticking point was CWS' insistence of the need for the rapid development in Ireland of winter dairying along Danish lines, a course rejected by Plunkett on grounds of its impracticality given the lack of capital of Irish farmers. This only reinforced CWS stereotypes of the 'backward' Irish farmer.[80] A nadir was reached when Plunkett roundly condemned the British wholesales for their policies in Ireland in a speech he delivered to the National

Co-operative Festival in August 1901. He specifically blamed them for damaging the growth of agricultural and producer co-operatives.[81] By this time, it clear that many in IAOS regarded the activities of the wholesales as symptomatic of British imperialist attitudes towards Ireland.[82] But it would be several more years before the differences were finally resolved.

CWS creamery activities were concentrated in south-west Ireland, particularly in Kerry and Limerick, and were controlled by three depots at Tralee, Cork and Limerick. A pattern of major creameries, supported by smaller auxiliary creameries that processed milk from farmers further away from the main creameries, ensured a reasonably reliable output of butter from the region. Advances of money to farmers facilitated a steady supply of milk. Considerable sums were invested in leases, plants and machinery, totalling almost £100,000 by 1900.[83] This had risen to £120,000 by 1903.[84] There was a conscious effort to learn from Danish methods and technology. Right at the beginning of the CWS venture into creameries, John Andrew in Copenhagen was asked to supply a plan of a Danish creamery, a copy of which was sent to Stokes as a blueprint for CWS Irish creameries.[85] Occasionally, CWS butter managers were sent to Denmark to witness Danish methods first-hand, as was the Limerick Depot manager in early 1899.[86] Comparisons of the prices and quality of Danish and Irish butter were regularly made.[87] By March 1905, CWS was operating 38 main creameries and 50 auxiliaries, although this was eclipsed by IAOS, which by 1901 led 236 dairy co-operatives with a total membership of 26,577.[88]

Yet for all this investment and effort, the Irish creamery initiative proved to be an expensive failure. The warning signs were apparent as early as 1899. The creameries showed a loss of £1,476 over the year to December 1899.[89] Unease among the membership was recorded at the June quarterly meeting in Manchester, and the leadership equivocated, claiming that the loss was a blip that would be rectified by the promotion of winter dairying.[90] But matters worsened dramatically. Losses spiralled in 1902 and 1903. The half year to June 1902 alone showed a loss of £10,271, and the same period in 1903 registered a loss of £11,822.[91] In March 1904, an annual loss of £12,369 was announced, followed by considerable soul searching and criticism of the leadership at the various CWS quarterly meetings.[92] Matters improved slightly in 1905, but even then losses for the year were £9,045.[93] By March 1908, the Manchester quarterly meeting were told that £52,000 had been lost on the CWS Irish creameries to date.[94] The effect on CWS policy was dramatic and certainly paved the way for a deal with IAOS. This came at a conference on 16 January 1909, at which CWS agreed to transfer its creameries over time to local dairy co-operative societies and established the principle of an arbitrator who would secure agreement on prices to be paid for the creameries.[95] In fact, the writing was on the wall three years earlier. In

October 1906, nine major creameries were identified as ones to be closed or sold off.[96] By April 1907, CWS had a list of creameries it was prepared to sell off to dairy co-operatives under the wing of the IAOS, if the price was right.[97] The disposals took place quite quickly. During 1910, eight main creameries and 14 auxiliaries were sold or closed.[98] By March 1913, CWS owned just five creameries and ten auxiliaries. It had ceased to be a major player in Irish butter production.[99] A brave face was put on the failure of the experiment. It was claimed that the CWS creameries had achieved a measure of success if only by curbing the near monopoly of butter supplies the Danes had carved out for themselves. It was contended that the experiment had at least limited the price that CWS would have had to pay for Danish butter if the CWS creameries had not been in operation.[100] Such claims were viewed with scepticism.

Why had the CWS initiative failed? Contemporaries blamed the backwardness of the Irish farmer, or the blinkered refusal of IAOS to effectively promote winter dairying, without which many CWS creameries had had to close during the winter months. Recent research has focused on the wider question of the relatively limited achievements of Irish co-operative dairying compared to its Danish counterpart. While this has not specifically examined the experience of CWS, some of the problems identified seem also to have been a hindrance for CWS. A key problem was the relative weakness of contract law in Ireland in respect of the legal obligation of farmer to supply milk under contracts with creameries of all description.[101] It was notoriously difficult to hold farmers accountable in the courts if they did not deliver. This was exacerbated by the crowded and varied field of creameries seeking to buy the milk of farmers. CWS, IAOS co-operative creameries and private creameries all competed fiercely with each other, and farmers were easily tempted to switch allegiance in response to short-term opportunities to secure a better price.[102] The private sector was especially powerful, with major players such as the Condensed Milk Company of Ireland Ltd, as well as a host of smaller companies.[103] Certainly the CWS' own records show that milk supplies became a problem, especially after 1900. Some farmers were slow to repay advances from CWS. From the opening of the first CWS creamery in 1895 until March 1899, £23,881 was advanced to farmers, but a substantial £6,258 had not been settled by either cash or milk delivered.[104] By July 1902, the Limerick depot manager was reporting a shortfall in milk supplies, simply because private creameries were paying the farmers more. The CWS Board allowed him to pay more to the suppliers.[105] But in November, when a similar plea was received from a depot manager, this was refused on the grounds that it might incur serious loss.[106] Meanwhile, debts owed by the farmers rose sharply, reaching £27,665 by the end of November 1902.[107] Managers of the Limerick and Cork depots were reprimanded for this. In December 1903, supply had become such an issue that the Board gave the Limerick depot manager instructions to close some creameries where milk supplies were inadequate.[108] The effect on profitability was laid out starkly by the Tralee depot manager in May 1904, when he attributed losses to the fact that he had to pay for milk at 3s-5d per gallon, while the low price of butter ensured a weekly loss of £90 per week.[109] The experience of CWS certainly indicates that fierce competition was an important factor in CWS failure. There may also have been some truth in the effects of a lack of winter dairying, but some historians have pointed out that the Irish climate was not particularly conducive to success in this field.[110] From a co-operative perspective, there were two fundamental flaws in the CWS strategy. Firstly, it never resolved the conflict between consumer and producer interests in creameries, and this not only led to the political conflict with IAOS but also created divisions within the CWS that arguably sapped commitment to the initiative. Secondly, in other contexts the CWS strategy of securing control of, or proximity to, the producers of commodities had achieved some success, but not in this one. This stemmed from the fact that competition for milk was so intense that the expected advantages of CWS creamery managers negotiating directly with farmers never really materialised. CWS hoped to bring the scale and efficiency of Irish butter production up to Danish levels. But this was simply not possible. Ultimately, CWS had little option but to withdraw wounded from the field.

The other area in which contraction rather than expansion resulted in this period was in shipping. The original motive behind CWS involvement had been the high freight rates charged by private shipping firms. The aim was that by running its own ships, CWS could pressure those firms to curb this tendency. But CWS found that the costs of running its own ships were very high indeed. The high level of capital investment in the ships themselves, the expense of maintenance and the tough competition for freights from other shippers all coalesced to inflict considerable losses. For example, for the year to September 1897, including depreciation of assets, a loss of £2,425 was incurred. Various factors were blamed, including low freight rates and a strike in Hamburg.[111] But 1898 and following years saw a recovery, with profits being returned in 1898, and bumper profits of over £10,000 in the year to March 1900.[112] Similar results were evident between 1901 and 1903, but another downturn in 1905 saw losses of £1,370 in the quarter to September 1905.[113] Herein lay the problem that nagged at CWS members: shipping could generate spectacular profits but equally spectacular losses. The unpredictability of international trade with the continent at a time when many European countries were protectionist, combined with the intensity of competition from private shippers and the high capital costs of building, buying and maintaining a fleet of ships, meant that CWS involvement always had its critics.

The fundamental reason for CWS shipping was to protect the organisation's import of continental commodities from exploitation by ruthless and ideologically hostile shipping companies. But profitability required that lucrative export cargoes for private enterprise would have to be carried on CWS ships. Coal was the backbone of this export trade, especially to Hamburg and Calais. Major contracts with coal producers were renewed annually. Among the largest CWS customers in the UK for Hamburg were Pope & Pearson, Richard Fosdick and Hemsworths, who between them shipped thousands of tons of coal on CWS ships.[114] To Calais, CWS exported for Hemsworths, Hartleys, Fosdick and Kittle & Co.[115] CWS also exported coal to Rouen from Swansea in the early 1900s for the French firm Leblanc, Charlemaine, Guian & Co.[116] On their return journeys, CWS vessels brought sugar from the continent, especially from Hamburg and Calais, as well as wheat, butter, vegetables and a wide range of goods bound for co-operative societies across the UK.[117] More controversially, CWS also supplied non-co-operative customers such as Hogg & Co. and McFie's, the Liverpool sugar refiner.[118] Superficially, reviewing profits in the 1890s and early 1900s, and the role shipping played in some of CWS' continental operations, this line of the business looked set fair for the future.

But CWS engagement in shipping was problematic for a variety of reasons. Firstly, CWS' fleet was simply not large enough to accommodate the expanding range of CWS overseas trading interests in Europe, let alone across the Atlantic, concentrated as it was on a few lines between the UK and Hamburg, Calais and Rouen. Dried fruit from Greece was imported on vessels chartered from other companies, such as Cunard.[119] When occasionally the question of a CWS ship being sent to Greece was considered, CWS decided that commitments elsewhere dictated chartering a vessel from a private firm instead.[120] Butter from Denmark—probably the most important branch of CWS commerce with the continent—was shipped via a range of private firms, not by the CWS' own vessels. The fact that it had to be shipped from ten different Scandinavian ports was a decisive factor.[121] Thus, CWS shipping was not seen as being quite as important to CWS overseas commerce as its advocates claimed. Besides, the growth of CWS trade meant that it was well placed to benefit from competition among shippers to carry its increasingly voluminous and lucrative trade. Secondly, shipping was an extremely competitive business, and relations with rival shipping firms were always tense. Efforts were made to prevent a self-defeating race to the bottom in freight charges through shipping conferences and other agreements, but making them stick proved fiendishly difficult. In 1895, bitter competition between CWS and the Goole Steamship Company (Goole SS) was softened by an agreement by both to 'pool' freights.[122] This involved a sharing of cargoes and profits between the two companies, especially on the Hamburg route. As similar deal was made among shippers in Hull in respect of imports of fruit from Hamburg later that summer.[123] But relations remained uneasy. In September 1897, CWS threatened legal action against the Harbour Master at Hull for allegedly showing favouritism to a rival shipping company.[124] So fractious were relations that in December 1900 CWS withdrew from the Humber Conference, a body that set freight rates among a range of competing shippers.[125] There were other signs of CWS concern. In September 1901, a proposal that CWS acquire two new steamships met with heated opposition at the Manchester quarterly meeting and at a meeting in Lincoln.[126] Then, in spring 1902, dissatisfaction with Messrs Fuhrmann & Co., the private shipping brokerage firm CWS had used in Hamburg since the 1880s, resulted in CWS taking over its own ship brokerage from its Hamburg depot.[127] Matters became tense when Fuhrmanns approached the General Steam Navigation Co. in London to commence a service between Goole and Hamburg. The firm declined when it ascertained that CWS did not intend to withdraw their own service, as implied to them by Fuhrmann.[128]

However, the decisive development in precipitating a CWS retreat from a major portion of its shipping commitments came in November 1903, when the Lancashire and Yorkshire Railway Company decided to branch out into shipping. It indicated its intention to put a Bill before parliament to enable it to run steamship services from Goole to Hamburg and other continental ports.[129] Both CWS and the Goole Steamship Company petitioned against the Bill—but were unsuccessful.[130] By summer 1905, the CWS leadership had concluded that on the Goole to Hamburg line, the best strategy was to seek a deal with Lancashire and Yorkshire, and withdraw the CWS service altogether.[131] On 15 November 1905, CWS sold its three steamships and goodwill in the Goole to Hamburg line to Lancashire and Yorkshire for £80,000.[132] A key condition of the deal was that Lancashire and Yorkshire would guarantee the lowest possible freight charges for CWS goods carried on its ships.[133] CWS shipping staff in Hamburg and Goole were transferred to Lancashire and Yorkshire, and the CWS shipping department manager, C.R. Cameron, also joined that company.[134] It was the beginning of a process of scaling back CWS shipping operations. The CWS Board were very clear about the reasons for this in its June 1906 report to the Manchester quarterly meeting. With its combination of rail and shipping, as well as its formidable capital resources, Lancashire and Yorkshire would quickly come to dominate shipping between Goole and the continent, and CWS would struggle to compete. Lancashire and Yorkshire had also bought the ships of the Goole Steamship Company, equipping it with a formidable fleet with which to undertake business. But other, wider changes argued for retrenchment. Hamburg had ceased to become as important a centre of CWS trade. As the German economy grew, it absorbed a greater proportion of the Kiel butter that had initially attracted CWS to the city. Furthermore, the Manchester Ship Canal had revolutionised shipping, making freight rates more competitive, and it became more important for CWS trade as it acquired factories and warehouses on its banks. Quite simply, CWS shipping had served its purpose. The CWS was big enough, and the private shipping sector competitive enough, for gradual withdrawal to be the most logical strategy.[135]

Both the Irish and the shipping examples demonstrate that while expansion was certainly the predominant theme of the period before the First World War, it was by no means one of untarnished success or thoughtless growth. The Irish experiment had been borne of the need to increase supplies of high-quality butter and bacon and to rebalance CWS bargaining power in its relations with Danish producers. It would be hard to argue, given the scale of financial losses incurred, that this had been anything other than a serious failure—and one that undermined unity within the wider co-operative movement. Yet it is hard to dismiss claims by defenders of the Irish strategy that it had some effect upon butter prices or in foiling the machinations of the London 'bacon ring'. More significant, perhaps, is that CWS at least managed to extricate itself from its Irish entanglements in a way that both limited long-term losses and rebuilt some bridges with the Irish movement. CWS had managed its way out of a difficult commercial and political position through some careful and shrewd negotiation and realistic retrenchment. This pragmatism and strategic acumen were even more apparent in its dealings with Lancashire and Yorkshire over the Goole–Hamburg line. Here, what had become a reasonably profitable field of activity was abandoned because of a prescient appreciation that in the long run Hamburg would become less important to CWS, and that a collaborative relationship with a formidable transport operator like Lancashire and Yorkshire would serve CWS and the movement much better than a futile and costly competitive struggle. In the end, both episodes showed that the leadership of CWS had developed an increasingly sophisticated commercial outlook, which allowed for strategies of orderly retreat as well as ambitious expansion. They show that CWS, by the first decade of the twentieth century, had matured as a business organisation.

IV

While there were abortive and abandoned initiatives, the period also saw major new areas of expansion and vertical integration that proved to be much more successful. As in the past, key drivers were competitive pressures from within the UK. One of the most important examples of how domestic commercial competition drove CWS towards stronger integration of overseas supply chains right down to the level of production was tea. As a household staple in Britain, co-operative societies were major purchasers of tea, and from its earliest days CWS sought to imprint itself as a major source of supply. But early CWS efforts to buy tea were unsuccessful, and many societies opted to buy from private suppliers. A turning point came in 1869, when the CWS leadership approached a London tea buyer, Joseph Woodin, to buy tea for CWS. Woodin was a Christian

Socialist with long connections with the co-operative movement, and his ideological commitment meant that CWS had secured a priceless ally in its early attempts to obtain a foothold in tea.[136] Woodin supplied CWS with tea throughout the 1870s, investing £25,000 and employing 30 staff just to operate CWS business. But there was always some unease at CWS dependence on a private firm for such an important commodity, even if it was owned by someone so close to the movement. The connection was reviewed on several occasions during that decade.[137] By the end of the 1870s, intensification of tea competition and difficulties in sustaining orders from societies prompted a move to set up a bespoke CWS tea department. Negotiations in 1879–80 resulted in the effective absorption of Woodin's CWS business into CWS, with his sons becoming CWS employees.[138] It proved to be but a first step into one of CWS' most enduring overseas businesses.

The first head of the new department, Charles Fielding, was appointed in August 1882 after a gruelling two-stage interview procedure involving seven other highly qualified candidates with long experience in tea. At 38 years old, Fielding was well established in the tea trade and had traded on his own account, but the decisive factor in his favour was that he knew the market for tea in Lancashire and Yorkshire extremely well, especially in the blends that tended to be preferred there.[139] It was indeed crucial experience, as much of Fielding's duties involved travelling around co-operative societies particularly in that part of the UK, trying to persuade them to buy CWS tea instead of fiercely promoted brands such as Hornimans, and gathering further intelligence of blends that would sell. In May 1882, the first joint meeting of the English and Scottish CWS to run the new tea department was held.[140] Various experiments were undertaken, including the direct import of tea from China.[141] In 1887, new premises were opened in Leman Street, East London following a fire that destroyed the first tea department. By then, the tea department employed 200 people.[142] From 1882, a joint partnership between CWS and SCWS made the CWS tea department effectively a flagship SCWS/CWS joint department, serving both countries' co-operative societies with coffee and cocoa as well as tea. In December 1923, this longstanding CWS/SCWS partnership was converted into a Joint Society, the English and Scottish Joint Co-operative Wholesale Society (E & S Joint CWS).[143] By the 1890s, the joint tea department employed 300 people in London. By then, it produced 350 different blends of tea to meet the varied tastes of co-operative societies and members, a sensitivity shaped by past preferences and the qualities of local water.[144] At any one time, the Leman Street department held £30,000 worth of tea in stock, an essential resource given the wide variation of blends required.[145] By then, some members of the tea committee began to advocate the acquisition by CWS of tea gardens in India and Ceylon as a way of both securing tea supplies and to break the command over supplies and prices enjoyed by the

London brokers from whom the department had to procure tea. But such a move was strongly resisted by Fielding, who contended that so varied were society tastes in tea that the cost of acquiring sufficient tea estates to supply these would be prohibitive.[146]

Nevertheless, within a decade this reluctance to vertically integrate down to production had been overcome. Co-operative societies stubbornly continued to do business with private companies in preference to CWS tea, and by 1893 this had been recognised as a major problem by both CWS and SCWS.[147] Some 56 societies did not buy any tea from SCWS/CWS at all.[148] Fielding and others made a concerted attempt to persuade societies to buy more, but with little effect.[149] By 1897, both SCWS and CWS were still concerned that many societies seemed immune to overtures pleading for co-operative loyalty.[150] Alarmingly, some societies enjoyed such a close relationship with Hornimans that they actively advertised and promoted their teas.[151] The problem was especially acute in the Manchester heartland of consumer co-operation.[152] Moreover, in 1897, the CWS Tea Committee noted that CWS had gone as far as it could in suppressing prices, warning that the business was at the very margin of profitability.[153] In these circumstances, the idea of a stronger CWS presence in the Indian sub-continent as a way of improving quality and reducing purchase prices was strongly revived towards the end of the decade. In July 1897, the Board instructed Fielding to buy tea directly in Calcutta through the firm of Lyall, Marshall & Co., to see if the high brokerage charges in London could be avoided by more direct trade with the sub-continent.[154] Then, in October 1898, Fielding and several directors formed a deputation to India to explore the purchase of tea plantations.[155] While this did not immediately lead to purchase, following several other visits a firm commitment to eventual acquisition was made once a more solid legal partnership between CWS and SCWS was confirmed.[156] By then, the wholesales were convinced that tea producers were actively engaged in limiting tea production to bolster prices. It was reported that in May 1900 a meeting of Ceylon tea producers had agreed to destroy a tenth of their tea to force up the price from 6s to 7d per lb. The Board pledged that CWS would never be party to this, and that one of the reasons to acquire tea plantations was to break down this kind of cartelised activity.[157] The upshot was that in December 1901, CWS/SCWS acquired the Nugawella and Wellaganga tea estates in Ceylon.[158] Other purchases followed. By January 1908, the Mahavilla estate, also in Ceylon, had been acquired.[159] By 1913, CWS had its own office and manager in Colombo, George Price.[160] Other estates were acquired, and by May 1915 CWS/SCWS owned eight estates in Ceylon and one in southern India, consisting of 5,000 acres and producing 211,780 lbs per annum.[161] This represented less than 1 per cent of total CWS purchases that exceeded 30 million lbs annually, but the purpose of tea estate acquisition was never that CWS should become self-sufficient in tea; the impracticalities and excessive costs identified by Fielding in 1892 still militated against this. The aim was rather to put pressure on both tea planters in India and Ceylon and tea brokers in London that it was well within the capacity of the wholesales to expand their operations if they felt that planters and brokers were organising to exploit them. As will be seen, the war triggered further estate acquisitions. Interestingly, similar pressures do not seem to have been experienced in relation to CWS' developing involvement in coffee and cocoa; although, as will be clear, by the eve of the First World War the progress of CWS interests in West Africa did lead to experimentation in relation to cocoa production.

Another area of new expansion was in dried fruit. As shown, Greece had become an important source of dried fruit for the CWS in the 1880s. As always, CWS leaders were aware that excessive dependence of any one source of a commodity exposed it to potential exploitation—as the experience of Danish butter had illustrated. Sporadic purchases of Spanish raisins began in the late 1880s.[162] Early in 1893, a CWS deputation proceeded to Spain to buy dried fruit.[163] In May 1896, it was decided that a depot would be opened in Spain.[164] By the following January, it had been opened at Denia.[165] In December 1898, *The Wheatsheaf* (monthly co-operative periodical) dubbed the town 'Raisinopolis' and applauded the dominance of the town's raisin trade by CWS.[166] By the end of 1899, CWS had two large warehouses in the town and was handling over 1,000 tons of fruit per year. CWS employed 500 Spanish workers and supplied oranges for the CWS jam works in Middleton, Manchester, making the production of CWS marmalade a vertically integrated supply chain in total.[167] But operating the trade in Denia at times proved difficult, as certain powerful local interests sought to maximise their own benefits from the trade at CWS' expense. Thus in 1905, local farmers held back fruit supplies to push up the price.[168] Later in the year, local farmers and merchants pressured local shipping companies to limit their movement of fruit to the UK to keep up prices there, and they tried to refuse shipments of fruit from companies that refused to comply with this. CWS had to face them down, and did so.[169] Conscious of the need to win local favour, early in 1906 CWS agreed to help fund certain events at the local festival.[170] Attacks on Denia also came at home. In October 1905, the Liverpool Dried Fruit Dealers Association was formed, with one of its aims to win the trade of CWS and end its involvement in direct purchasing in Greece and Spain. The CWS leadership pledged to resist this and threatened to close any accounts with CWS held by merchants who were members of the association, and in a circular urged co-operative societies to follow suit.[171] But so successful was the CWS depot that by 1909 it was in the process of erecting the largest warehouse in Denia.[172] The depot regularly returned healthy profits, rising from £1,070 in 1897 to £1,716 in 1907.[173] Denia supplemented the ongoing CWS trade in fruit with Greece and served to establish CWS/SCWS as among the most formidable suppliers of the UK market.

However, perhaps the most ambitious new CWS ventures came in 1897 with the establishment of a trading depot in Sydney, Australia, and a tallow works there three years later; and in 1913 with the establishment of a range of CWS depots and activities in Sierra Leone, the Gold Coast and Nigeria. As with many other such overseas initiatives, the driving force came from domestic UK developments and rivalry with private enterprise. The movement became embroiled in a major confrontation with Lever Brothers, the soap giant. Following the launch of Sunlight Soap in the mid-1880s, the firm became a giant, moving production to Merseyside and founding Port Sunlight, the model workers' village.[174] Through clever advertising and free gifts, Lever conquered the British market, even the co-operative societies, and in 1895 the firm became a limited company. But by the late 1890s, the soap industry—including the CWS itself, which was also a major producer—experienced new problems, largely resulting from the fact that new technological innovations meant that palm oil, coconut oil, tallow and the other fats used to make soap were now in demand to make margarine, lard and a range of new products. The high cost and shortages of raw materials pushed Levers into desperate measures. After attempting to reduce costs by shrinking the size of their soap tablets and increasing their price to wholesalers, in 1905 the firm took a step that was to plunge it into controversy, confrontation with the co-operative movement and ultimately costly and unsuccessful litigation. It approached glycerine producers in the north of England to establish what was essentially a cartel to reduce the costs of the soap industry, especially in reduced advertising costs, collective buying and combined manufacturing of key ingredients.[175] Almost half of the soap industry signed up. But when in September 1906 Levers took advantage of the deal to reduce advertising costs by cancelling its £6,000 advertising deal with the *Daily Mail*, it found that it had made a very powerful enemy. The *Mail* launched a major publicity campaign against the restrictive practices of what it dubbed 'the soap trust', urging retailers not to stock the produce of trust members and consumers not to buy them. This was so damaging that by the end of November 1906 the 'soap trust' was disbanded, with Lever allegedly having lost £500,000, in spite of a successful lawsuit against the *Mail*, which secured £91,000.[176] The unlikely beneficiaries were CWS, which had been developing its involvement in soap production since the establishment of its first small soap works in Durham in 1873. To keep up with Levers, in 1894 CWS opened a large soap works at Irlam, on the northern bank of the Manchester Ship Canal. But up to 1906, this ran at well below its 400 tons per week capacity, so popular were Levers' products with co-operative societies.[177] However, the trust scandal of 1906 boosted co-operative society purchases of soap from CWS, so that by the end of 1906 Irlam was being worked around the clock to produce well over 600 tons of soap per week.[178] The dramatic improvement in CWS soap promoted plans to open new CWS soap factories at Silvertown in London (opened 1908) and Dunston near Newcastle (1909).[179] In response to the soap trust scandal and to entreaties from CWS for societies to be loyal to CWS, by 1910 almost 400 co-operative societies were refusing to stock Lever soaps. This prompted Levers in summer 1910 to sue 38 co-operative societies on the false pretext that these societies were unlawfully passing off CWS produce as Lever soaps. Levers lost both the case and the ensuing appeal, but the aftermath of hostility poisoned relations, especially when Levers started to buy up its opponents, aiming to achieve a near monopoly position by acquisition instead of by trust.

Deepening competition in soap shaped CWS/SCWS policy in Australia from the last years of the nineteenth century. The initial establishment of the Sydney depot was driven by Australia's emergence as a supplier of commodities in demand in the UK, notably butter, wool and wheat.[180] The depot also became involved in supplying some Australian co-operative societies, notably tea. In 1899, CWS arranged for the supply to Australian societies of Ceylon tea.[181] In 1900, the Adelaide society, with over 3,000 members, was admitted as a member of CWS, with a view to purchasing CWS boots, shoes and clothes.[182] The establishment of the tallow factory in 1900 was in direct response to the shortages of soap-making raw materials mentioned earlier, and it was placed under the direct authority of the CWS' new soap works at Irlam, Manchester.[183] But there were serious problems with both the tallow works and the depot. The first manager of the depot, Mr Fairbairn continually incurred the displeasure of the Board for exercising too much initiative and involving CWS in transactions of which it disapproved. For example, in August 1901 Fairbairn was fiercely criticised for sending a speculative cargo of tobacco to Liverpool without prior consultation with the Board.[184] A few months later, the Board intervened to stop Fairbairn granting an unsecured loan of £2,000 to a Farmers Co-operative Society that was speculating in jute.[185] But CWS concern about the management of its Sydney interests came to a head in the spring of 1902. It emerged then that Fairbairn had been buying and selling on information to private companies in Australia.[186] At about the same time, it emerged that Benjamin Jones, senior manager in the CWS London branch, had a close personal interest in the firm of Ebdy & Co., which had been selling CWS goods on commission, through Jones' patronage.[187] Fairbairn resigned in May 1902 and Jones was asked to resign in September 1902, after it transpired that over £83,000 of business had been conducted through Jones' private connections.[188] Then, in November, Mr Pollitt, the manager of the tallow works was dismissed.[189] A major reorganisation of both the depot and the works followed, with a Mr Royle taking control of all administrative and financial matters relating to not the works and the depot.[190] But disillusionment was setting in. In November 1903, there was even discussion of closing the depot altogether.[191] Although CWS' growing trade in Australia wheat ensured it was kept open, CWS' view of it remained jaundiced, a factor that ultimately led to a major retrenchment during the First World War.

But perhaps the most dramatic and significant new CWS venture was in West Africa in 1913. It was CWS' bitter rivalry with Lever Brothers that triggered this initiative. The problems involved in securing stable supplies of palm oil led Lever Brothers to seek permission from the British Colonial Office to set up its own palm oil plantations in West Africa. The Colonial Office refused, and Lever Brothers turned to the Belgian Congo, which accommodated the firm.[192] But the approach caused consternation within the co-operative movement. A series of major articles in *Co-operative News* in the early months of 1913 traced the fortunes of Lever Brothers to secure a monopoly of palm oil extraction in West Africa, and while they acknowledged the failure of the initiative, it also noted that the Colonial Office had at times seemed to vacillate on the question.[193] The stories were firmly backed by an editorial article that noted information received that the CWS director were about to act on the issue.[194] Lever Brothers were still in negotiation with the Colonial Office about a possible grant, and it was not until early 1914 that their efforts to secure exclusive rights to process palm oil in southern Nigeria were refused, and they were persuaded to look elsewhere.[195] On 24 April, the Board resolved to seek rights to process palm oil in the Rokel River area of Sierra Leone, specifically on the same terms it understood to have been granted to Lever Brothers in another area of Sierra Leone.[196] Unlike Levers, CWS was far less insistent upon exclusivity, and as a result it was ultimately successful.[197] Negotiations had to be undertaken with local chiefs as well as the Colonial Office. On 4 November 1913, Lander, Thorpe and Green (manager of the Irlam soap works) of CWS, in the company of the District Commissioner (the local colonial official), met the ten most powerful local chiefs and 1,000 of their followers at Masungbo in Karene, Sierra Leone.[198] The result was the establishment of a range of CWS facilities, including a depot at Makene for purchasing palm oil from natives and selling them CWS produce in return, and a depot in Freetown to sell CWS produce.[199] CWS purchased land in Higher Irlam for a margarine factory that would utilise palm oil imports together with the soap works.[200] In September 1913, permission was sought from the CWS membership for £25,000 to set up these various facilities.[201] This was followed by an SCWS deputation to the Gold Coast in Spring 1914, which produced another joint CWS/SCWS depot in Accra, with several smaller satellites to buy cocoa as well as palm oil.[202] As with Sydney, there were serious personnel problems, not least because of the harsh environmental conditions. These will form an important part of a later chapter. But notwithstanding these difficulties, the West African palm oil trade grew in importance. The CWS depot in Liverpool took responsibility for managing West African imports, and the importance of the city in this branch of trade was reinforced when CWS acquired the African Oil Mill Company for £125,000 in November 1916.[203] The mill was tasked with processing all of the palm oil kernels sent back to the UK by CWS—yet another example of intense international vertical integration of production.[204]

The common theme in all these examples of new CWS global initiatives was that they were each a response to the intense competition, and hostility, which CWS encountered in the domestic market. The most extreme manifestation of this was the bitter conflict with Lever Brothers in respect of soap, which drove the West African initiative and the Sydney tallow works experiment. But an added complication was the ongoing question of the dubious loyalty of co-operative societies to the CWS as customers. Their fickleness—born of the need to maintain the loyalty of co-operative members and customers in the face of increasing competitive independent shopkeepers and emergent chains—meant that the wholesales had to maximise their competitiveness in terms of price and quality, especially in commodities where competition could be extremely fierce, such as tea and dried fruit. The wholesales' response was to vertically integrate key international supply chains as far as possible, in order to put pressure on producers of key commodities to offer CWS the best possible terms. The wholesales could not afford to leave the procurement of overseas commodities to the relatively disorganised sorties into purchasing depicted in so much of the business studies literature as typical of pre-1970s 'scientific' supply chain management. It will be seen in the next chapter that there was another asset that the CWS could employ in enabling it to exert control over its international supply chains—the financial resources of the CWS banking department, which could be used to facilitate the growth of key sources of overseas commodities. As will be alluded to in the final section of this chapter, the investments of the CWS Bank were arguably also an important tool in diminishing ideological and political opposition, especially in state authorities in the UK and overseas.

V

The international political environment in which CWS expanded its global interests between 1890 and 1914 was one of deepening international tensions that culminated, of course, in the outbreak of the World War of 1914 to 1918, which wrecked the international order. The growing friction between nations was economic as well as political, as emergent industrial powers such as Germany, Russia and the USA erected protectionist tariff barriers to protect their economies from foreign competition. As increasingly global commercial operators, the British wholesales could not avoid engagement with major international political questions that affected their commercial interests, notwithstanding the co-operative principle of political neutrality. The emergence of domestic enemies in private trade, which sought to use the law to tax co-operative dividends and to constrain the growth of co-operative trade meant that by the 1890s the movement had already entered the political fray through its own parliamentary committee. What factors shaped the attitude of the wholesales to political issues that affected their global trade links? How did the war of 1914 to 1918 further shape these?

Central to the concerns of CWS and SCWS about state policies affecting their overseas interests was the question of trade. The co-operative movement generally was strongly committed to free trade, for ideological as well as political reasons. As Katarina Friberg has argued, co-operators generally eschewed the state as an organ of social transformation and regarded voluntarism as the only truly effective method to create a more equal and prosperous society. They therefore equated free trade as an essential pre-requisite for the development of international co-operative trade and co-operation between co-operators across the globe. State protectionism was generally regarded as being anti-voluntarist and ultimately anti-co-operative.[205] From the point of view of the wholesales, this ideological commitment was reinforced by a hard-headed need to keep its increasingly important imports of foreign foodstuffs as cheap as possible, and therefore free of the burden of tariffs or other protectionist restrictions. In spite of the attacks upon it, the British co-operative movement was growing in confidence during this period, especially in light of the growth of co-operative movements across Europe, which nurtured real hope that a powerful international movement was in the process of being forged. By 1908, the rise of European wholesale societies provided ample evidence of the growing economic might of the new movement. In May 1908, a *Co-operative News* article noted that the turnovers of wholesale societies in several European countries had more than doubled between 1901 and 1907. Turnover for the German CWS rose from £756,888 to £2,993,311, the Danish CWS from £742,465 to £2,049,455 and the Swiss CWS from £167,035 to £574,182.[206] While these lagged well behind the turnover of the English CWS (which rose from £17,642,082 to £24,786,568 in the same period), the general growth of the consumer co-operative movement inspired confidence.[207] There were even initial discussions at the ICA Congress in Cremona in that year about establishing an International Co-operative Agency that would jointly buy commodities for the wholesales on the international market, an idea that would make more, if unsatisfactory, progress in the 1920s.[208] Indeed, the formation of the ICA itself in 1895 was itself a sign of this newfound confidence and willingness to co-operate across national borders.[209] While its actual achievements during the period were limited, it clearly signified that there was now an international voice for co-operation, a fact that undoubtedly helped make co-operators in the UK more assertive about policy issues.

The role of CWS in this deepening international (especially European) collaboration requires some comment. Cole acknowledges that CWS conducted some trade with co-operatives in Europe but dismisses it as being on such a small sale that it was insignificant.[210] But this is to severely underestimate the importance of CWS in not only trading with European co-operatives but also assisting the growth of the European wholesales. Certainly, CWS co-operative trading in Europe was geographically extensive. In 1901, CWS discussed with the Milan Co-operative Union the possible supply to the British wholesales of Italian co-operative produce.[211] By autumn 1903, CWS was supplying woollens to the Milan Co-operative Distributive Society.[212] So promising was this link that CWS sent showcards to the Milan society advertising CWS wares and arranged for a CWS display at an exhibition in Milan.[213] The *Wheatsheaf* trumpeted the achievements of the Milan society in May 1906, describing it as a "model society".[214] Moreover, the Association of Co-operative Societies of Milan were accepted as CWS members.[215] Orders were also sent to the Basle Society in Switzerland, especially CWS boots and shoes.[216] In 1907, a sub-department was even set up with CWS to deal specifically with trade with foreign co-operative societies.[217] Business was also done with foreign wholesales, including bran supplied to the Belgian CWS.[218] CWS also provided financial support for foreign wholesales, including £24,000 worth of assistance to the French CWS in November 1913.[219] Perhaps most poignantly, in the last days of peace in July 1914, the Austrian CWS pleaded desperately for a loan of £80,000 from CWS to help it bail out co-operative societies faced with massive withdrawals by co-operators called up to fight Serbia. But Britain was itself at war with Austria within days, and CWS had to refuse.[220] Although the volume of trade and financial help was small, it was nonetheless significant in building real confidence that co-operation had come of age and was at last capable of making itself heard politically. The confidence that instilled in the wider movement should not be underestimated.

As Trentmann has shown, the co-operative movement, including the wholesales, were an integral component of a wider social movement in Britain that saw free trade as not merely an economic issue but also an important aspect of British political culture.[221] The wholesales' commitment to free trade came to the fore politically in the wake of the South African War of 1899–1901, when the Conservative government introduced a duty on sugar to help pay for the war.[222] The move engendered a long and bitter struggle against the tax by the co-operative movement, which relied upon sugar from beet imports from the continent. Although initial action by the movement was muted, the wholesales kept up a long and steady lobbying campaign against it.[223] The parliamentary co-operative committee, which included several leading CWS directors, including T. Brodrick, met the Chancellor of the Exchequer in April 1903, complaining that it cost the movement £500,000 a year. The Chancellor remained unmoved, but the CWS continued its efforts.[224] In October 1905, the Board reaffirmed its desire to see the parliamentary committee resume its agitation on the question.[225] Then, in February 1908, the parliamentary committee urged local societies to write to their MPs to oppose the tax, pointing out that it had cost the movement almost £5 million since its introduction.[226] Early in 1910, it was pointed out that the CWS alone had paid £4.2 million in sugar duty since its introduction.[227] Another bone of contention for CWS that spurred it into action was the Brussels Sugar Convention of 1902.

Sugar was a commodity that had seen huge changes in the nineteenth century. Originally exclusively a tropical product, during the latter half of the century the development of sugar beet production in Germany, France, Russia, Austria and other European countries dramatically increased the supply and reduced its price. These European countries, still strongly influenced by rural landowners who were under pressure from the flood of cheap food from America, promoted sugar beet production by subsidies and bounties, which served to make sugar very cheap indeed on the world market compared to the middle of the century. With its policy of free trade, Britain's consumers benefitted hugely, as did the co-operative movement and the wholesales, for whom cheap sugar ensured low prices for CWS/SCWS jams, confectionary and sugar for the co-operative consumer. By 1900, about 80 per cent of British sugar was beet sugar, and 65 per cent of it came from Germany.[228] But by then the system of bounties and subsidies was being increasingly criticised as unfair. Those countries who paid the subsidies were finding the costs of this increasingly burdensome, while Britain, the major consumer, became increasingly sensitive that in the long run excessive dependence on the beet-producing countries might lead to overdependence on mighty continental sugar cartels that could just as easily push up prices. In addition, British imperial sugar producers in the Caribbean objected very strongly to what they saw as unfair competition from state-sponsored European producers. British adherence to free trade had always forestalled any international agreement, but these arguments persuaded the British government, with nine other countries, to set up the Sugar Commission, with the power to impose penalties on countries that subsidised or otherwise unfairly supported beet production. Britain even prohibited the import of subsidised sugar. Both Trentmann and Pigman see the convention as a significant first step to the creation of an international rule-based system of trade, in which countries collaborated to eliminate practices such as state subsidies that undermined the 'level playing field' for international trade.[229] But Britain's pro-free trade lobby argued fiercely and insistently against, ultimately leading to Britain's withdrawal from the Convention in 1912.

Their view was that the interests of the British consumer trumped all other considerations. If other countries were foolish enough to subsidise the British consumer, then it was not the job of the British government to put those foreign interests before the material interests of the British citizen. The co-operative movement, especially the wholesales, played a leading role in the agitation against the convention. In 1905, the *Co-operative News* published a long article listing the grievances of the wholesales against the Convention, arguing that it had cost CWS £1 million in additional costs since its introduction.[230] Indeed, CWS sought to circumvent the Convention by importing Peruvian sugar from New York, Peru not being a signatory to the convention.[231] A series of co-operative conferences followed, each of which roundly condemned the Convention.[232]

Unsurprisingly, the wholesales and the movement were also staunch opponents of Joseph Chamberlain's Tariff Reform League after 1903. Trentmann shows how the movement sided with powerful opponents of tariff reform such as the Cobden Club and organised meetings and demonstrations across the country against Chamberlain and his League.[233] CWS took a lead in this. At a major conference held at its Manchester headquarters in August 1903, John Shillito, Chairman of CWS, led the condemnations of Chamberlain's protectionist agenda.[234] In September, a joint co-operative–Cobden Club meeting against tariff reform was held at the Newcastle Branch of CWS.[235] SCWS also threw its weight in favour free trade. At a conference against tariffs in Glasgow that September, William Maxwell, Chair of SCWS, led the proceedings.[236] The wholesales' opposition to tariff reform was not just based on ideology. They were concerned about the impact on their financial position. CWS estimated that tariffs along Chamberlainite lines would cost it £1,265,000 annually, and SCWS £422,000.[237] Thus, despite their supposed political neutrality, the wholesales had actually come to play an important part in the politics of Britain's overseas trade in the years before the First World War. Given Chamberlain's strongly pro-imperial agenda and his ideas about imperial preference cementing the British Empire as a political and economic global entity, one might expect some co-operative diffidence about the Empire. But this was not so. Trentmann shows that for many pro-free traders, there was no contradiction between Empire and free trade, with the former sometimes paving the way for the latter.[238] The co-operative movement and the wholesales fell within this pro-imperial free trade milieu. The facts of such substantial investment in Indian tea estates, Canadian and Australian wheat and later West African imperial palm oil and cocoa demonstrated that co-operation was able to accommodate itself within Empire.[239] Indeed, CWS was developing substantial financial interests in Empire through the acquisition of imperial stocks and shares by the CWS bank in the decades before the war. Between 1912 and 1914, at various points, CWS held £100,000 in Alberta bills, £20,000 in Province of Saskatchewan bills, £15,000 in Government of

West Australia stock, £15,000 in New Zealand government debentures and £15,000 in Victoria state (Australia) stock.[240] These were but a few of the very large investments in Empire that CWS had taken on. CWS certainly supported prestigious imperial and national initiatives. CWS contributed £50 to Captain Scott's ill-fated Antarctic expedition in 1910, a decision that elicited the quip from a quarterly meeting delegate that perhaps Scott should open an ice cream depot for CWS at the south pole![241] Moreover, Rhodes shows that by the early 1900s, co-operatives were seen as important tools of imperial development in India and Burma by the India Office, though these tended to draw upon the traditions of credit and agricultural co-operations exemplified by Plunkett and Raiffeisen, rather than Rochdale consumer co-operation.[242]

The war was to prove a major turning point in the fortunes of British co-operation and a period of great turmoil. Initially, expectations that the war would be short meant that both state and firms pursued a 'business as usual' strategy, a policy that quickly proved to be horribly misjudged. The co-operative movement and the wholesales were also complacent. They refused an invitation in early August to be represented on a special Prices Advisory Committee established by the government, on the short-sighted principle that CWS directors should use their time exclusively for CWS affairs.[243] As a result, the wholesales were excluded from other government-led bodies that took on significant powers as the war dragged on and the state adopted an ever-more interventionist policy. Especially important were the Sugar Commission and the Grain Supply Committee, which came to control the prices and supplies of sugar and wheat—two vital foodstuffs in which the wholesales had massive interests.[244] When CWS realised its error, its efforts to secure representation in these bodies fell on deaf ears.[245] As early as October 1914, rising sugar prices was already a major concern for the wholesales and the wider movement.[246] The lack of political representation meant that the British government was influenced strongly by private interests, often hostile to co-operation. One consequence was that when the government introduced its Excess Profits Duty (EPD) in 1915, co-operative dividends were brought within its purview, something that had never happened before.[247] CWS subsequently paid almost £1 million in EPD, and for a time suffered serious losses. Meanwhile, the exclusion from key committees controlling food supplies and prices was felt all the harder as state control tightened in response to shortages, inflation and the indefinite duration of the conflict. A government food department was established in autumn 1916, and its powers were increased by Lloyd George, who replaced Asquith as Prime Minister in December 1916. The department was reorganised as the Ministry of Food and Lloyd George appointed Lord Devonport (formerly Sir Hudson Kearley) as Food Controller. It was an inflammatory appointment from a co-operative point of view, as Kearley's fortune had been made in the grocery wholesaling firm of Kearley & Tonge.[248] Devonport proved to be not only incompetent but also as hostile to co-operation as feared. He continued the policy of ignoring co-operative requests for better representation, as well as rejecting their views and those of others calling for the introduction of comprehensive food rationing in the face of spiralling food prices. By summer, food prices were identified widely as the cause of a rash of unofficial strikes and industrial unrest, prompting Devonport's replacement in June 1917 by Lord Rhondda.[249] Lord Rhondda introduced a much more comprehensive response to the food crisis. This included bread subsidies, the recruitment of co-operators and trades unionists as advisors, the incorporation of co-operative and labour leaders onto the 1900 or so local food committees across the country and the establishment in January 1918 of a Consumers Council, again with labour and co-operative representation (including Mary Cottrell, who would become the first woman on the CWS Board shortly after the war). During 1918, rationing was gradually introduced for sugar, lard, margarine and butter as well as bacon and ham. Much of what the co-operative movement had been lobbying for was conceded. In part, this reflected a major change in the co-operative movement's attitude to politics. Enraged by Devonport and what they saw as the deliberate disregard of co-operative interests by the British state, a groundswell of co-operative opinion—this time supported by CWS—called for co-operative representation in parliament. As a result, the Co-operative Party was launched in October 1917.[250] Political neutrality was a thing of the past, though it would take ten years before a working relationship with the main working-class political body, the Labour Party, would be established.

Inevitably, the war had a disruptive effect on the international trade of the wholesales. SCWS' extensive trade with Canada and its developing commerce with West Africa were hit by spiralling shipping costs, a problem relieved only by belated state control introduced in May 1917.[251] CWS also suffered in this way, though possession of its own ships provided some respite at first. But once German U-boats began to take their heavy toll, it also faced higher shipping costs as well as major losses. A cargo of butter worth £8,300 aboard the S.S. *Pallas* en route from Gothenburg to Hull was seized by the Germans in October 1915.[252] By 1915, shortages of shipping were impacting upon CWS' ability to conduct its overseas commerce. But shipping was not the only problem. The neutral Scandinavian countries were important for supplying Germany and the central European powers as well as Britain. In October 1915, L. Wilson, the CWS butter buyer, reported that the Germans were paying 252s for a cwt of Danish butter, compared to just 201s by British purchasers.[253] Butter purchases were suspended at Gothenburg in June 1916.[254] Moreover, scandal erupted just a few weeks later. The Foreign Secretary presented evidence to CWS that the manager of its Gothenburg depot had not only knowingly sold butter to merchants who intended to sell it on to German merchants but had also applied for export licences to Germany himself.[255] Both the manager and Wilson, the CWS butter buyer, were subsequently dismissed, and the Gothenburg depot closed.[256]

Gothenburg was not the only overseas CWS facility to suffer from the war. Shipping problems and the growing importance of West Africa as a source of palm oil led to the closure of the Sydney tallow works in June 1915.[257] Trade from the Sydney depot effectively ground to a halt.[258] In northern France, the Rouen branch was abandoned in September 1914 due to panic that it would fall into German hands.[259] But CWS was able to expand its activities elsewhere, as well as adjust its arrangements in certain countries to meet the challenges of war. In West Africa, land and buildings were purchased in Accra for £3,024 for cocoa production, and of course as shown earlier, a palm oil mill was acquired in Liverpool.[260] There was also expansion of tea estates in India. In 1916, the Mango Range and Murugalli estates were acquired in South India, and the Nagastenne and Bowhill estates in Ceylon, at a total cost of £16,016.[261] In part this reflected the emergence of the 'Shillito League', a pressure group within the co-operative movement that argued that the best way to promote co-operation further was by the acquisition of raw material production to a much greater extent than to date. A pamphlet by John Smith of Oldham (probably a pseudonym) entitled "The Case for Co-operative Ownership of Raw Materials" was published in 1916, and the league received extensive coverage in the *Co-operative News*.[262] That the CWS was strongly influenced by this thinking is clear from an article in the *Co-operative News* by the CWS director George Thorpe:

> Co-operators must own, gather and create their own raw material, as far as possible: and when they have succeeded in doing that, then they are a long way on the road towards governing output and controlling prices.[263]

In North America, major changes were also implemented by CWS. Orders were issued to focus wheat trade through the Winnipeg and New York depots, and steps were to be taken to increase CWS/SCWS co-operation in the wheat trade there.[264] This also led to the acquisition of land in Canada by the SCWS/CWS to grow their own wheat. In January 1917, 10,240 acres of land were acquired for $310,000 about 60 miles from Saskatoon, known as the Vietzen farm.[265] Indeed, CWS involvement in the Canadian economy had been deepening during the war. In December 1915, CWS lent £225,000 to the Canadian government in the form of CWS-owned Canadian dollar securities, for an interest payment of 0.5 per cent per annum.[266] The position of the wholesales was strengthened still further in August 1917 when John Gledhill was appointed adviser on North American trade to the Ministry of Food.[267]

Thus, the war forced CWS to not only revise its relationship with the British state at home but also take major steps to adjust its overseas commitments to meet the challenges of war. In some instances, this necessitated reluctant withdrawal from some activities—at least for the duration—but in other contexts advances in CWS ownership of production took place, particularly in Canada, West Africa and India. In this respect, it can be argued that the war, on balance, strengthened the presence of the wholesales within the British Empire. It was a trend that would become even stronger after the war, reflecting the much more difficult trading circumstances that would prevail then. Trade with Australia and New Zealand would recover from the wartime downturn, while the new political order in Europe created by the Treaty of Versailles and the Russian Revolution would open new opportunities—and difficulties. CWS overseas interests would change—but not in their vital importance to the British wholesales.

Notes

1. Wilson, Webster & Vorberg-Rugh, *Building Co-operation* 100–101.
2. Jefferys, *Retail Trading in Britain 1850–1950* 29; 163.
3. Wilson, Webster & Vorberg-Rugh, *Building Co-operation* 102.
4. Ibid., 108–109.
5. Kinloch & Butt, *History of the SCWS Ltd* 245–263.
6. Wilson, Webster & Vorberg-Rugh, *Building Co-operation* 111.
7. CWSBM 2 October 1891.
8. CWSBM 4 March 1892 and 28 April 1893.
9. CWSBM 28 September 1894.
10. CWSBM 8 February 1895 and 12 July 1895.
11. CWSBM 1 March 1895.
12. CWSBM 9 August 1895.
13. CWSBM 8 November 1895, 14 February 1896 and 2 October 1896.
14. CWSBM 29 July 1898.
15. CWSBM 23 November 1899 and 28 July 1905.
16. CWSBM 15 December 1899 and 26 December 1902.
17. CWSBM 25 August 1905 and 19 June 1914.
18. CWSBM 13 March 189 and 29 June 1914.
19. *Wheatsheaf* July 1902, 7.
20. Article by L. Wilson (manager of CWS butter department) "The Progress of an Interesting Industry", *Co-operative News* 18 January 1908, 61.
21. *Co-operative News* 17 March 1900, 283.
22. *Wheatsheaf* October 1899, 50.
23. CWSBM 12 July 1895.
24. CWSBM 7 May 1897.
25. CWSBM 2 June 1899.
26. CWSBM 27 October 1899.
27. CWSBM 17 November 1899.
28. CWSBM 30 August 1901.
29. *Co-operative News* 15 June 1901, 711.
30. CWSBM 13 September 1901.
31. *Co-operative News* 21 December 1901, 1510.
32. CWSBM 20 September 1902, 28 September 1905 and 3 August 1906.
33. CWSBM 8 March 1912.
34. CWSBM 2 June 1899.

35. CWSBM 16 April 190, 8.
36. *Co-operative News* 13 January 1912, 36.
37. CWSBM 15 April 1904.
38. CWSBM 25 July 1902.
39. CWSBM 10 November 899. For more information about this body, see P. Salmon, *Scandinavia and the Great Powers* (Cambridge, Cambridge University Press 1997) 133; S.E. Andersen, *The Evolution of Nordic Finance* (London, Palgrave Macmillan 2011) 89–90.
40. CWSBM 2 November 1900.
41. CWSBM 15 November 1901.
42. CWSBM 2 July 1897.
43. CWSBM 4 October 1901.
44. CWSBM 8 February 1895.
45. Lancashire Divisional Meeting, Report in *Co-operative News* 21 September 1912, 1171–1172.
46. P. Redfern, *The Story of the CWS 1863–1913* (Manchester, CWS 1913) 226.
47. Ibid., 227–230.
48. Ibid., 427–429.
49. Kinloch & Butt, *History of the SCWS Ltd* 120–121.
50. CWSBM 30 November 1894.
51. CWSBM 23 March 1900.
52. CWSBM 20 March 1903.
53. CWSBM 29 April 1894.
54. CWSBM 25 August 1905.
55. CWSBM 19 January 1906.
56. CWSBM 15 December 1905.
57. CWSBM 2 February 1906.
58. CWSBM 23 August 1906.
59. Kinloch & Butt, *History of the SCWS Ltd* 99.
60. CWSBM 15 January 1909.
61. CWSBM 14 April 1899.
62. CWSBM 29 November 1912.
63. For more on Plunkett see P. Bolger, "Horace Plunkett: The Man" in C. Keating (ed.), *Plunkett and Co-operatives: Past, Present and Future* (Cork, Bank of Ireland Centre for Co-operative Studies 1983) 14–22. For the development of the movement he led, see, in the same volume, Keating, "Plunkett, the Co-operative Movement and Irish Rural Development" 45–69.
64. Redfern, *The Story of the CWS* 297.
65. An excellent account of the growth of IAOS, and its troubled relations with CWS, is provided by P. Doyle, Civilising Rural Ireland: *The co-operative movement, development ad the nation-state 1889–1939* (Manchester, Manchester University Press 2019).
66. CWSBM 25 January 1895.
67. Doyle offers an especially insightful analysis of these philosophical differences.
68. CWSBM 4 June 1897.
69. CWSBM 8 October 1897.
70. *Co-operative News* 6 August 1898, 885.
71. L. Kennedy, "Aspects of the Spread of the Creamery System in Ireland" in Keating (ed.), *Plunkett and Co-operatives: Past, Present and Future* 92–110; 93.
72. CWSBM 7 October 1898.
73. Account of SCWS Quarterly Meeting September 1901, *Co-operative News* 7 September 1901, 1069.

74. CWSBM 23 June 1899; Account of Quarterly Meeting of London Branch of CWS, *Co-operative News* 17 June 1899, 661.
75. CWSBM 7 July 1899.
76. CWSBM 28 July 1899.
77. CWSBM 15 December 1899.
78. CWSBM 5 March 1900.
79. CWSBM 18 May 1900.
80. June Quarterly Meeting of CWS in Manchester, *Co-operative News* 23 June 1900, 682.
81. *Co-operative News* 24 August 1901, 1014–1016.
82. Wilson, Webster & Vorberg-Rugh, *Building Co-operation* 129.
83. Manchester Quarterly Meeting, *Co-operative News* 23 March 1901, 321.
84. Manchester Quarterly Meeting, *Co-operative News* 28 March 1903, 350.
85. CWSBM 8 November 1895.
86. CWSBM 9 December 1898.
87. CWSBM 27 August 1897 and 7 October 1898.
88. "Co-operation in Ireland" *Co-operative News* 2 November 1901, 1315.
89. CWSBM 16 February 1900.
90. June Quarterly Meeting in Manchester, *Co-operative News* 23 June 1900, 682.
91. CWSBM 21 August 1903.
92. Printed Report for Quarterly Meeting, CWSBM 19 March 1904; also Accounts of Branch Meetings in Newcastle and London, *Co-operative News* 19 March 1904, 313–315.
93. *Co-operative News* 4 March 1905, 245.
94. Manchester Quarterly Meeting March 1908, *Co-operative News* 21 March 1908, 325.
95. CWSBM 22 January 1909.
96. CWSBM 12 October 1906.
97. CWSBM 19 April 1907.
98. Printed Report for Quarterly Meeting, CWSBM March 1911.
99. Printed Report for Quarterly Meeting, CWSBM March 1913.
100. Discussion of CWS Irish Creameries at Newcastle Quarterly Meeting March 1907, *Co-operative News* 19 March 1907, 99.
101. Henriksen, McLaughlin & Sharp, "Contracts and Co-operation" 412–431.
102. Ibid., 414.
103. Ibid., 424.
104. CWSBM 14 April 1899.
105. CWSBM 18 July 1902.
106. CWSBM 7 November 1902.
107. CWSBM 28 November 1902.
108. CWSBM 4 December 1903.
109. CWSBM 6 May 1904.
110. Henriksen, McLaughlin & Sharp, "Contracts and Co-operation" 413.
111. Printed Reports for Quarterly Meetings December 1896, March 1897, June 1897 and September 1897, CWSBM.
112. Printed Reports for Quarterly Meetings September 1899 and March 1900.
113. Printed Reports for Quarterly Meeting September 1905.
114. For example, Pope & Pearson: CWSBM 23 December 1892; Fosdick: CWSBM 12 April 1895, 21 January 1897, 11 February 1898, 17 November 1899, 10 January 1902, 30 January 1903, 12 May 1903, 24 December 1903; Hemsworths: 20 January 1905.
115. For example, Hemsworths: CWSBM 24 May 1895, 2 September 1896, 10 March 1899, 27 September 1901; Hartleys: CWSBM 24 May 1895; Fosdick: CWSBM

42 September 1896, 26 August 1898, 10 March 1899, 23 June 1899, 23 January 1903, 26 April 1904; Kittle & Co.: CWSBM 15 May 1903.

116. CWSBM 6 June 1902, 20 November 1903, 15 April 1904, 13 January 1905.
117. Sugar: CWSBM 7 February 1896, 2 December 1898, 9 June 1899, 8 June 1900, 3 October 1902; Fruit: CWSBM 2 August 1895, 28 February 1896.
118. McFie's: CWSBM 12 April 1895; Hogg & Co.: CWSBM 29 April 1898.
119. CWSBM 29 July 1898.
120. CWSBM 18 May and 1 June 1900.
121. CWSBM 16 December 1904.
122. CWSBM 3 May 1895.
123. CWSBM 12 July 1895.
124. CWSBM 17 September 1897.
125. CWSBM 21 December 1900.
126. *Co-operative News* 21 September 1901 (Lincoln Meeting), 1131–1132; *Co-operative News* 28 September 1901 (Manchester Quarterly Meeting), 1164.
127. CWSBM 30 May 1902.
128. CWSBM 25 July 1902.
129. CWSBM 20 November 1903.
130. CWSBM 26 February 1904; 29 April 1904.
131. CWSBM, Quarterly Joint Meeting 24 August 1905.
132. CWSBM 17 November 1905.
133. CWSBM 23 March 1906.
134. CWSBM 27 April 1906 and 18 May 1906; *Co-operative News* 3 March 1906, 235.
135. Printed Report to Manchester Quarterly Meeting June 1906, CWSBM 16 June 1906; also see *Wheatsheaf* June 1906, 182.
136. Redfern, *The Story of the CWS* 120.
137. Ibid.
138. CWSBM 20 November 1880.
139. GPCM 29 July 1882, 2/0/4, 7.
140. Redfern, *The Story of the CWS* 121.
141. Ibid.
142. Ibid., 122.
143. Redfern, *The New History of the CWS* 338.
144. Article: "The Wholesale Societies' Tea, Coffee, Cocoa and Chocolate Department" in *CWS Annual 1892* 459–473; 464.
145. Ibid., 465.
146. Ibid., 467–468.
147. CWSBM 10 March 1893.
148. CWSBM 17 March 1893.
149. CWSBM 12 October 1894, 16 and 30 November 1894.
150. CWSBM 24 September 1897.
151. CWSBM 14 October 1898.
152. *Co-operative News* 3 December 1898, 1331.
153. Minutes of CWS Tea Committee 8 November 1897.
154. CWSBM 16 July 1897.
155. CWSBM 21 October 1898.
156. CWSBM 6 November 1899.
157. *Co-operative News* 23 March 1901, 322.
158. Joint Meeting, CWSBM 22 November 1901; *Wheatsheaf* October 1902, 57.
159. *Wheatsheaf* January 1908, 106.
160. Joint Meeting, CWSBM 30 March 1910; CWSBM 13 March 1913.
161. "Our Tea Consumption" *Co-operative News* 1 May 1915, 570–571.
162. CWSBM 20 December 1895.

163. CWSBM 23 June 1893.
164. CWSBM 8 May 1896.
165. CWSBM 22 January 1897.
166. *Wheatsheaf* December 1898, 34.
167. Article about the Denia Depot, *Wheatsheaf* November 1899, 72–73.
168. CWSBM 27 January 1905.
169. CWSBM 6 October 1905.
170. CWSBM 16 February 1906 and 16 March 1906.
171. CWSBM 27 October 1905.
172. *Co-operative News* 16 October 1909, 1364.
173. CWSBM 29 July 1898 and 24 April 1908.
174. J.D. Jeremy, "The Enlightened Paternalist in Action: William Hesketh Lever at Port Sunlight before 1914" *Business History* 33:1 (1991) 58–81.
175. C. Wilson, *The History of Unilever: A Study in Economic Growth and Social Change*, vol. 1 (London, Cassell 1954) 80–82.
176. Ibid., 87–88.
177. Redfern, *The Story of the CWS* 241.
178. Ibid., 243.
179. Ibid.
180. CWSBM 24 September 1897 (wheat) and 24 June 1898 (butter) and 6 October 1899 (wool).
181. CWSBM 14 July 1899.
182. Report on June 1900 Quarterly Meeting in Manchester, *Co-operative News* 23 June 1900, 680.
183. CWSBM 21 December 1900.
184. CWSBM 23 August 1901.
185. CWSBM 6 September 1901.
186. CWSBM 16 May 1902.
187. CWSBM 9 May 1902 and 25 July 1902.
188. CWSBM 29 May 1902 and 19 September 1902.
189. CWSBM 7 November 1902.
190. CWSBM 28 November 1902.
191. CWSBM 6 November 1903.
192. A.G. Hopkins, *An Economic History of West Africa* (London, Routledge 1973) 210–212.
193. *Co-operative News* 8 February 1913, 162; 15 February 1913, 196; 22 February 1913, 226; 1 March 1913, 260.
194. *Co-operative News* 1 March 1913, 269.
195. For information on Lever Bros correspondence with the Colonial Office, see "Palm Oil Grant in West Africa: Official CO Correspondence 9 December 1913 to 31 March 1915" CO879/115/8 National Archives 4, 67 & 68.
196. CO879/115/8 23; CWSBM 24 April 1913.
197. CWSBM 12 June 1914.
198. *Co-operative News* 11 February 1914, 212.
199. CWSBM 15 January 1914.
200. CWSBM 7 November 1913.
201. Printed Report for Quarterly Meetings September 1913.
202. *Co-operative News* 4 July 1914, 860–861; CWSBM 5 August 1914.
203. CWSBM 23 July 1915 and 3 November 1916.
204. CWSBM 8 December 1916.
205. K. Friberg, "A Co-operative Take on Free Trade: International Ambitions and Regional Initiatives in International Co-operative Trade" in M. Hilson, S. Neunsinger & G. Patmore (eds.), *A Global History of Consumer Co-operation since 1850: Movements and Businesses* (Leiden, Brill 2017) 201–225; 202.

206. *Co-operative News* 2 May 1908, 501–502.
207. Wilson, Webster & Vorberg-Rugh, *Building Co-operation* 99.
208. *Co-operative News* 28 March 1908, 368.
209. Cole, *A Century of Co-operation* 254–255. There are also excellent general histories of ICA: J. Birchall, *The International Co-operative Movement* (Manchester, Manchester University Press 1997); R. Rhodes, *The International Co-operative Alliance during War and Peace 1910–1950* (Geneva, ICA 1995).
210. Cole, *A Century of Co-operation* 255.
211. CWSBM 8 March 1901 and 12 April 1901.
212. CWSBM 20 November 1903.
213. CWSM 9 February 1906.
214. *Wheatsheaf* May 1906, 163–165.
215. CWSBM 2 March 1906.
216. CWSBM 26 February 1904; 21 September 1906.
217. CWSBM 19 July 1907.
218. CWSBM 4 October 1912.
219. CWSBM 28 November 1913.
220. CWSBM 31 July 1814; 5 August 1914.
221. F. Trentmann, *Free Trade Nation* (Oxford, Oxford University Press 2008) 13–15.
222. Ibid., 56.
223. Ibid., 46.
224. *Co-operative News* 18 April 1903, 450.
225. CWSBM 13 October 1905.
226. *Co-operative News* 15 February 1908, 193.
227. *Co-operative News* 15 January 1910, 62.
228. Trentmann, *Free Trade Nation* 155.
229. See Trentmann, *Free Trade Nation* 154–161; G.A. Pigman, "Hegemony and Trade Liberalization Policy: Britain and the Brussels Sugar Convention of 1902" *Review of International Studies* 23 (1997) 185–210.
230. *Co-operative News* 14 January 1905, 41.
231. *Co-operative News* 4 February 1905, 118–121.
232. Conferences Was held in Pendleton, London, Newcastle and Kettering, *Co-operative News* 4 February 1905, 118–121; 11 February 1905, 160–161; 18 February 1905, 192–193.
233. Trentmann, *Free Trade Nation* 46–50.
234. *Co-operative News* 22 August 1903, 1018.
235. *Co-operative News* 5 September 1903, 1080.
236. *Co-operative News* 12 September 1903, 1102.
237. *Co-operative News* 21 November 1903, 1398.
238. Trentmann, *Free Trade Nation* 141–142.
239. R. Rhodes, *Empire and Co-operation: How the British Empire Used Co-operatives in Its Development Strategies 1900–1970* (Edinburgh, Birlinn 2012) 49.
240. CWSBM 12 July 1912, 25 July 1913 and 14 November 1913.
241. *Co-operative News* 25 June 1910, 813.
242. Rhodes, *Empire and Co-operation* 94–130; A. Webster, "Co-operatives and the State in Burma/Myanmar 1900–2012: A Case Study of Failed Top-Down Co-operative Development Models?" in R.A. Brown & J. Pierce (eds.), *Charities in the Non-Western World: The Development and Regulation of Indigenous and Islamic Charities* (Abingdon, UK, Routledge, 2013) 65–87.
243. Wilson, Webster & Vorberg-Rugh, *Building Co-operation* 153.
244. Ibid., 153–154.

245. CWSBM 13 October 1916.
246. *Co-operative News* 3 October 1914, 1257.
247. Wilson, Webster & Vorberg-Rugh, *Building Co-operation* 157.
248. Ibid., 158–159.
249. Trentmann, *Free Trade Nation* 197.
250. Wilson, Webster & Vorberg-Rugh, *Building Co-operation* 156–165.
251. Kinloch & Butt, *History of the Scottish Co-operative Wholesale Society Ltd* 270–271.
252. CWSBM 15 October 1915.
253. *Co-operative News* 16 October 1915, 1375.
254. CWSBM 9 June 1916.
255. CWSBM 7 July 1916.
256. CWSBM 15 September 1916 and 27 October 1916.
257. CWSBM 18 June 1915.
258. CWSBM 10 December 1915.
259. CWSBM 10 September 1914.
260. Printed Report for Quarterly Meetings June 1916.
261. Ibid.
262. *Co-operative News* 17 July 1915, 962–963.
263. *Co-operative News* 12 June 1916, 806.
264. CWSBM 1 December 1916.
265. CWSBM 5 January 1917.
266. CWSBM 30 December 1915.
267. Wilson, Webster & Vorberg-Rugh, *Building Co-operation* 161.

4 Dealing With Dictators and Developing the Empire

The Zenith of British Co-operation and the World 1918–1945?

I

The co-operative movement, and particularly the wholesales, emerged from the First World War much strengthened in terms of membership and political influence. Membership of co-operative societies rose from 2.9 million in 1913 to 4.5 million in 1920, reaching about 10 per cent of the British population by the latter date.[1] However, both CWS and SCWS had some pressing concerns about the new post-war environment, created by the swift and largely unexpected victory of the Allies in November 1918. Some wartime problems showed no signs of abating. Rampant inflation continued into the peace for several years, imposing heavy costs upon co-operative societies and wholesales alike. But one issue above all others perhaps explains why there was a great deal of anxiety within the movement generally about the future. It emerged from the war bitterly divided about the shape and organisational structure of the movement in the future.

In 1914, the Co-operative Congress had launched a major survey into the commercial interests of the movement. From the outset, its deliberations became a source of friction, especially when in October 1914 both the CWS and the SCWS declined to participate in the Survey Committee established under the auspices of the Co-operative Union.[2] The decision represented not only a legacy of deepening tension between the wholesales and the Co-operative Union, the national commercial and political wings of the movement, but also a shrewd (and accurate) suspicion on the part of the former that the Survey would be critical of both the methods of the wholesales and their prominence within the movement. Sure enough, the third of its four reports, the Interim Report produced in 1918, attacked the wholesales' *de facto* leadership role within the movement and the concentration of so many branches of co-operative commerce under their control, especially through the CWS banking department. The quality and structures of management were attacked as overstretched, outdated and out of touch with the wider movement.[3] The report contended that a new federal society should be created to take control of the bank, with the wholesales becoming just one voice in its governance among the wider institutions of the movement.[4] Other steps were recommended to reduce the wholesales' influence, including re-establishing the Co-operative Insurance Society (taken over by CWS several decades earlier) as an independent society and the transfer of key activities such as auditing and legal services to the Co-operative Union.[5] Coming so soon after the war, in which the wholesales had come to play an influential part in shaping state policy on food procurement, the interim report infuriated the wholesales and galvanised them into action. In 1919 and 1920, representatives of the wholesales met with both the Survey Committee and the Central Board of the CU and made clear their opposition to all of the proposals that sought to curtail CWS activities and interfere with its internal organisation. The dominant position the wholesales enjoyed within the movement because of their command of wealth and resources ensured that they won the day, and the final report, published in 1920, omitted the call for a new federally controlled co-operative bank and most of the other changes that the wholesales found objectionable.[6] The question of radical organisational reform was effectively postponed for over 30 years.

In fact, the leaderships of the wholesales were bullishly optimistic about the future, and as will be seen, this partly reflected confidence in the global supply chains that had been developed over the previous half century, notwithstanding the disruptions inflicted by the war upon them and on the global economy more generally. This confidence was especially apparent over the question of whether wartime state controls over the food supply and process should be continued into peacetime. It was consistently argued by the trade unions and indeed the wider co-operative movement that the Ministry of Food should become a permanent government department and that price controls should be continued for the foreseeable future.[7] But the wholesales dramatically broke ranks with this position in September 1919, calling for wartime controls to be dismantled as soon as possible.[8] William Lander, a leading CWS director, explained to a sceptical London meeting of co-operators that the CWS was well placed to ensure a plentiful supply of wheat, bacon and other essential foodstuffs from as far afield as the USA and even Soviet Russia. "If the Government would take their fingers out and get out as quickly as possible", said Lander, "they would be able to protect the interests of the consumer".[9] A bitter row about this continued within the co-operative movement into 1921, but by then the direction of government policy was clear. In March of that year, the Ministry of Food was closed, and by the middle of 1922 virtually all wartime controls had been fully dismantled.[10] For its part, the English CWS confidently sought to prepare for what it believed would be a period of sustained British and global reconstruction and economic recovery, in which its global supply links would provide it with a competitive edge in the British market, regardless of the growth of multiple retail chains and the historic fickleness of its retail society members and customers. This confidence was exemplified by ambitious investment plans. It decided to raise capital through the issue and sale of 'Development Bonds' to co-operative retail societies, trade unions and other bodies supportive of the movement. The first tranche in 1919 was for £2.5 million and the second for £4.5 million. The monies were used to fund £3.7 million of capital investment, contributing to an expansion of CWS productive works from 54 to 76.[11] Though SCWS lacked its English counterpart's financial resources, it opened the Springside Tomato Farm, the Falkland Floor-cloth Factory and the Eastfield Paper mill in 1919–20.[12] The wholesales were thus relatively undeterred by the challenges of the peace, and the English CWS was very confident about its prospects.

Such optimism would certainly have been tempered had the leaders of the wholesales enjoyed an inkling of what the next quarter of a century would bring for its interests, both at home and abroad. In Britain, the post-war boom would rapidly give way to a severe economic downturn in 1921, which would see unemployment rise to 2 million and obdurately remain above 1 million until after the outbreak of the Second World War in 1939.[13] The industrialised regions, which were the heartlands of consumer co-operation, would be especially badly affected, inflicting severe losses on retail societies and even resulting in a loss for the CWS of £3.4 million between March and September 1921, and a loss of almost £250,000 for the SCWS in 1921 as a whole.[14] While both wholesales quickly returned to profit as the 1920s progressed, the decade remained challenging, as industrial relations deteriorated and culminated in the General Strike of 1926. Just as trade appeared to be recovering, an even greater calamity befell the British economy in 1929, as a major stock market crash in the USA plunged the world into the Great Depression, with unemployment rising to over 3 million in Britain by 1931. The decade that followed saw a recovery in the British economy, especially in the south and midlands of England, where new industries such as motor vehicles, electrical goods and chemicals generated a significant rise in living standards for many, especially in the context of falling global commodity prices. For the co-operative movement, this produced mixed results—just as the ongoing problems of mass unemployment in the north inflicted losses and difficulties on societies there, so societies in London and the south, traditionally seen as weak areas for the movement, grew from strength to strength. As a result, the overall position of the wholesales and the movement in general remained reasonably stable during the inter-war period, and as will be seen, the international connections of the former were to prove invaluable for the war effort after 1939.

In terms of the wholesales' global links and the impact of worldwide developments in trade and international relations, the period may be divided into three distinct periods, and the organisation of this chapter reflects these. The next section of this chapter will examine developments between 1918 and 1929. Notwithstanding the downturn in British fortunes in 1921, this period was one of international reconstruction and recovery, led primarily by rapid growth in the economy of the USA and fuelled by that country's leading role as a food and manufacturing producer, as well as its position as the new main source of international loans and credit.[15] Britain sought to re-establish its position as a major centre of international finance by returning to the Gold Standard in 1925, after having being forced to leave it during the war. But this caused its own problems, as it overpriced British manufactures on the global market and contributed to industrial strife and unemployment. The war and the Treaty of Versailles had radically altered the political context for international commerce. A tranche of newly independent states was created in Eastern Europe, including Poland, Czechoslovakia, Hungary and Yugoslavia, joining the Baltic states of Estonia, Latvia and Lithuania, which had been liberated from Russian rule by the revolutions of 1917 and the Bolshevik peace treaty with the Germans at Brest-Litovsk in 1918. There were large projects of state and economy building here that had to be undertaken, as well as one of reconstruction in the war-ravaged economies of Belgium, France, Germany and Austria. It will be seen that the wholesales, especially the English CWS, were determined to play a role in these schemes of recovery and reconstruction, seeing in them opportunities for both commercial advantage and co-operative advancement by supporting co-operative movements across the continent. Indeed, the wholesales at least nominally supported the efforts of the ICA to promote co-operation, especially through the creation of an International CWS, which it hoped would eventually service co-operatives and wholesales around the world with jointly procured commodities. The most controversial aspect of CWS policy in the field of reconstruction was the wholesales' enthusiasm for building commercial and financial links with the Soviet Union, especially after the end of the Russian Civil War of 1918–21, and the launch of the regime's New Economic Policy (NEP), which sought to accommodate an element of market economics and a certain prioritisation of overseas trade as a source of essential commodities and precious foreign exchange. For the wholesales, this was in part an ideological commitment to supporting what seemed to be the world's first workers' state. The British Empire also became an important focus of wholesale activity, especially Canada, Australia and New Zealand. This was again prompted by commercial aims and ideological commitment, though in this case it also reflected efforts by the British state to redefine its relations with its Empire in a context of increasing resistance to British rule in India and a continuing drift of the 'white dominions' towards independence. The 1920s saw British governments groping towards the notion that the Empire was a project of economic and social development rather than one of pure exploitation. Ultimately, this resulted in the Colonial Development Act of 1929, which set up a Treasury resource for the funding of development projects in the Empire.[16] It will be seen that the wholesales commercial involvement in Empire became more significant during the 1920s, and that some of its most sophisticated initiatives to secure its supply chains were developed there.

The third section of the chapter then turns to the period from 1929 to 1939, in which the Great Depression wreaked havoc across the world and then ushered in a phase of 'de-globalisation', as the major industrial economies of Europe and North America abandoned aspirations to free trade and scrambled to protect their markets, forming a series of trading and currency blocs within which trade and investment tended to cluster. By 1937, when some measure of international recovery was under way, the volume of international trade was still only 97 per cent of its 1929 level.[17] In terms of Britain's international trade after 1929, the situation was especially stark, given the country's historic position as a leader of trade liberalisation and a major exporter of manufactures. In terms of exports, the British economy had already been struggling to recover even its 1913 position before the onset of the Great Depression. As late as 1929, the value of British exports of goods and services were only about 80 per cent of the 1913 level; and by the end of the 1930s, they were only 75 per cent of the 1913 level.[18] In contrast, Britain's dependence on imports of raw materials and food meant that imports grew in value, to 20 per cent higher than 1913 in 1930, and nearly 40 per cent higher than 1913 by the outbreak of war in 1939.[19] The resultant deficit in the trade in goods and services was alleviated by falling commodity prices in the 1930s, and by invisible earnings from interest and dividends earned overseas. In addition, it became British policy to focus its trade with the Empire and the 'Sterling Area', a bloc of countries (mostly but not exclusively in the Empire) that tended to base their currencies on Sterling.[20] A central theme of this section will be how the wholesales adapted to this increasingly difficult context for international commerce in the 1930s, and the strategies they employed to contend with a period of effective retreat for the globalised economy.

The final section then turns to the Second World War, when, as between 1914 to 1918, international trade was disrupted (even more so than in the First World War), and the state intervened to control the economy, involving policies such as state control of international trade and rationing. It will be seen that the co-operative movement—especially the wholesales— was to play a much more prominent role in facilitating international trade, and indeed in shaping state economic policy, than was the case between 1914 and 1918. The nature of the co-operative role—and some consideration of its legacy—will be the central issue in this section.

II

Although the wholesales fiercely resisted the reforms suggested in the third General Survey Committee Report, they were certainly not impervious to a case for pragmatic change under their own control. Its leadership had been aware of the growth of competition from multiple chains (chains with more than nine shops), which as early as 1915 commanded 7 to 8.5 per cent of the retail trade, compared to the co-operative societies' share of 7.5 to 9 per cent. Their concern well founded, as the multiples' share grew even faster than the co-operatives in the next 25 years, reaching 18–19.5 per cent by 1939, compared to the co-operative retail societies' 10–11.5 per cent.[21] The wholesales believed that a significant advantage could be gained by strengthening its overseas supplies of produce, especially given the immediate post-war boom and ongoing difficulties of price inflation. Thus, just a couple of months after the end of the war, the CWS Board set out preparations for centralised purchasing of a range of commodities, moving away from the prevailing practice of individual CWS departments and productive factories being able to purchase their requirements.[22] The belief was that this would not only keep prices as low as possible by bulk purchase deals but also enable the CWS to co-ordinate its buying activities systematically, rather than leaving procurement to the preferences and foibles of individual CWS managers. The commodities to be subject to this new policy included sugar, dried fruit, rice, tapioca, maize, cereals, canned goods, butter and cheese. Individual CWS managers were assigned specific roles. Mr Mastin of the Manchester Head Office was to take responsibility for sugar and tapioca purchases. Mr Thomas of the Brislington butter factory was placed in charge of butter procurement. Mr Gough of Bristol would supervise cheese, while Mr Oldham of Manchester would lead on canned goods and Mr Andrew of the Green Fruit department in Manchester would buy American and Canadian apples. The purchase of dried fruit in Turkey and Greece would remain in the hands of the regular annual deputations to those countries.[23] It was also the intention to centralise wheat purchasing, which in fact was the first commodity earmarked for the new system. But as wheat imports remained subject to state control in January 1919, it was agreed that the system for this would be settled at a future date.[24] In addition, because it was anticipated that many new opportunities would emerge for trade with foreign co-operative organisations, the existing Export Committee was reformed, with three representatives each from the Grocery and Drapery Committees as opposed to two as previously.[25]

It will become apparent that these were just the first two changes in the CWS' methods of handling overseas trade, and by no means the most radical. Trade with the Soviet Union and co-operative movements across Europe—new areas of wholesale international commerce—and with Australia and New Zealand saw some of the most radical innovations. Before turning to developments here between 1919 and 1929, a review of the well-established lines of wholesale commerce in North America and Europe will illustrate that these links remained as important as ever. West Africa and India also provided a strong element of continuity, as will become clear in a later chapter.

Some branches of CWS commerce seem to have continued in the 1920s with relatively little change. CWS trade with Greece and Turkey for dried fruit appears to have continued along pre-war lines, with few problems. The Denia depot in Spain also provided reliable and continuing service in supplying fruit, and significant investment was made in 1919 to construct an apricot pulping plant.[26] At the end of the decade a further £2,000 was invested in machinery for apricot pulping.[27] That great staple of the wholesales' overseas supplies, Denmark, also continued to be vital in the 1920s, though here there were challenges. Butter imports remained as important as ever, and in the first half of 1921 the weekly credit facility of the Esbjerg depot was doubled from £20,000 to £40,000, a move that also represented the increasing price of butter on the world market.[28] By the mid-1920s, Germany and the central European countries had emerged as major competing importers. Whereas in 1913 93.3 per cent of butter exports went to the UK, by 1926 this had fallen to 69.6 per cent, with Germany's share rising from just 1.4 per cent in 1913 to 24.1 per cent by 1926. Prices movements reflected this increased demand. Butter was 212.08 Kroner per 100 kilos in 1913, then rose to the dizzying heights of 614.51 Kroner per 100 kilos in 1920–1, at the end of the high post-war inflationary period. Although it fell to 424.34 Kroners in the following year, by 1924–5 it was 531.93 Kroner per 100 kilos.[29] Competition from rival private firms in the UK also intensified. In September 1920, the CWS Board sent a special deputation to discuss with their buyers in Denmark how to counter a major propaganda offensive by private traders seeking to win trade from the CWS in the butter import trade.[30] Some domestic Danish organisations also sought to cut out the CWS, through agents able to deal directly with co-operative societies in the UK. By 1928, Danish Co-operative Dairies, which controlled 40 per cent of dairies in the country, sent commission agents to Manchester and Birmingham, from where they sent out circulars to co-operative societies, offering lower prices than CWS. Another CWS deputation was hurriedly dispatched to Denmark to discuss counteractive strategies.[31] But by then, the wholesales were already seeking to develop alternative supplies of butter, from the Baltic states, Finland, Sweden, New Zealand, Australia and even Argentina.[32] CWS bacon interests in Denmark fared better. In June 1920, £10,000 of extensions and improvements were agreed for the Herning bacon factory.[33] On their completion in 1926, the factory could process 90,000 pigs per year.[34] However, even this was not enough to meet growing demand. In July 1928, the need for additional capacity of 50,000 pigs was recognised, and the result was a second, subsidiary factory about 25 miles from Herning at Skjern, which opened in November 1929.[35] So buoyant was the bacon trade that in February 1930 it was announced that the capital invested at Skjern could be written off much faster than anticipated.[36] But as will be seen in the next section, major problems were lying in wait.

North America also continued to satisfy the needs of the wholesales in the 1920s. The New York depot, and CWS/SCWS operations in the USA, surged during the immediate post-war boom of 1918–21. The manager of the New York depot, John Gledhill, had built a close relationship during the last year of the war with the Allied governments, and although in February 1919 the formal arrangement for collaboration between the CWS New York depot and the British Ministry of Food was terminated, it continued to occasionally process Ministry of Food orders, such as for bacon and lard in September 1919.[37] The post-war boom resulted in new initiatives to develop business, especially in California, where canned fish and dried fruit were in especially strong CWS demand.[38] Growing British demand for bacon prompted a deal by CWS in November 1919 to purchase as an experiment the whole bacon output of the Farmers Terminal Packing Company, a co-operative that had just opened a plant near St Paul in Minnesota and was equipped to process 1,000 pigs per day.[39] In March 1920, senior managers of CWS boot and shoe factories, including their new plant in Northampton, were sent to the USA to purchase £250,000 worth of leather.[40] The weakness of Sterling, and the consequent high cost of exchange, compelled CWS to allow the CWS depot to borrow locally to meet its increasingly heavy purchases. For February and March 1920 alone, the New York depot estimated it would need $1 million (c£300,000) to meet its obligations.[41] Even after the British slump of the early 1920s, purchases in the USA remained buoyant, prompting Gledhill's successor in New York, William J. Murphy, and his deputy, Andrew M. Duggan, to become representatives on the Chicago Board of Trade in summer 1922.[42] When the 50th anniversary of the establishment of the New York depot was celebrated in 1926, there was much reflection on its success. Since its establishment, the depot had shipped over £57 million of commodities to the UK, and 1924 was cited as the record year, with a turnover of £4,543,374.[43] It had even achieved a position of significance in the US economy for certain products. In 1925, the depot shipped 19.4 per cent of American lard exports and 20 per cent of oleo oil and rice.[44] Even after the crash of 1929, it will be seen that New York and the USA would continue to play an important role in the wholesales' overseas commerce.

The wholesales' interests in Canada also developed rapidly in the 1920s. In 1927 CWS agreed to bulk purchase the output of the Quebec cheese factories, having been approached to do so by the commercial agent of the Quebec government.[45] But wheat continued to be central to their concerns. Probably the most significant development in Canada, as was the case in Australia, was the emergence of wheat pools, farmer-led co-operative organisations that sought to reduce the dependence of farmers on middlemen to sell their produce and to prevent gluts and falling prices by a more controlled release of grain onto the market. By 1926, there were three major wheat pools in Manitoba, Saskatchewan and

Alberta, with a total of 125,000 members, commanding 65 to 70 per cent of the exportable surplus of Canadian wheat.[46] The reaction in many parts of British commercial opinion and the press was quite negative, viewing the pools as an exploitative attempt by a few vested interests to push up the price of grain. This was a suspicion that even infected the British co-operative movement, notwithstanding the co-operative credentials of the pools. There was particular concern when representatives of the Canadian wheat pools visited Australia to discuss synchronisation of marketing activities in order to prevent gluts caused by Canadian and Australian wheat landing simultaneously at British and other ports.[47] These worries prompted a series of visits to London by wheat pool leaders to soothe ill feeling and reassure British customers.[48] At one of these in February 1928, A.H. Hobley, the central wheat buyer for CWS, speaking for what by then was the largest buyer of wheat in the UK, welcomed the wheat pool as a legitimate response by farmers to the threat of 'capitalistic domination', but stressed the importance of keeping prices reasonably low.[49] Later that year at the Third Annual International Wheat Pools Conference in Saskatchewan, representatives from both CWS and SCWS stressed the importance of wheat pools collaborating closely with the consumer co-operative movements in the UK.[50] As will be seen, the CWS' relations with the Australian wheat pools was even more ambitious. CWS also developed close relations with specific Canadian societies. Sixteen societies in Saskatchewan purchased over 1,000 lbs of tea every month from the CWS, as well as sundry other goods.[51] In March the following year, the Saskatchewan Grain Growers Association Ltd opened negotiations with CWS to supply them with consumer goods, and by November an agreement was in place, backed by £5,000 of credit granted by CWS.[52]

Food prices, especially of commodities such as wheat and butter, were a major concern for all wholesalers and provisions retailers in the immediate post-war period. This partly resulted from the effective cessation of wheat and other supplies from Russia until the early 1920s because of revolution and civil war. The high inflation, stimulated by the post-war recovery at least until the early 1920s, also heightened anxieties about food. In fact, the late 1920s saw the prices of wheat and other foods fall with increased production, facilitated by the spread of new technologies and the opening of more land for production.[53] But earlier in the decade, so pressing were concerns about shortage and prices that the wholesales took some quite innovative and controversial steps to increase food supplies.

The most controversial were moves from the early 1920s by CWS and SCWS to try to develop trade with the Soviet Union, especially with those co-operative organisations that had survived the revolution, albeit with severe interference from the Soviet state. Russia had seen the rapid development of co-operation in the ten years before the revolutions of

1917. By 1920, there were 26,000 consumer societies, which together with dairy and credit co-operatives ensured that most of the population was either a member of, or linked in some way to, a co-operative.[54] It was strongly claimed by some pre-revolutionary co-operative leaders that during the war the co-operatives were essential in supplying the population with food, and that this position became even more pronounced after the March 1917 revolution.[55] But the movement rapidly fell foul of the new Bolshevik regime for a number of reasons. The first was essentially ideological; Lenin regarded co-operatives as essentially a form of 'capitalist collectivism' that needed to be replaced by state institutions firmly under the control of the Soviet state.[56] A second factor was that in the deepening economic and social crisis caused by the civil war from 1918, the Bolshevik strategy was based on the imposition of state rule through force ('War Communism') and the ruthless suppression of any independent bodies that might form a focus of opposition. The fact that many Russian co-operatives tried to continue their operations across the fast-moving territorial divisions created by the Civil War inevitably fuelled Bolshevik suspicion of potential co-operative treachery.[57] As a result, during 1919 the Bolsheviks moved to destroy the independence of the co-operatives and to bring them under communist control, effectively nationalising major co-operative bodies such as Centrosoyus (The All Russian Union of Co-operative Societies) and the Moscow Narodny Bank, the Co-operative Bank, by merging it with the State Bank.[58] The takeover became deeply repressive when, in autumn 1920, 11 leaders of Centrosoyus were sentenced to a total of 125 years imprisonment.[59]

The repression of the Russian co-operators became an issue within the British co-operative movement, which, since 1917, had viewed the revolution as a moment when co-operation would be liberated from the restrictions of tsarism and could develop deep and lasting links with the British and global movements. The British wholesales were motivated by commercial opportunities as well as ideology. As early as April 1917, the wholesales and several Russian co-operative organisations had set up the Russo–British Information Bureau based in London to promote greater collaboration between the two movements.[60] Early in 1919, there was a flurry of pro-co-operative and pro-Soviet activity and articles, especially in the *Co-operative News*, with opposition to British intervention in the Civil War being a strong theme.[61] By July, CWS was negotiating with the Rostock-on-Don Co-operative Society to develop £150,000 of trade with southern Russia and was preparing to send representatives out there.[62] But by January 1920, these efforts had been abandoned, chiefly because of the dangers of the civil war, although a delegation representing various Russian co-operative organisations visited the CWS in Manchester. Perhaps unwisely, one of the visitors pointed out that co-operatives were functioning in Siberia, where opposition to the Bolsheviks was in control.[63] Thereafter came the Bolshevik clampdown. In October 1920 a CWS shipment to southern Russia worth c£65,000 was lost when the Soviet government seized control of local co-operatives and refused to honour debts to the CWS.[64] Then, Edward Owen Greening, a prominent co-operator working closely with Russian co-operators in London facing Bolshevik oppression, wrote a series of four articles in the *Co-operative News* (three on the front page) in November and December 1920, savagely condemning the repression of the co-operative movement in Russia.[65] The situation was even more confused by war between the Soviet Union and Poland, which raged from spring 1919 to August 1920 and ultimately ended in Soviet defeat. During this conflict, however, Lenin decided that a revival of trade with the western powers was essential, given the escalating economic and social problems caused by the civil war and the conflict with Poland. He identified the British specifically as likely to be tempted by the prospect of a trade deal, and to this end, in August 1920, a Soviet delegation arrived in London to negotiate a deal with the British government. A key member of the delegation was Leonid Krasin, a man with extensive business experience as well as a fierce commitment to the communist cause.[66] Krasin was one of ten people 'elected' by the Soviets to lead Centrosoyus, effectively replacing the non-Bolshevik leadership of the organisation.[67] The negotiations ultimately bore fruit with the signing of an Anglo–Soviet Trade Treaty in March 1921.

If Greening voiced fears about Soviet treatment of the co-operative movement, his reservations were nothing compared to the deep hostility harboured towards the Soviet regime by the British Security Services and leading figures in government, such as Lord Curzon. Throughout the 1920s, the Security Services offered deep and bitter political resistance to all efforts at rapprochement with the USSR, as well as strenuous efforts to unearth, arrest and deport all Soviet citizens suspected of espionage against Britain—which in effective amounted to virtually all Russians in the UK.[68] The result of this was that throughout the interwar period, those involved in commerce with Russia, especially the co-operative wholesales, were subject to deep state suspicion and the danger of disruption as a result of security operations. In the 1920s, there were three times when this proved to be especially difficult. Following the departure of Lloyd-George in 1923, Lord Curzon, with the support of the new Conservative PM Andrew Bonar Law, issued an ultimatum to the Soviets to cease their clandestine activities in the UK, which only died down when Bonar Law's resignation due to illness in May 1923 resulted in a restraining hand being imposed by Stanley Baldwin, the new PM.[69] Then, during Labour's first administration of 1924, relations were damaged (and Labour catapulted out of office in a General Election) as a result of an almost certainly counterfeit letter from a senior Soviet leader, Zinoviev, that suggested some parts of the Labour administration were unacceptably close to Moscow.[70] In May 1927, the Security Services conducted a raid on the premises of ARCOS (the All Russian Co-operative

Society, a Soviet creation), which threatened to disrupt trade for a while but ultimately backfired from the Security Services' perspective.[71] What this meant was that the wholesales themselves would court the disapproval of the political right and the British state as it sought to develop commerce with the Soviet Union.

The Greening warning about engaging with a Soviet regime apparently hostile to independent co-operatives was superseded by events. In the spring of 1921, Lenin launched the New Economic Policy (NEP), which conceded a substantial role for small-scale private enterprise, including co-operatives, as necessary for economic recovery in the wake of the civil war and the terrible famine that ravaged the Soviet Union in 1921.[72] The British movement received the news with great enthusiasm, and in April 1921 a *Co-operative News* editorial proclaimed "Russian Co-operators Again Free" and urged the rapid development of trading links with the Soviet co-operative movement.[73] An uneasy settlement was even reached early in 1922 between the Soviet regime and the previous leaders of Russian co-operation outside the Soviet Union, who reluctantly conceded that Centrosoyus would now be headed by a representative of the Soviet regime.[74] Thus, from 1921 the wholesales began to tentatively develop commerce with the Soviet Union and its co-operative organisations. In July 1921, CWS agreed to undertake trade with ARCOS, but only on a limited, cash basis.[75] By April 1922, deals were being struck with Centrosoyus (through their UK London Office), provided the latter agreed to settle outstanding debts and that all trading would be on a cash basis. Centrosoyus' request that the CWS Bank allow them credit terms was, at this stage, refused.[76] But, in due course, a more liberal relationship emerged. As early as October 1922, CWS agreed to sell skins and furs valued at £90,000 sent by Centrosoyus through their own tannery manager at Grappenhall, with the CWS bank advancing a small percentage of the value to Centrosoyus.[77] As will be seen, this role for the CWS Bank in promoting trade would prove to be a very important component of CWS' overseas trade and procurement strategy. Confidence in Russian trade was boosted by Centrosoyus (UK) paying down a significant part of its debts, and with its appointment of E.F. Wise, a former senior British Civil Servant, as an economic adviser.[78] Wise wasted no time in emphasising the rapid recovery of Soviet trade, with Soviet exports having grown fivefold between 1921 and 1922, and he stressed that the Soviets had a preference for trading with the co-operative movement over capitalists.[79] Trade grew rapidly. Between 1922 and 1924, Centrosoyus sold goods for a total of £4,006,768 and bought CWS and British produce worth £1,572,533.[80]

In 1924, CWS and Centrosoyus devised a new method for undertaking its trade in wheat, barley and a range of other crops that would prove profitable for both organisations. A new company, the Russo–British Grain Company, was established with CWS and Centrosoyus (UK) as the principal shareholders, together with some private shipping and brokerage organisations.[81] Its business was the import of grains from co-operative and other producers in the Soviet Union, and their sale to purchasers in the UK. A crucial point was that the wholesales were intended to be just one of many customers for the imports; Russo–British Grain would sell to the wider market, not just the co-operative sector. Some customers were in continental Europe, including in Hamburg, Warsaw, Paris, Genoa and Copenhagen. From the CWS' point of view, this was a way of increasing supplies of wheat but also of deriving profits (as a shareholder) from a wider market than just the co-operative sector (sales to non-co-operatives directly by the CWS itself were still unacceptable to some sections of the movement), while ensuring as large a market as possible to facilitate the economic advantages of buying in bulk. In addition, the CWS Bank became the principal supplier of credit to Russo–British, charging interest on its loans to the company. For example, in July 1925, it contributed 80 per cent of a £500,000 loan to Russo–British for it to pay for the import of 500,000 tons of grain (33.3 per cent to be wheat) from Exportkhleb, the Soviet export agency, at an interest rate of 11.5 per cent per annum. Repayment was to be by 1 July 1926. In fact, the export target was exceeded and repayment was received in full before the due date. In return, a further loan of £800,000 at 10 per cent interest was then arranged in July 1926.[82] As will be seen, this strategy of setting up intermediary companies and funding their activities through CWS Bank resources was replicated in other branches of overseas commerce. Russo–British imports and sales were considerable in the following years. In the year ended 30 June 1927, Russo–British sold 550,350 tons of grain, some 421,259 tons to the UK market. Of the British sales, 53.7 per cent was wheat and 23.09 per cent was barley. CWS purchased just 19.8 per cent of Russo–British sales, mostly wheat.[83] The composition of trade changed significantly in the following years, as wheat prices began to recede internationally and other sources of wheat on the international market, such as Australia, began to expand output. In the year ended 30 June 1928, 214,055 tons of grain were contracted for, but in this year only 13.24 per cent was wheat, while soya beans formed 61.45 per cent the bulk of the exports.[84] In the following year (ended 30 June 1929), the quantity of imports fell to 139,424 tons and the dominance of soya beans became more pronounced, at 75.77 per cent of contracted sales. CWS imports were restricted to just 12,272 tons of wheat and were not included in the overall figures cited above, suggesting that this was by now the only wheat imported. CWS shares of the overall figure cited above was zero.[85] The soya imports were mainly from Vladivostock and represented part of thriving trade with Siberia enjoyed by CWS.[86]

The late 1920s saw an expansion of CWS deals with a range of Soviet organisations, with the CWS frequently supplying credit and loans to facilitate trade. The deals involved both buying Russian produce and exporting CWS and other commodities to the USSR. Herrings and other fish, packed or canned in the CWS' own facilities, were sold to a range of Russian bodies, including ARCOS, Centrosoyus, Selosoyus (the main Soviet agricultural co-operative organisation) and Ukrainian Co-operatives, which represented a range of co-operatives in that state.[87] In December 1926, the CWS Bank made £150,000 available in credit for this branch of trade.[88] Mazlocentr (the leading co-operative organisation for the production and export of butter) struck a deal with CWS whereby it received credit of £100,000 for the export of 80,000 casks of butter, for 6 per cent interest and commission. This was in addition to 20,000 casks already handled by CWS.[89] Ukrainian Co-operatives was granted credit of £25,000 in 1927, mainly to enable its purchase of CWS textiles, at interest of 2 per cent above bank rate, with a minimum of 6 per cent.[90] Centrosoyus also bought substantial supplies of tea from the wholesales, increasing from £23,194 in 1924, £57,865 in 1925 and £212,422 in 1926 to £396,711 in 1927.[91] During the difficult months following the ARCOS raid in May 1927, CWS even agreed to export the produce (cutlery) of a private firm, John Kenyon & Co., for a commission of 2.5 per cent on the invoice price, as at that time only the co-operative wholesales were still trading with the USSR on a systematic basis.[92] By the end of the 1920s, trade between CWS and the USSR, either directly or through the Russo–British Grain Co., was substantial and represented probably the most important channel of commerce between the two countries, in spite of a politically and ideologically hostile and unstable relationship between the two countries. In the 1930s, in light of the dramatic and tragic developments that afflicted Soviet agriculture, the wholesales' relations with Russia were, with hindsight, to appear even more controversial.

The CWS Bank also played a vital role in another major area of wholesale commercial expansion in the 1920s: with the British Empire Dominions of New Zealand and Australia. CWS trade with New Zealand was identified as important from the end of the war, given that country's emerging reputation for dairy produce and meat. In February 1920, a deal was struck between CWS and the New Zealand Dairy Association to establish a new company, in which they would be the main joint shareholders.[93] The move triggered alarm among private traders, and it was even alleged in the House of Commons that the initiative aimed to secure CWS and the New Zealand Dairy Association an effective monopoly of all butter and cheese exports from New Zealand.[94] The accusation was rejected fiercely by the London office of the New Zealand Dairy Association, which pointed out that 65,000 tons of cheese and 20,000 tons of butter were available for export.[95] W.E. Dudley, a member of the CWS deputation sent to New Zealand to build relations with the Dairy Association and the farmers, also denied any monopolistic intentions, stressing instead that the move was in keeping with the longstanding CWS policy of going directly to the producer and partly resulted from the strong co-operative traditions among New Zealand's farmers.[96] In New Zealand itself, the Dairy Association led the way to forming the New Zealand Co-operative Marketing Company, consisting of a wide range of dairy producers and firms, with the objective of focusing as much of its trade as possible through the joint Dairy Association–CWS company.[97] The latter was named the New Zealand Produce Association (NZPA) and was London based, dealing with the import of butter and cheese from the home country. The Board consisted of equal representation from the Dairy Association and CWS. The CWS managed to persuade member societies (especially in London) to actively promote New Zealand butter and cheese in their stores, using posters designed and distributed by CWS.[98] As with the trade with Russia, the CWS Bank supplied much of the credit with which NZPA traded. The amounts were substantial. For example, by October 1920, £179,000 had been extended by CWS bank in credit to NZPA.[99] In August 1926, £94,000 credit was arranged to fund butter and cheese purchases over 12 months.[100] Credit was regularly supplied by CWS via a range of different local banks in New Zealand and Australia.[101] The bank also occasionally lent money to firms for capital investment through NZPA, for example to a freezing company in July 1927.[102] By the late 1920s, NZPA had extended its promotion of New Zealand exports to meat, especially mutton and lamb.[103] In October 1927, CWS agreed to share profits with the NZPA on an experimental purchase of 100,000 to 120,000 carcasses.[104] The arrangement placed CWS in a very powerful position in relation to the export trade in New Zealand agricultural produce.

CWS activity in Australia also grew rapidly in the 1920s and involved the CWS Bank and new, innovative activity to secure control over commodity supplies. The failure and abandonment of the Sydney depot persuaded CWS leaders that if trade with Australia were to be revived, a different approach was required. The advance of both consumer and producers' co-operation in Australia persuaded CWS that it might be most effective to work through emergent Australian co-operatives to access the Australian market for both exports and imports. Thus, in 1920, the Australian Producers Wholesale Co-operative Federation indicated its willingness to help CWS build its commerce in both Australia and New Zealand.[105] But it was in the mid-1920s that major new initiatives were launched. In 1925, CWS brought into Liverpool its largest cargo of Australian wheat to date (12,400 tons), and it was then recognised that this could prove to be a major new source for CWS.[106] At the same time, a new opportunity emerged for CWS. Several wheat pools had been formed in Australia and had taken responsibility for negotiating the advances from the banks in Australia that their members needed to operate as wheat farmers. In 1924, however, many of those banks were reluctant to lend to the pools without a government guarantee of repayment, and several of the pools were fearful that an anti-co-operative political environment would prevent it.[107] As a result, the Wheat Pool of Western Australia (formed in 1922) turned to CWS for funding. It was the beginning of a long relationship involving advances of millions of pounds. The Western Australia Wheat Pool dominated the export of wheat in that state, handling 15 million bushels compared to 6.5 million handled by other organisations.[108] At the time, wheat prices had risen because of relatively weak harvests in USA and Canada, which was one reason why CWS embraced the deal so quickly. As a result, CWS advances to the Western Australia Pool were substantial and revised from £1 million in March 1926, to £1.75 million in October 1926, then £2.5 million in December 1926 and finally to £3.5 million to cope with a larger harvest than expected.[109] The relationship continued year on year, with another £3.5 million being pledged for the forthcoming season in October 1927, the same in September 1928 and £3 million in October 1929.[110] CWS also funded the activities of another co-operative organisation in Western Australia, Westralian Farmers. Westralian Farmers was established in 1914 by the Farmers and Settlers Association of Western Australia to provide a wide range of services for member farmers, from tools to bags to transport and warehousing facilities.[111] CWS agreed to help fund the Westralian scheme for supplying tractors and other equipment to farmers.[112] As will be seen, these relationships with the West Australian Wheat Pool as well as Westralian Farmers would survive and thrive, even in the difficult years of the early 1930s. A similar but much more temporary relationship was struck with the Wheat Pool of South Australia early in 1927, with CWS advancing £1.5 million to this organisation.[113]

CWS interests in New Zealand and Australia were regarded by its leaders and supporters as ground-breaking, as they should also be by business historians. There are three reasons for this. Firstly, the creation of a separate company in the case of NZPA marked an important new strategy for CWS in its pursuit of taking its supply chains as close as possible to the supplier. It represented a unique alliance between local business interests and the CWS that was designed to channel a very large portion of local produce into CWS control through its joint role in NZPA. Moreover, it enabled CWS to secure the advantage of profiting from selling to a wider market than just the co-operative movement without incurring ideological opposition within the movement, which tended to frown upon the wholesales serving any customers other than the co-operative societies. Secondly, the role of the CWS Bank in funding and providing credit was at the heart of the deals and relationships that made the impressive advances in Australasia possible. Just as in its relations with the Soviet Union, this proved to be a major strategic advantage for the CWS in securing overseas supplies and growing trade. Moreover, CWS leaders and co-operators were aware that this was a strategic approach to securing supply chains and not mere accidental opportunism. In February 1926, an article appeared in the *Co-operative News* entitled "Trader and Banker: How the CWS is cheapening the food of the people". It was a report of a speech given by J. Oliver, CWS director, in which he lauded the unique role of the CWS Bank in promoting CWS commerce in Australia and New Zealand, and he stressed the unique nature of the role of the bank and how it successfully utilised bank resources in a way that enhanced the success of CWS.[114] It was seen as strategy and not mere opportunism. Thirdly, the growth of CWS Australasian commerce was seen increasingly both within the wholesales and across the movement more widely as indicative of the positive role the movement was acquiring within the British Empire. The *Co-operative News* and the *Producer* carried numerous articles and reports of activities that hailed the benefits and contributions of co-operative trade for the Empire. Thus, in October 1926, the eminent co-operator Sir Thomas Allen, the CWS director, spoke to a Co-operative Party Summer School about how it was the responsibility of co-operators to buy Empire produce, and how co-operation was promoting the development of the colonies.[115] Allen had been recently appointed to the newly created Empire Marketing Board, recognition in itself just how important to the Empire the British co-operative movement and wholesales were seen as by even a Conservative government.[116] In April 1928, a special dinner was hosted by CWS and SCWS in London, attended by an array of politicians, Whitehall civil servants with imperial responsibilities, soldiers, officials from the colonies and representatives from the Empire Marketing Board. They were regaled with speeches about the value of co-operation and especially the trade of the wholesales to the Empire. It was pointed out that in 1927 the CWS imports from the Dominions were worth £6.7 million.[117] In December 1928, the Secretary of State for the Dominions, L.S. Amery, even described the wholesales as "a great imperial organisation".[118] Notwithstanding its continuing support for the principle of free trade, the co-operative movement was, by the end of the 1920s, increasingly pro-Empire, and this party reflected the growth of the wholesales' imperial commerce.

The First World War had of course left a legacy of destruction and political change as new states emerged in Eastern Europe. For the international co-operative movement, this presented opportunities as well as problems, as it was perceived that co-operation could provide a solution to some of the problems caused by war. The CWS, as the wealthiest and largest European wholesale, was best placed to lead in a policy of co-operative reconstruction and saw commercial opportunities in such a role. Once again, the role of the CWS Bank was central to this policy, with the granting of credit and loans to co-operative organisations and wholesales across Europe. In the weeks after the end of the war, CWS received requests for financial help and new trade deals from both the Belgian and French co-operative movements.[119] CWS granted £100,000 in goods on credit to the Belgian CWS, and its request for a loan was eventually agreed (at 3 per cent interest) in April 1919.[120] In summer

1919 CWS arranged for generous credit trade terms to supply several European co-operative organisations, including £200,000 maximum rolling credit for the Polish CWS (Warsaw Federation); £100,000 for the Polish CWS (Country Federation) that was guaranteed by the Polish government; a massive £500,000 credit for the Polish Co-operative Union, again government backed; £20,000 for the Finnish CWS; and a staggering £400,000 in credit for the Rumanian CWS (£250,000 of which was government guaranteed). A special Export Sub-Committee was set up to work with foreign co-operatives as well.[121] The Serbian and Czech wholesales followed, with credit of £200,000 and £100,000 respectively, both government guaranteed.[122] Political sensitivities prompted refusal of requests from the German and Austrian wholesales.[123] The strategy was certainly designed to promote co-operation in the new states of Eastern Europe; indeed, there was a lively campaign in the Co-operative Press and within the wider movement to develop trade with co-operators abroad, if necessary through barter.[124] It was also, of course, guided by a desire to develop new markets for CWS produce there. But problems quickly emerged. In February 1920, CWS complained bitterly that both the Polish CU and the Warsaw Federation had yet to pay anything, having received a total of £266,879 in CWS goods. A battle ensued to secure repayment.[125] Caution began to be urged by CWS representatives to those campaigning for an extension of co-operative international trade by any means. Trade must be prudent and conducted on commercial principles. There was no room for "meddling sentiment".[126] More problems followed. By summer 1921, the Rumanian CWS had run up debts of £440,000, and negotiations in Bucharest resulted in a postponement of repayment for two years.[127] An agreement was eventually made with the Rumanian government whereby the debt (£565,000 by now) would be paid off in instalments with 5.5 per cent interest (£65,000 per year for 25 years), but this was only reached in July 1926.[128] The Warsaw Federation and other Polish co-operative bodies had also run up high debts to CWS by the summer of 1922, and CWS was moving towards approaching the government for it to honour its guarantee.[129] But the case dragged on, with the Polish government prevaricating over its commitments, and political crisis in that country caused yet further delays.[130] Ultimately, the matter was only settled in June 1930, and the CWS had to write off half of the debt in return for the Polish government repaying the rest over five years.[131]

Not all debtors were in the East. In August 1928, the Antwerp Co-operative Federation only agreed to pay its £84,126 debt to CWS in instalments.[132] While these problems did not stop trading by the British wholesales with continental co-operatives (the Latvian, Estonian and Lithuanian wholesales bought herrings, sugar, spices and even bicycles from CWS during this period), they did have negative consequences for more ambitious multilateral co-operative trading initiatives.[133]

A powerful idea that emerged after the war, and one especially within the ICA, was the creation of an International CWS (ICWS), jointly run and funded by national co-operative wholesales and/or Co-operative Unions, which would share intelligence about commerce between national movements and ultimately trade and sell to co-operatives across the world. Using bulk purchasing power on an unprecedented scale, this would ensure the cheapest prices for consumer co-operatives, enabling them to defeat capitalist opposition and provide a large market for co-operative production. It was an idea given extra momentum by the successful creation in July 1918 of *Nordilsk Andelsförbund* (NAF), which made joint purchases for societies in Denmark, Sweden and Norway, and Finland, from 1928. Its trade grew quickly in the 1920s, and it proved pivotal to Scandinavian co-operative success.[134] It was the work of Albin Johansson and Väinö Tanner, leading Swedish co-operators, and Johansson went on to become a major promoter of the idea of an International Co-operative Wholesale Society (ICWS). In 1919, CWS and SCWS both supported the initiative and participated in early discussions.[135] But progress in establishing such a practical body proved difficult, partly because of questions over how to resource it, but also because of the problems of international trade instability fomented by exchange difficulties and the collapse of the German Mark in 1923.[136] When the body was eventually formed in 1924, it was merely a medium for exchanging information.[137] In 1927, Johansson and others tried to move the ICWS into more practical steps such as co-ordinating co-operative production and even moving into trade.[138] Pressure for this mounted when, in 1928, the Finnish wholesale societies joined NAF.[139] But, in October 1928, CWS made clear its opposition to such a move. While it did not object to other wholesales engaging in collaborative purchasing and selling, it rejected that this be done under the auspices of the ICWS.[140] There were several reasons for this stance. Firstly, CWS was concerned that a successful ICWS might usurp CWS' aspiration to be the main if not sole supplier to British consumer co-operatives. Consumer society loyalty to CWS had long been an issue, without compounding the problem with a thriving ICWS. Secondly, as the largest wholesale in the world by a substantial distance, CWS leaders believed, probably correctly, that the financial burden of a trading and growing ICWS would fall upon it, and it doubted whether its member societies would tolerate this for long. And, crucially, CWS experiences in Eastern Europe with wholesale societies, and even with some in western Europe, gave rise to grave doubts about whether other societies could provide the sound commercial leadership a successful ICWS would need. This would prove to be a crucial factor in the disappointing progress ICWS would make in the inter-war period, though as will be seen, in the 1930s other forces would contribute to the problem.

The 1920s was a decade in which, despite the problems identified, the British wholesales, especially CWS, were confident that they had the resources and the methods to strengthen and manage the international supply chains on which the movement relied. In addition to the initiatives already cited, CWS trade spread into new parts of the world with which links had previously been slight or non-existent. One of the best examples was CWS trade with Argentina. Argentinian butter was purchased through the services of Nicolas Largo, a local agent, and a shipping company, Messrs Elowson & Wester.[141] In November 1927, Largo was granted credit of £50,000 by the CWS bank to supply 40,000 boxes of butter.[142] By November 1926, Hobley, the CWS wheat buyer, was pressing to secure 16,000 tons of wheat from Rosario through E & E Pillitz, CWS agents in Buenos Aires.[143] Orders for butter and wheat continued throughout the inter-war period. Argentinian co-operative societies also affiliated with CWS to procure CWS produce. *El Hogar Obrero*, a consumer society in Buenos Aires, purchased for Argentinian $16,920 a range of CWS produce, especially cloth.[144] Another customer was the Icelandic society *Mjokurfelag Rekjavikur*, which ordered maize and other supplies in 1928 and would become heavily dependent on CWS for credit.[145] These were just two key developments; there were others. But the optimism and expansion of the 1920s would be challenged by the much more difficult years of the 1930s.

III

Historians of globalisation have shown that the flourishing of global commerce and migration, and the emergence of worldwide cultural, political and legal commonalities, was neither as recent nor as 'all-conquering' as some have assumed. Rather, globalisation is now regarded as a series of 'waves' across hundreds of years that ebbed and flowed, with periods of strong globalising activity punctuated by periods of retrenchment (usually wars or economic depression and dislocation).[146] The international supply chains and global strategies of the wholesales had been constructed during a period of intense globalisation, in which Empires, industrialisation, population growth and migration created a global economy that was unprecedented in the degree of its integration.[147] While the protectionism of some countries had proved a barrier (Germany in particular), and there was major disruption caused by the First World War, generally the expansion of the wholesales' global commerce reflected this flourishing of globalising forces. But after 1929, a very different and much more difficult period of 'de-globalisation' unfolded that would last well into the 1950s before new global leadership and institutions revived the globalising trend seen before the 1930s. It will be seen that while the wholesales tried, with some success, to adapt to this much more difficult environment, ultimately barriers to trade and the war that followed (1939–45) would combine with other factors to degrade and ultimately break up the wholesales' global system of trade and procurement during the post-war world.

The stock market crash on Wall Street in 1929 began a startling deterioration of global economic conditions. It led to the recall of large US loans to countries like Germany, precipitating economic collapse and the rise to power of Nazism by 1933. One by one, the developed economies of Europe introduced tariffs on trade to protect their domestic markets. By the early 1930s, even Britain, the historic citadel of free trade, resorted to protectionism. The fiscal crisis caused by economic downturn and spiralling unemployment forced the minority Labour government of 1929–31 to introduce deeply unpopular cuts in social spending, in a desperate rear-guard action to protect British commitment to the Gold Standard. In the event, the government split and fell, giving way to a Conservative-dominated National Government that went on to win a landslide election victory later in the year, but that nonetheless abandoned gold in the autumn. To try to prevent what could have been a disastrous collapse in Sterling, the National Government introduced emergency legislation to protect the balance of payments by curbing imports. The Abnormal Importations Act (1931) was followed by the Import Duties Act of February 1932, which eventually imposed duties of 10 per cent on manufactured imports in general, rising to 33.3 per cent on imported steel. Imports of most foodstuffs and goods from the Empire were exempt, but the following years would see a tightening of other rules that would impact further on supplies of food from outside the Empire.[148] British policy on foreign trade was quite nuanced in its objectives. While a sufficient fall in currency value to increase the competitiveness of British manufactures in foreign markets was welcome, the escalation of raw material and food prices was not. As a result, in the 1930s the British increasingly sought to maximise as much of its trade as possible within what came to be known as the 'Sterling Area'.[149] This consisted of many countries within the British Empire, but also some countries in Europe, including Denmark, the Baltic states and Portugal. These countries exported largely to the UK and were heavily dependent on its market. Consequently, they tried to shadow the value of Sterling in terms of the value of their own currency to ensure stability for their exports. In 1932, Britain negotiated a major agreement with the Dominions (Australia, New Zealand, Canada, South Africa) at Ottawa in Canada, which was designed to maximise trade within the Empire and Sterling Area (though Canada, due to the scale of its trade with the USA, was part of the dollar bloc). In practice, because the depression and falling commodity prices had hit primary producing countries such as Australia very hard, the agreement favoured the Dominions rather than Britain, as the former were desperate to afford some protection for their emerging industrial sectors. Nonetheless, trade within both the Empire and the Sterling Area did intensify in the 1930s. Exports from the UK to Dominions (except Canada) fell from £143 million annual average between 1925 and 1929, to £111 million between 1934 and 1938.[150] But exports to the Empire as a whole rose as a percentage of total British exports, from 35.2 per cent annual average for 1924–9, to 39.7 per cent in 1937.[151] Imports showed a much more successful intensification, with imports from the Dominions rising from £183 million annual average in 1925–9, to £189 million in 1934–8.[152] As a percentage of total imports, imports from the Empire as a whole grew from 26.8 per cent (1924–9 annual average) to 37.3 per cent in 1937.[153]

Ottawa was followed by a series of bilateral agreements with specific countries, trying to both increase exports and limit some imports. An important one of these was with Denmark, signed in 1933, which guaranteed quotas for Danish exports in return for reduced tariffs on British exports. The impact was significant. In 1932, Britain imported nearly five times as much from Denmark as it exported to that country by value, a ratio that fell to just double imports over exports by 1937.[154] As will be seen, all of these shifts in UK government policy had consequences for the trade of the wholesales with the wider world, as did the more general effects of the worldwide depression.

As seen, one of the fastest growing and increasingly important branches of CWS and SCWS trade was with Australia and New Zealand, and here the impact of the problems of the early 1930s was dramatic. In Australia, the commodities that it exported fell in price by 23 per cent in 1929–30 and continued to fall for the next three years. Because Australia had borrowed heavily in the London financial markets, the loss of export income threatened the possibility of default, and reluctantly the Australian government followed a policy of deflation and retrenchment that hit living standards hard in the 1930s.[155] The Ottawa agreement did help, however, and Australian exports to the UK grew from £59.2 million (quinquennial average 1925 to 1929) to £61.8 million (quinquennial average 1934 to 1938).[156] New Zealand also experienced a severe collapse in the prices of its exports, which fell by 40 per cent between 1929 and 1932, though because its debts were not as pressing as Australia's, it avoided the same level of severity experienced there.[157] Exports began to recover after 1932, especially as prices rose, but significantly, exports to the UK did not quite match their 1920s peak, with quinquennial averages falling from £47.9 million 1925–9 to £43.8 million 1934–8.[158] How did the wholesales respond to the crisis in Australasia?

In fact, CWS was strategic in its response to the growing difficulties in both Australia and New Zealand. Early in 1930, a CWS and NZPA deputation undertook a tour of CWS and NZPA interests in Australia and New Zealand and returned with key recommendations that would reshape their trade policies in the 1930s. As world commodity prices fell, and as both New Zealand and Australian producers looked desperately to bolster their markets overseas, there were opportunities for non-co-operative merchants and wholesalers to challenge the wholesales. The deputation's attention was drawn to the efforts of private traders to strike exclusive supply deals with meat freezing companies that would cut out the co-operative wholesales entirely from this source of supply. The Board of CWS debated how best to respond. One faction supported the establishment of the CWS' own freezing plant in New Zealand, but the majority baulked at the high cost of this at a time when the economic situation was so difficult at home and in New Zealand. Perhaps there were also memories of the intense local hostility the movement had encountered in Ireland when it started to invest heavily in its own creameries at the turn of the century. As large sections of New Zealand farming were organised into marketing and other co-operatives, the possibility of antagonism seemed real if CWS became a competitor for New Zealand enterprise. Instead, the Board opted for the relatively new strategy of securing a financial stake in key local businesses and working as closely as possible with native co-operative and other organisations. Of course, since the establishment of NZPA, CWS had already pioneered the former approach, and through that body it worked closely with the New Zealand Dairy Association and the New Zealand Marketing Association. Significantly, when the deputation was approached by the Farmers Co-operative Organisation of New Zealand, who wanted to sell directly to CWS rather than go through the New Zealand Marketing Association, the deputation politely refused, stressing that it was their policy to work through the local association.[159] But the idea of taking a stake in local businesses appealed, and the deputation identified a number of meat freezing companies in New Zealand who were likely to welcome such an approach, either because of financial difficulties or the need for new investment. These included the Patea Farmers Co-operative Freezing Company, which had incurred serious losses of £135,000 and desperately needed a loan of £55,000, and which after due consideration by CWS was rejected as an investment opportunity.[160] But it did pursue investments in other recommended partners, notably Southland Frozen Meat and Produce Company (£5,000 in shares) and Hawkes Bay Company (£10,000), both of which were much more stable organisations.[161] A similar approach was taken with the Co-operative Dairy Producers Freezing Company Ltd, by a £100,000 loan and by CWS taking a seat on the board. It reinforced its alignment with key New Zealand organisations by asking William Fisher of the New Zealand Marketing Association to represent it.[162] Supplying meat from New Zealand was identified as an area of difficulty, and a special deputation was sent out to address this in June 1931.[163] The result was a decision late in 1931, with the full support of the New Zealand Marketing Association, to appoint a CWS representative in New Zealand to buy meat directly from the farmers: A.G. Hodder, the first CWS representative, supported by a William Maxwell as deputy, who was employed by the New Zealand Marketing Association.[164] As with butter, CWS kept its options open in terms of sourcing meat in New Zealand. As with butter and cheese, though it continued to buy from the NZPA, and indeed provided loans and credits for NZPA to conduct many of its purchase operations, it retained the right to source from elsewhere also.[165] The presence of Hodder and a dedicated team of buyers did serve to increase CWS meat procurement over the next few years. In season 1931–2, CWS only imported 62,214 carcasses of lamb and mutton on its own account. By 1935–6, this had risen to over 500,000 carcasses—and CWS even introduced after freezing its 'Congress' and 'Raydex' brands on the meat that became well known among purchasing societies in the UK.[166] This was in addition to other supplies secured through NZPA, which in the case of meat seems to have exclusively supplied the wholesales.

CWS also moved to address the reduced income of NZPA as the prices of commodities fell. In January 1931, it approved a 10 per cent reduction of directors' fees, and in the following month lent £15,000 to the organisation to help it through short-term financial problems.[167] NZPA was still valued as an organisation that not only could support the co-operative market for dairy produce in the UK but also could and did sell to a wider UK market, enabling it to achieve economies through even greater bulk buying. Thus, NZPA regularly identified portions of CWS credit and loans used to source butter or cheese for non-co-operative buyers. For example, in February 1932, NZPA used £2,500 of the £90,000 credit allocated by CWS to secure 40 tons of 'Gorge Cheese' for Allied Suppliers Ltd, who in turn had to meet all costs of transport, exchange and import charges.[168] In February 1933, £4,000 credit was used to supply 2,000 boxes of best Northern Wairoa Brand Butter to four different traders and wholesalers in Glasgow.[169] Similar transactions appear throughout the 1930s in the Board minutes. The minutes of the NZPA are even more illuminating. Between 1 November 1934 and 7 August 1935, 67.31 per cent of NZPA butter sales and 58.53 per cent of cheese sales went to the co-operative wholesales, with the rest to the private trade.[170] By summer 1936, NZPA was in overall profit once more, though its butter and cheese trade tended to subsidise some losses on meat. It had paid £47,000 to CWS in its 15 years of existence and promised even larger profits in the future.[171]

In Australia, the strategy of attempting to work through trusted co-operative partner organisations was repeated. One of the most important deals struck by CWS was with the New South Wales Co-operative Wholesale Society (NSWCWS) in 1930, under which NSWCWS agreed to procure butter, fruit and other commodities for CWS. NSWCWS was the most reputable secondary co-operative in Australia at the time, having been established in 1912 and attracting 15 affiliates by 1934.[172] CWS paid NSWCWS £1,000 a year and £5 per week for this service and provided credit to facilitate its purchases.[173] It also agreed to promote CWS trade with other parts of Australia, especially Queensland.[174] In February 1932 alone, it sent £13,000 of goods to CWS, predominantly flour and butter.[175] Other co-operative organisations that agreed to either buy for CWS or sell CWS produce included the Gippaland and Northern Co-operative Company in Victoria, Adelaide Co-operative Society, Port Adelaide Co-operative Society and Kudunda Farmers Co-operative Society.[176] In Western Australia, CWS chose to work through Westralian Farmers, which, as shown, had been substantially funded by CWS since the mid-1920s, especially in respect of its warehousing scheme for farmers. In Western Australia, there were 58 co-operatives who wanted to buy a range of commodities from CWS, including crockery, cotton piece goods, brushware, hardware, herring and fish paste. Westralian Farmers had close contacts with most of these societies, and were placed to take orders and vouch for the financial viability of the societies and their ability to meet debt.[177] At the same time, in the early 1930s CWS continued to provide loans and credit to both Westralian Farmers and the Wheat Pool of Western Australia. Thus, in October 1931, CWS agreed to provide £1.5 million for the Wheat Pool, charging 5 per cent interest and 0.125 per cent commission.[178] Westralian Farmers were granted £150,000 in credit in the following month, and continued to receive CWS support for the rest of the decade.[179] But problems arose as the declining value of the Australian pound and the slump in the price of wheat continued. Within weeks of granting Westralian Farmers £150,000, the latter asked for this to be increased to £200,000. CWS agreed, but so concerned were they about the financial state of Western Australian Farmers that Sir Thomas Allen even met the Australian High Commissioner to obtain better insight into the problems faced by the farmers.[180] In the following April, CWS even refused a request for a loan of £463,000 to invest in new equipment for the bulk handling of wheat.[181] Further difficulties arose in Westralian Farmers efforts to recover advances of CWS funds it had made to farmers that had not been used by them. Many farmers, already in dire straits, were slow to pay. In April 1933, only 15 per cent (£26,000 Sterling, £34,000 in Australian pounds) of overpayments for the 1929–30 season had been recovered, and CWS had to extend the time due for repayment several times.[182] In May 1933, CWS also agreed to reduce interest on Westralian outstanding debts from 5.25 to 5 per cent.[183] Matters did improve for Westralian Farmers as the decade progressed and the Australian rural economy slowly recovered, enabling it to reduce debts significantly.

But relations with the Wheat Pool of Western Australia proved less durable. By 1933, it complained that CWS' interest and charges (5 per cent interest and 0.125 per cent commission) compared unfavourably with the Commonwealth Bank of Australia, which charged 4 per cent and no commission. Reluctantly, CWS reduced its interest to 4.5 per cent and waived its commission.[184] But the Wheat Pool tried to push CWS further, pointing out that local banks were willing to lend to them now, in contrast to the difficulties experienced in the early years of the Pool in the 1920s. CWS refused any further concessions.[185] In fact, the last advance

by CWS to the Wheat Pool was for 1933–4, when the last £83,000 of
the annual total £800,000 was released in August 1934.[186] Thereafter,
the Pool secured funding elsewhere, as they explained to a CWS deputation in 1936.[187] Another change in direction was also evident in the
mid-1930s. In late 1935, CWS decided to revive its Sydney depot, and it
sent its representative, a Mr Marsland, to set up an office. A CWS deputation to Australia was criticised by NSWCWS because they had not been
informed about it by CWS. The deputation tried to reassure NSWCWS
that CWS still intended to direct a lot of trade through them.[188] But it was
an empty pledge, and in September 1936, CWS diverted all the business
it did with NSWCWS and several other agents to it.[189] In the following
month, it instructed Mr Marsland, the Sydney depot buyer, to act for
SCWS, and in December the agreement with NSWCWS was formally
terminated.[190] The reasons for this sudden alteration in policy are not
clear from the records, but most likely there was some dissatisfaction
with the performance of NSWCWS, in respect of either the quality or
price of its services. Another factor may have been the limited geographical coverage that NSWCWS could offer, as it was strong mainly in New
South Wales. Certainly the new depot wasted little time in increasing
business in Queensland. In August 1937, £30,000 in credit was arranged
for Marsland to buy eggs there.[191] Then, in January 1938, £5,000 was
arranged for the purchase of Queensland butter.[192]

In both New Zealand and Australia, CWS attempted in the 1930s to
develop and adapt strategies to ensure adequate supplies of key commodities at the best possible prices, in economic circumstances that were difficult and exacting. The results contrasted in consistency and success. In
New Zealand, the strategy of using the NZPA to bulk buy dairy produce
was tested in the early 1930s but ultimately withstood the difficulties
encountered. It was augmented by the twin new strategies of direct support
to meat freezing companies and the establishment of direct meat buying
operations by CWS. In total, these adjustments enabled CWS to sustain a
strong performance in securing supplies of meat and dairy produce. The
record in Australia was less impressive; the loss of the Wheat Pool business
for Western Australia and the ultimately aborted arrangement with NSW-
CWS in favour of restoration of a depot and a direct CWS buying operation represented a dramatic change of policy in the mid-1930s, although
the arrangement with Westralian Farmers certainly represented a strong
element of continuity in policy. But the important point is that in both
Dominions, notwithstanding the challenges of the decade, a clear (if changing in the case of Australia) strategy was deployed by CWS that combined
various arrangements in an attempt at coherence. Once again, even under
duress, CWS was trying to manage its supply chains. It was not merely
reactive, and it was certainly not unplanned in its approach.

Similar strategic approaches were evident in the wholesales' activities in North America and elsewhere in the 1930s. Probably one of the

most sophisticated involved the supply of tinned salmon to the British co-operative market, a highly prized luxury item for the Sunday tea table in the middle-class as well as the affluent working-class inter-war home. In January 1931, a CWS deputation was sent to British Columbia to seek a deal to ensure canned salmon supplies.[193] The deputation identified the Canadian Fishing Company as one in which CWS should seek a financial stake, and the Board sanctioned a return to Canada for the deputation, empowering it to take a controlling shareholding in the company, with authority to spend £375,000 on the task.[194] In the event, the New England Fish Company (based in Boston) was unwilling to sell a share in Canadian Fishing, let alone relinquish control, but they were in desperate need of financial assistance, at a time when the American banking system was in crisis. The deputation negotiated a $500,000 CWS Bank loan deal with New England, the terms of which entitled CWS to the output from Canadian Fishing cannery on the Skeena River on the Pacific Coast, as well as all the shares in Canadian Fishing if New England defaulted on the loan. The interest of 5 per cent would have contributed considerably to the cost of the salmon for CWS, and the whole deal effectively secured a supply of tinned salmon for CWS.[195] In 1934, CWS' financial clout was also deployed in its relationship with another US company in need of financial support, this time in California and in fruit canning. CWS secured 1,450 shares in Messrs Schuckl and Co. (£28,500) in exchange for a guarantee that the company would sell to CWS 50 per cent or 500,000 cases of assorted canned fruit (whichever was the greater).[196] Two years later, CWS granted Schuckl and Co. a loan of $150,000 to advance to fruit growers, in exchange for 450 of a new 500 share issue in the company.[197] The policy of buying into partner companies to secure supplies, or securing partnership with other organisations, was also applied in a major project in Argentina in the 1930s. As shown, in the 1920s Argentina became an increasingly important supplier of meat, wheat and butter, and CWS took important steps to consolidate this position through external partnerships. In January 1936, CWS agreed to acquire 52,000 shares in the Smithfield and Argentine Meat Company, a company with which CWS had undertaken much business in the past. Again, this was seen as a way of securing essential supplies.[198] Even more significant was a deal later in the year with I.E. Pillitz, a firm that supplied CWS with wheat from Argentina, to set up a joint limited company to purchase and operate warehouses and a quay berth for handling wheat in Rosario.[199] The move coincided with the modernisation and expansion of CWS flour milling capacity in Hull and London.[200] Apparently the deal fell through because of the CWS' unwillingness to go above £45,000 in the purchase price for the facilities.[201] Another deal was struck with the Anglo–Mexican Trading Company to enable CWS to sell to private firms overseas, especially in Denmark.[202] But perhaps the most controversial of such deals was CWS' decision to take up shareholdings in Tate & Lyle Ltd in order to secure supplies of sugar. The move had been contemplated as early as October 1929, partly in recognition that CWS took 73.5 per cent of its sugar supplies from that company.[203] CWS bought 88,000 shares at 30s per share (£132,000) in January 1930, and a special liaison officer was appointed to co-ordinate the policies of the two companies.[204] Then, in 1934, CWS and the co-operative movement generally became deeply alarmed at a proposed Sugar Marketing Scheme, which sought to impose a tax on sugar consumption, restrict sugar production via a quota system, and organised through a board dominated by 22 private companies.[205] The measure was seen as anti-co-operative, and to protect its supplies of sugar, CWS signed an exclusive deal with Tate & Lyle in April 1935 that conferred upon that firm the exclusive right to supply CWS with sugar for 21 years, provided that company agreed to meet CWS needs at published prices less certain discounts.[206] Collaborative deals between co-operatives and private companies of various kinds have been recognised as important components of the armoury available to co-operatives to meet needs such as fresh capital, access to expertise and consolidation of essential supplies. 'Hybridisation', where a co-operative strikes a deal or arrangement with private enterprise for mutual benefit, has been recognised by co-operative analysts, though the tendency has been to see such initiatives as being quite recent in origin, such as by the 'New Generation Co-operatives' in US agriculture from the 1980s onwards.[207] What is clear is that the CWS had pioneered various manifestations of hybridisation to deal with various global supply chain challenges during the inter-war period.

Inevitably, a great deal of CWS and SCWS concern in North America focused upon wheat supplies. As wheat prices fell, it made sense for CWS buyers to take full advantage by buying large quantities while the commodity was plentiful on the market. The centralisation of wheat buying within CWS in the 1920s enabled a strategic approach to be adopted. A complicating factor in the early 1930s was the instability of exchange rates, which meant that sudden shifts in currency values could impinge upon the ability of CWS buyers to buy as much as they required. To address this, in December 1931 both the Montreal and New York depots were granted overdraft facilities of £150,000 to ensure that they could react promptly on the market.[208] A similar policy had been applied in Argentina in March 1931, with a £100,000 overdraft being made available.[209] A similar provision was made for Australian wheat purchasing in December 1933, for £50,000.[210] In Canada, the overdraft facility was raised to $1 million with the Dominion Bank of Canada in August 1932.[211] Hobley, the head of wheat purchasing, also traded in wheat futures in an attempt to provide some degree of certainty in relation to the costs of wheat. But, in 1934, the policy went badly wrong, and losses of nearly £40,000 resulted.[212] Hobley was roundly criticised, and he had to give assurances that he would be cautious in his purchase of futures henceforth.[213] But it marked the end of Hobley's career. While he took retirement late in 1934, he felt humiliated and that he had been driven from office.[214] Inevitably, given the severe impact of the Great Depression on the USA and North America generally, the 1930s were difficult for the wholesales. In 1932, the New York depot briefly suffered a loss, and Murphy, the manager, was called back to London to explain why.[215] But both New York and Montreal recovered as North America was gradually restored to growth, and generally the wholesales held their own. In Canada, CWS traded with and supported co-operatives. They purchased cattle from the Saskatchewan Co-operative Livestock Producers Ltd and Canadian Livestock Co-operative Ltd.[216] CWS Bank funded the sales of honey by the Fédérée de Quebec.[217] It also lent £8,000 to the Grand Falls Co-operative Society of Newfoundland.[218] CWS also opened a new depot in Vancouver in June 1937 to buy fruit and wheat, a move that signalled that CWS remained bullish about its future in North America.[219]

However, the position in Europe proved to be much more difficult to manage during the 1930s. Even CWS interests in Denmark, for so long arguably the strongest part of CWS' overseas Empire, suffered. The introduction of tariffs and import quotas in 1932–3 was felt acutely. Sir Robert Stewart, Chair of SCWS, lamented that the 10 per cent tariff would inflate the cost of Danish imports for his organisation by £1 million per annum.[220] CWS despatched a deputation to Denmark in June 1932 to ascertain the effects of tariffs on the Danish trade.[221] By 1934, import quotas had reduced weekly sales of bacon by CWS to 17,000 cwts per week, compared to 20,000 per week in the previous year, though higher prices meant that income from sales had actually increased.[222] Results for the rest of the decade were frustrating for CWS. But political events across Europe were to devastate CWS interests even more seriously. CWS trade with the Soviet Union initially remained buoyant at the beginning of the 1930s. Trade in Russian wheat, Siberian butter, herrings and other produce continued as it had in the 1920s, much of it conducted on CWS credit.[223] Textiles, CWS margarine and leather, and even cattle were imported into USSR.[224] But with the consolidation of Stalin's rule in the Soviet Union by 1929, dramatic changes were implemented that would transform the Russian economy in the 1930s, increasing industrial production but also ravaging agriculture, creating mass famine and inflicting a reign of political terror that would eventually affect CWS commerce and relations with the USSR. The forced collectivisation of agriculture began in 1929, forcing millions of peasants to join state-run collective farms and creating a man-made famine that killed millions in the Ukraine and elsewhere in 1932–3.[225] Rapid industrialisation and urbanisation resulted from a series of Five-Year Plans, and the social and economic upheaval these changes caused, combined with growing Soviet fear of Nazi Germany and Stalin's ruthlessness, set off the Great Terror of the late 1930s, in which millions of Soviet citizens were killed or imprisoned on trumped up charges of treachery. While public knowledge of events in Russia was limited in the UK, it remains the case that CWS was unwittingly involved in funding Soviet wheat exports at a time when millions of the country's citizens were being starved as a direct result of state policy. In 1930, right-wing newspapers such as the *Daily Express* and the *Morning Post* attacked CWS for importing Russian wheat, condemning this as 'dumping' on the British market to the detriment of British farmers. It was also implied that CWS involvement with the Soviet Union was essentially ideological, and that this suggested that the co-operative movement was disloyal and even sinister. The CWS and the *Co-operative News* rigorously rebutted these attacks, arguing that the transactions were purely commercial and that private interests also imported Russian goods.[226] It is certainly the case that CWS Bank had made vast amounts from its loans to Soviet trade institutions. Between June 1924 and July 1933, it earned in interest and commission £975,365.[227] CWS' defence that its commerce with Russia was driven by commercial priorities rather than ideology was certainly true. But one claim by the Co-operative Press Agency would prove hideously misleading, when it stated that "the Russians do not starve themselves to send the wheat".[228] If this might have been true in 1930, it would certainly not be for very long.

The changing situation in the USSR did begin to affect the wholesales' trade. In spring 1933, the arrest of British engineers in the Soviet Union on accusations of espionage resulted briefly in a British embargo on trade, at least until they were released.[229] However, by the summer of 1933, tensions between the wholesales and their Russian partners began to emerge. The Russian contingent of the Russo–British Grain Company began to press for a reduction of the 10 per cent interest CWS wanted to charge on an advance of £800,000, but the latter initially refused.[230] But Exporthleb put pressure on CWS, and eventually it was reduced to 8 per cent.[231] Exporthleb kept up the pressure, forcing CWS to reduce the interest on a £100,000 loan for 80,000 casks of Siberian butter from 7 to 6 per cent.[232] By June, CWS and SCWS had set up a joint committee to review the Russian commerce of the wholesales, especially the pressure being encountered in respect of reducing interest and commission charges.[233] In the end, though, SCWS and CWS largely decided to concede to Russian demands.[234] Then, at the end of 1934, the Russian authorities insisted that all purchases of British produce would have to be paid for in cash. This would inevitably reduce imports from the UK.[235] In the same month, CWS was compelled to reduce interest charged on credits and loans to the Russo–British Grain Company and the Moscow Narodny bank.[236] In the following year, wheat exports from USSR fell so drastically that the decision was taken to wind up the Russo–British Grain Company, and its remaining operations were taken over by Exporthleb.[237] Meanwhile, as state oppression in the Soviet Union gathered momentum in 1936, the Soviet government effectively took over the co-operative societies, incorporating them into the state.[238] In summer 1936, Centrosoyus ceased trading and its activities were taken over by Rasnoexport and Rasnoimport, essentially newly constituted state organisations.[239] By 1937, the CWS deputation to the Soviet Union had to concede that as the Soviet Union industrialised, its need for imports from the UK was receding, and the internal demand for Soviet foodstuffs meant that there was less available for export.[240] The recession of British exports to USSR was already evident. The value of CWS exports to the country had fallen from £846,684 in 1934 to £453,904 in 1935.[241] Matters took a turn for the worse when in October 1937—the height of the Terror—the chairman of Centrosoyus in the USSR, Isaac A. Zelinsky, was denounced as an 'enemy of the people' in *Pravda*.[242] Zelinsky was subjected to a show trial at which he 'confessed' to having conspired with A.V. Alexander MP, Secretary of the Parliamentary Committee of Co-operative Congress, in plotting to overthrow the Soviet regime. Alexander vehemently denied the accusation, but the episode illustrated that by the late 1930s co-operative-Soviet relations were at a very low ebb indeed.[243] Unsurprisingly, a request for a short-term loan of £500,000 by the Moscow Narodny Bank was refused by CWS in March 1938 "in view of the unsettled international situation".[244]

The rise of fascist and authoritarian regimes in the 1930s also disrupted CWS trade. The rise of Hitler in 1933 led to discussions with the TUC and the Co-operative Union about a possible boycott of trade with Germany.[245] The Southampton and Dudley societies also called for a boycott.[246] But CWS refused, and though the quantum of trade with Germany was small in the 1930s, it continued virtually up to the outbreak of war. A steady but small export trade in woollen goods was undertaken by CWS throughout the decade, right up to July 1939.[247] Delegates continued to be sent to the annual Leipzig Toy Fair.[248] In December 1937, CWS even sent representatives to a dinner at the Savoy, London, organised by the German Chamber of Commerce.[249] Stubborn resistance to pleas by the co-operative and Labour movements to use commercial sanctions to counter international aggression was also evident when Japan attacked China in July 1937. Numerous societies called publicly for a boycott as well as approaching CWS directly.[250] CWS offered several reasons for refusing to comply. Firstly, while in 1936 CWS imports from Japan represented only 0.5 per cent (£187,000) of CWS overseas purchases, the sum was not negligible, and though alternative supplies could be found elsewhere, they would be more expensive. Secondly, CWS claimed that many retail societies had specifically required Japanese goods, and that their needs had to be respected.[251] The pressure continued into 1938, but CWS took the line that any boycott should be the work of those individual retail societies who purchased Japanese commodities.[252] CWS never gave ground on this position. To a large extent, its reluctance to engage in politically inspired commercial boycotts reflected CWS' deepening concern that such action would only worsen the environment of protectionism and international friction, and potentially contribute to the ever-growing likelihood of another war. It would also invite retaliation and make the already deteriorating international context for global trade even worse. By the late 1930s, it already had direct experience of how war could cut off sources of supply entirely. Shortly after the outbreak of the Spanish Civil War, the Denia depot was abandoned, and the CWS managers were 'rescued' by a British warship.[253] This abandonment of commercial interests paradoxically freed CWS to respond positively to calls from the British and international co-operative movements to help the Republican government. Thus, in early 1937 CWS sent the first of many shipments of food and medical supplies to aid the Republican cause.[254] The contrast between Spain on the one hand and Germany and Japan on the other was that in the latter two cases commercial considerations trumped ethical and ideological factors that might otherwise have favoured sanctions. In the case of Spain, commerce had effectively been removed from the equation.

It was commercial worries that continued to inspire CWS obstructionism to the idea of a trading ICWS. In 1938, the ICA established the International Co-operative Trading Agency (ICTA) to try to make the idea a reality.[255] CWS made it plain that it could not support the organisation and withdrew its membership within months of it being established.[256] It feared that ICTA would take away existing CWS trade and customers, and that individual co-operative societies might even be tempted to trade directly with ICTA in due course, making the perennial problem of retail society disloyalty to CWS even worse. But this did not mean that CWS was hostile to other national co-operative movements. At moments of crisis, it proved itself capable of strong commercial solidarity. For example, in 1934 the French Co-operative Bank (*Banques des Co-operatives*) and the French Wholesale Society (*Magasin de Gros de France*) got into major financial difficulties.[257] CWS stepped in and arranged a loan of £100,000 that rescued both organisations.[258] The French CWS was stabilised, and by October 1935 had repaid the loan.[259] SCWS also displayed an ability to co-operate internationally. In 1938, in collaboration with the Swedish Co-operative Union (*Kooperativa Förbundet*—KF), it set up the Luma Co-operative Electric Lamp Society Ltd, which was housed in its own Art Deco building, Luma Tower.[260] But international collaboration tended to be on the terms of the British wholesales, an attitude that probably resulted from the strong element of competition within the British co-operative movement, which was manifested in the reluctance of retail societies to show the loyalty to the wholesales the latter felt they deserved. It also partly reflected the fact that the wholesales and the British movement were the largest and wealthiest in the world, a position that they were reluctant to surrender, even in the name of international co-operative solidarity.

The 1930s had been, in many ways, a decade of retreat and retrench-ment for the international connections developed by CWS and SCWS. Yet they had fought a rear-guard action to try to preserve or adapt the supply chain strategies and networks they had taken so long to build. That they were in many instances overtaken by events and were unsuc-cessful should not disguise the fact that strenuous efforts were made to maintain a strategic approach to managing supply chains. It is certainly the case that some of the adaptations were sophisticated and innovative, even when they failed. But the invasion of Poland by Nazi armies in Sep-tember 1939 was to escalate deglobalisation dramatically as well as the degradation of the wholesales' global supply networks.

IV

The British government, the co-operative movement and the wholesales were in many ways far better prepared for war in 1939 than they had been in 1914. There was a much better understanding that major war between industrial powers would inevitably be one that depended on the maximum utilisation of national resources and would affect the whole population. This time there would be no attempt at 'business as usual'. In fact, preparations for war in which the British state would take control of whole areas of economic activity were undertaken long before 1939. Whereas the co-operative movement had been outsiders for much of the First World War, they were actively engaged in planning for war as early as the mid-1930s. In September 1936, the senior civil servant, Sir Ernest Gowers, arranged a secret meeting with A.V. Alexander MP, the leading figure in the Co-operative Parliamentary Committee, to discuss how the movement, and especially the wholesales, could help in a national crisis by helping stock and control the supply of essential foodstuffs. Alexander informed Gowers that in response to his invitation to meet, a confiden-tial joint CWS/SCWS committee had been set up to consider that very question. He advised that Hobley could provide especially useful help in respect of wheat supplies.[261] Further meetings took place on 1 October, 22 October and 26 November 1936, at which storage arrangements for a range of commodities (including meat and butter as well as grains) were discussed.[262] Though no clear agreement was reached at these meet-ings, they did lead in due course to more solid arrangements. In 1938, CWS was, along with Spillers and Ranks, given the task of acquiring and maintaining a national wheat reserve.[263] Especially significant was the implicit recognition that CWS was important not only as a domestic Brit-ish distributor of food and goods but also as a major global trader that procured a very large proportion of the nation's food.

The new position of the movement and the wholesales close to state policy makers became even clearer when war broke out. During the war, the British state effectively took over international trade in the most important commodities but farmed out the operation of international purchases and sales to those firms and organisations that had been doing this before the conflict. CWS knowledge and expertise in managing global supply networks, combined with local knowledge gleaned from local depots, representatives or agents, was used by the state to meet the global trade demands of a wartime economy. Thus, in 1940, CWS was asked by the state to lead in purchasing Canadian wheat for the British economy.[264] In 1943, they took control of a large share of imports from Canada of tinned and frozen fish.[265] CWS also supplied Allied organisations, notably the exiled Polish government's Poland Supply Co., which served Polish troops and civilians in Russia.[266] On the domestic front, it was especially well placed to promote rationing as an essential policy, through prominent co-operative spokesmen such as A.V. Alexander, First Lord of the Admiralty in the wartime coalition.[267] Many CWS and SCWS factories were requisitioned for war production on SCWS/CWS advice, and SCWS and CWS were represented on a wide range of government advisory committees.[268] The CWS Bank also lent to local authorities desperate for money to deal with bomb damage.[269] At no other time in its history had the co-operative movement generally, and the wholesales specifically, enjoyed such political and economic influence.

This led to accusations that this closeness to the state bred complacency, and that this contributed to a refusal to address flaws within the structure and practise of the co-operative movement that contributed to its long-term post-war decline, both in terms of membership and market share.[270] But there is strong evidence that though its efforts at reform and change were unsuccessful in this period, neither the wholesales nor the wider movement were heedless of the need for change. Both the CU and the wholesales promoted the creation of 'District Societies', joint bodies consisting of local retail societies with the aim of co-ordinating activities and even promoting amalgamations to create larger and better resourced retail societies, able to organise and locate stores more competitively within larger geographical areas. In 1943, it participated in a major co-operative national forum, the Advisory Committee on Post-War Problems, on the changes that would be needed to meet the challenges of peace. This is in turn prompted CWS to conduct its own internal review of preparations for the post-war environment, spearheaded by a fast-rising strategic thinker and Head of the CWS Market Research Bureau, Fred Lambert, who seems to have been the main drafter of the *Report by the CWS on its Policy and Programme for Post War Development* (1944). The report called for the modernisation of CWS factories and production; promotion of retail society amalgamations and the strengthening of District Societies; the creation of a motor trade and pharmacy branch of CWS; the establishment of more CWS Bank branches across the country; and, perhaps most controversially, the merger of CWS and SCWS. Ultimately, most of the recommendations were not implemented, largely because of resistance by retail societies and the SCWS, jealous of their independence.[271]

Interestingly, neither the CWS report nor one by the CU, *Co-operative Reorganisation* (Second Interim Report 1945), identified the wholesales' international commerce as central to reform. The focus of both reports was exclusively on the domestic organisation of co-operation. This seems to have been the result of two factors. Firstly, there was a general assumption that this was not a primary source of concern, and one that tended to require adaptations and policies specific to parts of the world with which the wholesales traded. Sweeping, 'one size fits all' reforms were simply not seen as appropriate. Secondly, if there was uncertainty about domestic commercial conditions in the UK post-war, it was as nothing compared to the impossibility of speculating what the global economy would resemble once the fighting stopped. This is unsurprising. Only in 1944 was agreement reached at Bretton Woods on the creation of new institutions such as the International Monetary Fund (IMF) and the International Bank for Reconstruction and Development (the 'World Bank') tasked to gradually restore the world trading system to a more orderly one than the 1930s, based on free trade and the elimination of exchange control. Even then, the actual process of negotiating down the barriers to trade erected in the 1930s and the war only really began once the war was over, and it only produced tangible results with the signing of the General Agreement on Tariffs and Trade (GATT) in 1947.[272] In addition, the sheer physical devastation of much of the European economy and political uncertainties about future relations between the capitalist and communist worlds, notwithstanding the formation of the United Nations, made reliable prediction nigh impossible. If Bretton Woods began the journey back towards globalisation, it looked a long, rocky and winding road in 1944, and for a good part of the trail thereafter.

While the wholesales did not abandon their international trading activities during the war, they now largely carried them out on behalf of the British state. This produced both changes in practice and difficulties in measuring performance. The general principle was that while the whole control of trade and CWS facilities had nominally passed to the state, they would operate as far as possible as they had before the war.[273] But this was an aspiration that would prove difficult to sustain. Special government companies were established that took over the assets of different companies producing specific commodities—thus, in July 1940, MARCOM Ltd was set up that took control of all margarine production, including by CWS.[274] Similar arrangements were made for bacon (BINDAL Ltd) and milk and butter (BACAL).[275] Only a few weeks after war broke out, the NZPA had to secure a running overdraft arrangement with the CWS Bank for £50,000 because butter imports had been taken over by the Ministry of Food, which demanded immediate payment on delivery of the butter.[276] By 1940, this facility had been raised to £100,000.[277] In New Zealand itself, the CWS purchasing depot was now buying on behalf of the British government and had to buy meat "for cash rather than on credit terms. It would be reimbursed in due course by the New Zealand government, but in the meantime the CWS Bank would need to provide a running overdraft facility of £150,000 for the CWS New Zealand depot.[278] Significantly, when the CWS was considering who to appoint as manager for the Longburn Freezing Works (New Zealand North Island) it acquired in 1940, the CWS meat department manager in London declared himself unable to judge the capabilities of W.E. Wilson, the main contender for the post, as he had been working at a time of government control over trade, and thus Wilson's abilities had not been tested by the demands of a truly competitive market.[279]

Inevitably, the war itself damaged CWS commerce. The Nazi occupations of France, Denmark and much of mainland Europe severely disrupted CWS commerce and created uncertainty about the repayment of wartime debts. CWS did take steps to minimise problems. Its Danish facilities, especially its bacon factories, were placed into the ownership of holding companies to provide some measure of anonymity as British concerns and legal protection in the event of a German invasion.[280] But losses were incurred and uncertainty about how and whether trading connections could be re-established after the war remained. Some branches of trade were sustained and even flourished. CWS had been developing a thriving trade with Palestine (then a troubled British protectorate in which Jews and Arabs fought over land and the political future) since 1934, acting as agents supplying the Palestinian CWS (*Hamashbir–Hamerkazi*) with US-made agricultural machinery.[281] During the war, this trade continued and remained controlled by CWS.[282] CWS also advanced £90,000 to the Palestinian fruit exporter, Thuva Export Ltd, though problems of wartime commerce and shipping did result in a loss of £21,000 for CWS.[283] In Canada, it renewed a £100,000 loan to the Fédérée de Quebec.[284]

While, as shown, there was little in the way of a really concerted attempt to develop a coherent overall plan for post-war international trade, the topic was not ignored, and there were a variety of initiatives and discussions that did try to address the question, albeit by reference to specific geographical areas. The Palestinian CWS, for example, signalled in May 1943 that it would like to continue its employment of CWS as agents to import US machinery into the post-war period, as well as to develop both the purchase of CWS produce and the utilisation of the CWS Bank's services.[285] In November 1944, meetings between the CWS and representatives of the Czech and Yugoslav governments in exile were arranged to discuss supplying CWS produce and financial services to them after the end of the war.[286] The drapery committee was instructed to convene its own sub-committee to consider the likely development of trade with the USA and Canada after the end of hostilities.[287] In terms of concrete steps, the acquisition of the New Zealand Longburn Freezing Works in 1940 for £175,000—and subsequent further investments in it—was undertaken with an eye on the post-war world, as was the acquisition of half of the shares in Ocean Beach Freezing Company for £100,000.[288] In December 1943, it opened negotiations with the Canadian government about a possible CWS bacon factory there.[289] In March 1944, CWS sent delegates to the Swedish Co-operative Congress with a view to sourcing furniture from KF after the war.[290]

But the truth was that the sheer uncertainties about what the post-war world would look like precluded any coherent plan for reconstructing the wholesales' global networks once the war was over. Planning remained piecemeal. As will be seen, the turbulence of the post-war world, with the onset of the Cold War and the extreme challenges of rebuilding national economies and international trade from the physical devastation of global war, would mean that there would be no easy or rapid reconstruction of the wholesales' global supply networks.

Notes

1. Trentmann, *Free Trade Nation* 210.
2. Wilson, Webster & Vorberg-Rugh, *Building Co-operation* 170.
3. General Survey Committee Interim Report (GSIR) (1919) 18–21.
4. GCSIR 178–183.
5. Wilson, Webster & Vorberg-Rugh, *Building Co-operation* 174.
6. Ibid., 176.
7. Ibid., 167.
8. CWSBM 19 September 1919.
9. *Co-operative News* 10 January 1920, Supplement.
10. S. Pollard, *The Development of the British Economy 1914–1990* (London, Arnold 1992) 18–19.
11. Wilson, Webster & Vorberg-Rugh, *Building Co-operation* 178.
12. Kinloch & Butt, *History of the SCWS Ltd* 291 and 297.
13. R. Middleton, *Government Versus the Market: The Growth of the Public Sector, Economic Management and British Economic Performance c.1890–1979* (Cheltenham, Edward Elgar 1996) 276.
14. Wilson, Webster & Vorberg-Rugh, *Building Co-operation* 179; Kinloch & Butt, *History of the SCWS Ltd* 284.
15. A.G. Kenwood & A.L. Lougheed, *The Growth of the International Economy 1820–1990* (London, Routledge 1993) 183.
16. M. Havinden & D. Meredith, *Colonialism & Development: Britain and Its Tropical Colonies 1850–1960* (London, Routledge 1993) 146–147.
17. Kenwood & Lougheed, *The Growth of the International Economy* 209.
18. Middleton, *Government Versus the Market* 272.
19. Ibid.
20. An excellent outline of the Sterling Area and its development can be found in P.J. Cain & A.G. Hopkins, *British Imperialism 1688–2000* (Edinburgh, Pearson 2001) 464–488.
21. Pollard, *The Development of the British Economy 1914–1990* 85.
22. CWSBM 20 February 1919.
23. CWSBM 28 February 1919; 2 May 1919; 16 May 1919.

24. CWSBM 28 November 1918; 23 January 1919.
25. CWSBM 14 February 1919.
26. CWSBM 8 May 1919.
27. CWSBM 26 November 1929.
28. CWSBM 14 April 1921; 18 July 1921.
29. *The Producer* December 1925, 44.
30. CWSBM 3 September 1920.
31. CWSBM 27 January 1928.
32. *The Producer* November 1927, 22.
33. CWSBM 11 June 1920.
34. CWSBM 25 November 1926.
35. CWSBM 5 July 1928; 5 November 1929.
36. CWSBM 11 February 1930.
37. CWSBM 20 February 1919; 19 September 1919.
38. CWSBM 6 November 1919; 26 February 1920.
39. CWSBM 6 November 1919.
40. CWSBM 31 March 1920.
41. CWSBM 11 February 1920.
42. CWSBM 27 July 1922.
43. *Co-operative News* 29 May 1926, 17.
44. *The Producer* May 1926, 210.
45. CWSBM 3 February 1927; 25 February 1927.
46. *Co-operative News* 20 February 1926, 5; 27 February 1926, 4.
47. *Co-operative News* 20 November 1926, 1.
48. Ibid.
49. *The Producer* February 1928, 97.
50. *The Producer* June 1928, 200.
51. *The Producer* April 1925, 151.
52. CWSBM 26 March 1926; 25 November 1926.
53. Kenwood & Lougheed, *The Growth of the International Economy* 164–165.
54. Birchall, *The International Co-operative Movement* 52.
55. Typed article on behalf of the Joint Committee of Russian Co-operative Organisations in London, 8 April 1920, 2–4; "Russian Co-operative Crisis", Papers of E.O. Greening, NCA.
56. Birchall, *The International Co-operative Movement* 52.
57. Evidence of co-operative efforts to continue operation in non-Bolshevik areas is found in an article, "Co-operation in Russia", about a statement by Alexander Berkenheim, the then-Vice President of the All Russian Union of Consumer Societies, Moscow. *Co-operative News* 5 April 1919, 248.
58. Birchall, *The International Co-operative Movement* 52–53; Z. Stencel-Lensky, *Co-operation in Soviet Russia* (London, Co-operative Printing Society 1920)—printed for the Joint Committee of Russian Co-operative Organisations in London.
59. Letter from E.O. Greening, *Co-operative News* 9 October 1920, 4.
60. CWSBM 20 April 1917.
61. *Co-operative News* 4 January 1919, 1–2; 8 February 1918, 98–99.
62. CWSBM 25 July 1919; 8 August 1919.
63. CWSBM 23 January 1920; *Co-operative News* 10 January 1920, 4.
64. *Co-operative News* 9 October 1920, iii.
65. *Co-operative News* 27 November 1920, 1; 4 December 1920, 1; 11 December 1920, 1; 18 December 1920, 3.
66. A very good account of the delegation and Anglo–Russian relations leading to the signing of an Anglo–Russian Trade Treaty in March 1912 can be found in R. Service, *Spies & Commissars: Bolshevik Russia and the West*

(Basingstoke, Macmillan 2011). On Krasin see 251; on the negotiations and the Treaty see 300–314.

67. See Secret Political Report on Soviet Russia, Helsingfors 21 July 1920, Files of MI5, KV2/500, 96 National Archives (NA).
68. Probably the most vivid account of the ongoing battle between British Security Services and Soviet espionage in the UK is T. Phillips, *The Secret Twenties: British Intelligence, the Russians and the Jazz Age* (London, Granta 2017).
69. Ibid., 142–162.
70. Ibid., 181–191.
71. Ibid., 270–320.
72. Service, *Spies & Commissars* 314.
73. *Co-operative News* 2 April 1921, 8.
74. Letter from Russian Consulate General to Mr Jackson, 15 February 1922, KV2/500, NA; *Co-operative News* 4 March 1922, 7; 29 April 1922, 4.
75. CWSBM 14 July 1921.
76. CWSBM 27 April 1922; 4 May 1922.
77. CWSBM 13 October 1922.
78. *Co-operative News* 13 January 1923, iii; 10 March 1923, 2.
79. *Co-operative News* 24 March 1923, 3.
80. *The Producer* May 1925, 194.
81. *Co-operative News* 12 January 1924, 8.
82. CWSBM 2 July 1926.
83. Minutes of the Russo–British Grain Company, 11 July 1927, NCA.
84. Minutes of the Russo–British Grain Company, 13 September 1928, NCA.
85. Minutes of the Russo–British Grain Company, 15 July 1929, NCA.
86. CWSBM 13 April 1927.
87. *Co-operative News* 13 February 1926, 2; CWSBM 30 July 1926.
88. CWSBM 3 December 1926.
89. CWSBM 6 January 1927.
90. CWSBM 12 May 1927.
91. *Co-operative News* Russian Supplement 7 May 1927, 1.
92. CWSBM 21 July 1927.
93. CWSBM 11 February 1920.
94. *Co-operative News* 3 July 1920, 4.
95. *Co-operative News* 17 July 1920, 11.
96. *Co-operative News* 7 August 1920, 3.
97. *The Producer* November 1922, 15.
98. *The Producer* March 1923, 153.
99. CWSBM 7 October 1920.
100. CWSBM 19 August 1926.
101. CWSBM 7 October 1927; 13 October 1927.
102. CWSBM 21 July 1927.
103. CWSBM 26 August 1927; 7 October 1927.
104. CWSBM 21 October 1927.
105. CWSBM 3 September 1920; 1 October 1920.
106. *The Producer* July 1925, 247.
107. *Co-operative News* 20 February 1926, 4.
108. *The Western Australian* 23 June 1922, 6 at https://trove.nla.gov.au/newspaper/article/28171992; *The Producer* November 1925, 11.
109. CWSBM 18 March 1926; 22 October 1926; 17 December 1926; 13 April 1927.
110. CWSBM 13 October 1927; 27 September 1928; 29 October 1929.

111. *The Midlands Advertiser* Western Australia 7 November 1913, 3 at https://trove.nla.gov.au/newspaper/article/156493197.
112. CWSBM 25 November 1926; 20 January 1927.
113. CWSBM 20 January 1927.
114. *Co-operative News* 20 February 1926, 4.
115. *Co-operative News* 2 October 1926, 9.
116. Imperial Economic Committee to L.S. Amery MP 19 May 1926, Empire Marketing Membership File, G/11, NA.
117. *The Producer* May 1928, 175–176.
118. Co-op News 15 December 1928 4.
119. CWSBM 23 December 1918; 16 January 1919.
120. CWSBM 30 January 1919; 18 April 1919.
121. CWSBM 17 July 1919; 20 February 1920.
122. CWSBM 22 August 1919.
123. CWSBM 14 August 1919; 1 April 1921.
124. *Co-operative News* 12 February 1921, 2.
125. CWSBM 20 February 1920.
126. *Co-operative News* 14 May 1921, 2.
127. CWSBM 19 August 1921.
128. CWSBM 16 July 1926; *Co-operative News* 17 July 1926, 1.
129. CWSBM 16 June 1922; *Co-operative News* 15 July 1922, 7.
130. CWSBM 18 June 1926.
131. CWSBM 3 June 1930.
132. CWSBM 16 August 1928.
133. For example: CWSBM 5 September 1927 (Estonia); 15 October 1927 (Latvia); 10 September 1929 (Lithuania).
134. M. Hilson, "Consumer Co-operation in the Nordic Countries, c1860–1939" in M. Hilson, S. Neunsinger & G. Patmore (eds.), *A Global History of Consumer Co-operation since 1950: Movements and Businesses* (Leiden, Brill 2017) 121–144; 128–129.
135. CWSBM 28 August 1919; 6 November 1919.
136. *Co-operative News* 28 April 1923, 1.
137. K. Friberg, "A Co-operative Take on Free Trade: International Ambitions and Regional Initiatives in International Co-operative Trade" in Hilson, Neunsinger & Patmore (eds.). *A Global History of Consumer Co-operation* 201–228; 220.
138. Ibid., 219–220.
139. *Co-operative News* 24 November 1928, 5.
140. CWSBM 5 October 1928.
141. CWSBM 27 July 1926.
142. CWSBM 20 January 1927.
143. CWSBM 25 November 1926.
144. *The Producer* July 1929, 182.
145. CWSBM 10 August 1928.
146. See the essays in A.G. Hopkins (ed.), *Globalization in World History* (London, Pimlico 2002).
147. P. Gervais & C.S. McWaters, "Globalisation" in J.F. Wilson, S. Toms, A. de Jong and E. Buchnea (eds.), *The Routledge Companion to Business History* (London, Routledge 2017) 316–330.
148. Pollard, *The Development of the British Economy 1914–1990* 93–94.
149. Cain & Hopkins, *British Imperialism* 464–478.
150. Cain & Hopkins, *British Imperialism* 471.
151. Pollard, *The Development of the British Economy 1914–1990* 95.

152. Cain & Hopkins 471.
153. Pollard, *The Development of the British Economy 1914–1990* 95.
154. Cain & Hopkins 474.
155. Ibid., 498–505.
156. Ibid., 502.
157. Ibid., 512.
158. Ibid., 502.
159. CWSBM 29 April 1930.
160. CWSBM 21 October 1930.
161. CWSBM 29 April 1930.
162. CWSBM 27 January 1931.
163. CWSBM 19 May 1931.
164. CWSBM 16 December 1931.
165. *The Producer* September 1936, 264.
166. *The Producer* November 1936, 331.
167. CWSBM 13 January 1931; 3 February 1931.
168. CWSBM 23 February 1932.
169. CWSBM 21 February 1933.
170. Minutes of NZPA, Managing Directors Report 7 August 1935, NCA.
171. Minutes of NZPA, Report by R. Ellison of Delegation to New Zealand November 1935, 5.
172. See N. Balnave & G. Patmore, "Rochdale Consumer Co-operatives in Australia and New Zealand" in Hilson, Neunsinger & Patmore (eds.), *A Global History of Consumer Co-operation* 456–480; 460–461; N. Balnave & G. Patmore, "Rochdale Consumer Co-operatives in Australia: A Case of Rural Survival" *Journal of Co-operative Studies* 41.1 (April 2008) 11–21.
173. CWSBM 13 May 1930.
174. Ibid.
175. *The Producer* May 1932, 139.
176. CWSBM 29 April 1930.
177. Ibid.
178. CWSBM 6 October 1931.
179. CWSBM 10 November 1931.
180. CWSBM 24 November 1931.
181. CWSBM 12 April 1932.
182. CWSBM 5 April 1933.
183. CWSBM 30 May 1933.
184. CWSBM 3 October 1933.
185. CWSBM 24 October 1933.
186. CWSBM 14 August 1934.
187. *Report of CWS Deputation to Australia, Tasmania and New Zealand, 12 October 1935 to 11 March 1936* (Manchester, CWS 1936) 15, NCA.
188. Ibid., 19.
189. CWSBM 1 September 1936.
190. CWSBM 27 October 1936; 22 December 1936.
191. CWSBM 31 August 1937.
192. CWSBM 18 January 1938.
193. CWSBM 31 January 1931.
194. CWSBM 23 May 1933; 30 May 1933; 31 May 1933.
195. CWSBM 15 August 1933; 24 February 1942.
196. CWSBM 16 May 1934.
197. CWSBM 5 May 1936.
198. CWSBM 21 January 1936.
199. CWSBM 13 October 1936.

200. *The Producer* July 1936, 195.
201. CWSBM 22 June 1937.
202. CWSBM 13 July 1937.
203. CWSBM 1 October 1929.
204. CWSBM 7 January 1930; 13 May 1930.
205. *The Producer* August 1934, 229–231.
206. CWSBM 9 April 1935.
207. F. Chaddad & M.L. Cook, "Legal Frameworks and Property Rights in US Agricultural Co-operatives: The Hybridization of Co-operative Structures" in P. Battilani & H.G. Schröter (eds.), *The Co-operative Business Movement, 1950 to the Present* (Cambridge, Cambridge University Press 2012) 175–194; 183.
208. CWSBM 8 December 1931.
209. CWSBM 10 March 1931.
210. CWSBM 13 December 1933.
211. CWSBM 23 August 1932.
212. CWSBM 20 February 1934; 10 April 1934.
213. CWSBM 31 July 1934.
214. *The Producer* December 1934, 364; CWSBM 8 January 1935.
215. CWSBM 11 July 1933.
216. CWSBM 2 September 1930; 17 February 1931.
217. CWSBM 2 November 1934.
218. CWSBM 15 October 1935.
219. CWSBM 22 June 1937.
220. *Co-operative News* 19 March 1932, 1.
221. CWSBM 31 May 1935.
222. *Co-operative News* 11 August 1934, 8; *The Producer* August 1934, 229–231.
223. CWSBM 15 January 1930; 11 November 1930; 5 August 1931.
224. CWSBM 28 August 1929; 30 September 1930; 3 August 1932; 31 May 1932.
225. For a recent account of the famine see A. Applebaum, *Red Famine: Stalin's War on Ukraine* (London, Penguin 2018).
226. *Co-operative News* 4 October 1930, 1; 18 October 1930, 1; 25 October 1930, 1.
227. CWSBM 17 October 1933.
228. *Co-operative News* 18 October 1930, 1.
229. *Co-operative News* Editorial article 29 April 1933, 12.
230. CWSBM 25 July 1933.
231. CWSBM 3 October 1933.
232. CWSBM 6 February 1934; 13 February 1934.
233. CWSBM 5 June 1934.
234. CWSBM 14 August 1934.
235. *Co-operative News* 8 December 1934, 10.
236. CWSBM 12 December 1934; 18 December 1934.
237. CWSBM 5 June 1935.
238. *Co-operative News* 11 January 1936, 8; 22 January, 14.
239. CWSBM 21 July 1936; *Report of Deputation to Russia, 3 to 30 June 1937* (Manchester, CWS 1937) 14–17, NCA.
240. Report of Deputation to Russia, 3 to 30 June 1937, 15–16.
241. Ibid., 12.
242. *Co-operative News* 16 October 1937, 1.
243. *Co-operative News* 12 March 1938, 1.
244. CWSBM 22 March 1938.
245. CWSBM 27 June 1933.
246. CWSBM 15 August 1933; 19 September 1933.

247. CWSBM 18 July 1939.
248. CWSBM 25 January 1938.
249. CWSBM 30 November 1937.
250. CWSBM 5 October 1937; Co-op News 9 October 1937, 1.
251. CWSBM 12 October 1937.
252. CWSBM 12 April 1938.
253. *Co-operative News* 22 August 1936, 10.
254. Co-op News 6 March 1937, 1.
255. M. Anderson, "'Cost of a Cup of Tea': Fair Trade and the British Co-operative Movement, c.1960–2000" in L. Black & N. Robertson (eds.), *Consumerism and the Co-operative Movement in Modern British History: Taking Stock* (Manchester, Manchester University Press 2009) 240–259; 246.
256. CWSBM 14 June 1938.
257. *Co-operative News* 30 June 1934, 12.
258. CWSBM 28 April 1934.
259. CWSBM 1 October 1935.
260. *The Producer* February 1937, 42, www.theglasgowstory.com/image/?inum=TGSA05075.
261. Note of interview between Gowers and Alexander 29 September 1936 MAF 72/669 NA.
262. Notes of all these minutes can be found in MAF 72/669 NA.
263. Sir W. Richardson, *The CWS in War and Peace 1938–1976* (Manchester, CWS1977) 83–84.
264. CWSBM 21 May 1940.
265. CWSBM 8 June 1943.
266. CWSBM 14 October 1941.
267. J. Tilley, *Churchill's Favourite Socialist: A Life of A.V. Alexander* (Manchester, Holyoake Books 1995) 57.
268. CWSBM 25 March 1941; Richardson, *The CWS in War and Peace* 87–90; Kinloch & Butt, *History of the SCWS Ltd* 313; 322–323.
269. CWSBM 8 April 1941.
270. See M. Cohen, *The Eclipse of 'Elegant Economy': The Impact of the Second World War on Attitudes to Personal Finance in Britain* (Farnham, Ashgate 2012) 154; L. Sparks, "Consumer Co-operation in the UK 1945–93" *Journal of Co-operative Studies* 79 (1994) 1–64; 27.
271. Wilson, Webster & Vorberg-Rugh, *Building Co-operation* 217–220.
272. Kenwood & Lougheed, *The Growth of the International Economy* 235–240.
273. CWSBM 19 September 1939.
274. B. Wubs, *International Business and National War Interests: Unilever between Reich and Empire, 1939–45* (Oxford, Routledge 2008) 150; CWSBM 2 July 1940.
275. P. Nicol, *Sucking Eggs: What Your Wartime Granny Could Teach You about Diet, Thrift and Going Green* (London, Vintage 2010) 31.
276. CWSBM 26 September 1939.
277. CWSBM 23 April 1940.
278. CWSBM 12 December 1939.
279. CWSBM 6 February 1940.
280. CWSBM 12 December 1939.
281. CWSBM 20 December 1934.
282. CWSBM 23 July 1940; 23 February 1943.
283. CWSBM 14 January 1941.
284. CWSBM 1 August 1944.
285. CWSBM 4 May 1943.

286. CWSBM 14 November 1944.
287. CWSBM 21 December 1943.
288. CWSBM 6 February 1940; 25 November 1941; 29 September 1942.
289. CWSBM 21 December 1943.
290. CWSBM 28 March 1944.

5 Retreat and Deconstruction
The Decline of the Global British Co-operative Wholesale Networks 1945–1980 and West Africa and South Asia—Two Case Studies of the Wholesales Overseas

I

The wholesales emerged from the Second World War in a position that superficially appeared to have been significantly strengthened. They had played a central role in both shaping and implementing wartime economic policy, especially in developing and implementing rationing and in controlling aspects of international trade on behalf of the government. Commercially, they appeared to be much stronger. Sales of CWS had risen from £125,015,316 in 1939 to £166,834,649 in 1944, with profits rising from £2,891,485 to £5,845,869; these were impressive results, notwithstanding wartime inflation. Membership of member retail societies of CWS had grown from 6,765,194 in 1939 to 7,544,315 in 1944.[1] SCWS sales rose from £24,617,902 in 1939 to £37,677,558 in 1944.[2] Moreover, improvements in the trading position of the wholesales continued initially into the peace. There was generally a sense of optimism about the future, which initially strengthened in the post-war period, notwithstanding the continuing hardships of rationing, austerity and the demands of reconstruction.

In terms of the international supply networks of the wholesales, there were grounds for the expectation that in the foreseeable, though not immediate, future, the long record of innovation and leadership British co-operation had enjoyed would resume. The overseas depots outside Europe remained in place, and the coming of peace in Europe promised the re-establishment of key factories and depots in Denmark and France, just as the fruit depot at Denia in Spain had been re-opened after the end of the Spanish Civil War. The liberation of Eastern Europe, and the initially close alliance with the Soviet Union, seemed also likely to re-open opportunities there. In the first few years after the war, there were of course some uncertainties. By 1948, relations with the Soviet Union had severely deteriorated, and with the refusal of Stalin to relinquish control of those Eastern European states his forces had 'liberated', commercial prospects there for the wholesales (and British business generally) receded. Also, the weakness of the British economy and its dependence on the large US loan negotiated in the wake of the sudden termination of lend-lease in 1945 triggered the severe foreign exchange crisis in spring 1947 and resulted in a tightening of rationing and exchange controls in Britain for a much longer period than had been hoped. This represented a continuing barrier to a 'return to normality' in terms of the wholesales' overseas supply and trade system. This was compounded by a retreat from key imperial possessions, including India, Ceylon, Burma and Palestine in 1947–8. CWS/SCWS had extensive interests in tea estates in Ceylon and India, as well as developing links with the Palestinian CWS, and independence created uncertainty about wholesale interests there. It was a concern that would be repeated when more widespread decolonisation gathered momentum a decade or so later.

But against this, there were also promising developments that seemed to indicate that while some global opportunities might be closed, they would be compensated by emerging ones elsewhere. Crucial was the indication that the new framework for international trade established at Bretton Woods would in due course create a much freer and more liberal trading environment than had existed in the 1930s. Even the onset of the Cold War had a positive side, with the massive injection of $11 billion into Europe after 1947 in the form of Marshall aid, which promised to speed up western European recovery, underpin a new spirit of European co-operation and promote international trade. British government policy towards what remained of the Empire also seemed to offer opportunities for co-operation. British governments, faced with the severe economic problems of war and its aftermath, looked to the Sterling Area and the Empire as an essential economic resource that could earn desperately needed dollars for vital imports from the US. However, if the Empire was to be a successful dollar earner, many African colonies would need to be developed economically and socially. The Colonial Development and Welfare Acts of 1940 and 1945 set aside funds to develop the poorest colonies, while the Colonial Development Corporation and Overseas Food Corporation, established in October 1947, was to take the lead in pioneering specific development projects.[3] Co-operatives as a vehicle for colonial economic development had a long history in the British Empire, and the post-war Labour government saw the development of co-operatives in the colonies as highly desirable. To this end, in 1946–7 the Co-operative College, after negotiation with the Colonial Office, established a course for people from the colonies and colonial officials involved in development co-operatives within the Empire.[4] In addition, a CWS director sat on the economic advisory board of the Colonial Office from 1947.[5] In this context, one might have expected that such continued alignment with state priorities would have afforded new opportunities in the developing colonies. Of course, by the 1950s the post-war recovery was well under way and ushered in an unprecedented rise in living standards across the developed world, with full employment and rising purchasing power stimulating a huge expansion of global trade. By the end of the 1950s, globalisation was once again in full bloom, and would continue to be so for the rest of the century—indeed, up until the Great Crash of 2008. Surely this would augur not only a revival of the co-operative wholesales' global networks, but their further development and extension?

However, this was not to be the case. By the 1970s, most of the wholesales' overseas depots and productive facilities had been either closed or sold off. Increasingly, the international procurement strategies and operations of the wholesales (or wholesale, after CWS and SCWS merged in 1973) came to resemble those employed by the large multiple firms, as did many of their commercial operations. Like the multiples, the unified CWS would adopt many of the modern and mainstream supply chain management strategies that were becoming ubiquitous across the world. How and why did this happen? The next section of this chapter will trace the deconstruction of the wholesales' global supply network and explore the reasons for its abandonment. It will be seen that many of the reasons for this lay within the co-operative movement and within Britain itself, although other factors, including a loss of enterprise and global political developments, also played a part. The final sections of the chapter will examine two key case studies of wholesale activity within the British Empire: the palm oil and cocoa operations in West Africa, and the tea plantations run by the E & S Joint CWS in India and Ceylon. This will highlight both the interweaving of wholesale interests with the British Empire and the lifespans of two of the most celebrated branches of wholesale overseas operations. It will set out the 'life cycles' of these theatres of wholesale activity, from their inception to their demise. In the process, it will reinforce some of the key observations of the earlier chapters.

II

For over a decade after the war, many co-operators were slow to realise that the movement faced challenges more serious than ever before in the shape of well-resourced multiple store competitors and shifting consumption patterns in which the fastest growth and highest profits lay in lines in which the CWS and retail societies did not excel (dry goods,) as well as shifting social behaviours that were quite inimical to co-operation as a social and business movement. The performance of the movement suggested some element of decline but was initially hardly catastrophic. In terms of overall market share, the movement fell from 12 per cent in 1951 to 10.8 per cent in 1961, with the share in food declining from 17.1 to 15 per cent in this period and non-food from 6.5 to 5.6 per cent.[6] To many, while this was a cause for concern, it did not represent calamitous or irreversible decline. Yet more perceptive observers of the national scene within the movement were becoming increasingly aware—especially as the post-war recovery gathered pace in the 1950s—that Britain was changing irrevocably and quickly into a country that was very different to the one in which British co-operation had flourished, and one much more hostile to its values and traditional methods of operation. What were these changes? Why would it prove so difficult for British consumer co-operation to adapt to them?

Firstly, the rise of multiple chain competitors gathered pace in the immediate decades after the war. Chains such as Tesco, Sainsburys, Marks & Spencer and Woolworths had been making major strides in the inter-war period, with multiples growing their market share from 7–10 per cent in 1920 to 18–19.5 per cent in 1939. Moreover, their share of retail sales grew much faster than did the co-operative movement between 1930 and 1952.[7] In terms of market share, the proportion enjoyed by the multiples and the co-operatives changed, respectively, from 23 and 12 per cent in 1950 to 33 and 9 per cent in 1966.[8] As highly centralised bodies, many of which were enlarged by mergers and were much better placed to raise capital from the banks or from the City via PLC status, the multiples were able to build larger, more modern and technologically sophisticated shops in locations that reflected the movement of population from town and city centres to the suburbs.[9] The thousand or so co-operative societies that ran their stores across the UK tended to be highly localised and autonomous. Both their financial and political capital were heavily invested in their local shops and their status as independent and democratic co-operatives. Nobody within the movement had the authority to impose change upon a co-operative society; its autonomy was complete. This meant that any attempt to reform the organisation of individual societies—or indeed the structure of the movement more widely—had to be achieved by persuasion and consent. If, for example, two societies were to amalgamate to form a larger society, covering a larger geographical area, and with greater resources, this could only be achieved with the democratic consent of both societies. Such a democratic system of decision-making had the disadvantage that it made rapid adaptation to a quick changing environment often difficult to achieve. Centralised 'command and control' private capitalist multiple chains were not so constrained. If circumstances required the closure of several small stores and their replacement by a larger and modern store, this could be accomplished quite quickly, and the larger multiples could command the financial resources to carry such changes through relatively easily. Co-operative reform, as will be seen, would prove very difficult to enact.

Secondly, Britain experienced major sociological and cultural changes in the decade after 1945 that would also impact negatively upon the consumer co-operative movement. The two decades after the Second World War saw an unprecedented period of full employment and rapidly rising living standards, even among working-class families who traditionally had formed the bedrock of co-operation's members and customers. With full employment came material trappings that made the home much more central to the lives of British people: central heating, indoor bathrooms, refrigerators, radio and later TV, modern, attractive but inexpensive furnishings and of course the motor car. This created a much more individualised working-class culture, in which conspicuous consumption, especially among the young, became an arbiter of status and self-confidence.[10] The effect of this was to erode traditional loyalties, such as to the co-operatives, and to put in its place notions of individualism and consumer choice.[11] The effect was to erode the spirit of collectivism upon which co-operation depended to renew itself ideologically from generation to generation.[12] This was manifested at first not by falling membership (though this did become the case in the 1960s), but rather by non-attendance at meetings, disengagement from social and other events and a decline in interest in the internal democratic process within the co-operative.[13] This was not mere impression. The Co-operative College commissioned an academic study of the movement in the mid-1950s that provided evidence that a corrosive apathy had indeed set in.[14] The result was an aging membership wedded to practices of the past and reluctant to countenance change.[15] The dividends societies paid to their members proved to be one issue on which many retail societies dug in their heels. The multiples proved to be strong competitors on price, and many retail society members were reluctant to suppress dividends to enable their societies to compete more effectively on price.[16] These were hardly favourable circumstances in which reform could flourish.

The leaders of both the CU and the CWS realised that reform was needed for the movement to meet the twin challenges of the multiples and the transforming market. In 1955, with the support of CWS, the Co-operative Congress agreed to the establishment of an independent commission to investigate the movement and make recommendations to make it more competitive. Composed of a wide range of co-operators, politicians and academics, the Co-operative Independent Commission (CIC) convened in 1956 and reported two years later. The report called for numerous changes, including the amalgamation of retail societies to reduce their number to 200–300 large and well-resourced regional co-operatives. The idea was that this would enable them to support other key objectives of the CIS report, namely: reorganisation of the movement's store property portfolio to meet the needs of fast changing communities, investment to modernise 'drab' stores, more professional training for store managers, and major reform of the governance of CWS to empower managers and confine members' representatives to a general supervisory role. Crucially, the report called for a special body to be created, the Co-operative Retail Development Society (CRDS), to lead the modernisation and amalgamation programmes, as well as pave the way for a string of specialist co-operatives stores focusing upon such commodities as shoes.[17] But resistance to change from retail societies was fierce, and by 1960 both the membership of CWS and Co-operative Congress had rejected the idea of a CRDS and indeed most of the proposed reforms.[18]

It was a pattern that was to be repeated. In 1963, CWS itself tried to lead a new initiative for reform. A sub-committee of the CWS' Policy Committee was set up to review the position of CWS within the movement, including its relations with retail societies and many of the issues raised by CIC just five years earlier. The work of this sub-committee was channelled into a special Joint Reorganisation Committee convened in November 1964, consisting of representatives from the CWS and major societies. It reported in 1965, and this was circulated to societies across the country.[19] It was approved and adopted by CWS in October 1965, which began to implement its recommendations. One of these involved the appointment of full-time Executive Directors supported by a part-time Board, together with major internal reforms in the structure of CWS, especially the creation of three internal sub-divisions, for food, non-food and administration. But central to the plan was the idea of forging a new relationship between CWS and the retail societies, in which CWS would aspire to become a *buyer for* the retail societies rather than one that made and sold to them. It was recognised that such a relationship could not be created in the short term, and it represented a long-term aspiration rather than an immediately realisable goal. But the policy was given some purchase by the launch of *Operation Facelift*, a massive CWS-led investment in retail society stores to not only update them but also try to create a recognisable, national 'Co-op' brand. Some 1,300 shops were so improved in the next few years. At the same time, the CU produced its *Regional Plan for Co-operative Societies*, based upon the findings of the 'Amalgamation Survey' it had launched in the wake of the CIC Report of 1958. This called for even more radical amalgamation, aimed at the eventual creation of about 50 large and well-resourced regional retail societies. It was believed that this would make CWS engagement with retail societies more manageable. Many of the new changes were implemented by Philip Thomas (appointed January 1967), the first CWS Chief Executive to be appointed from outside the movement. He was to die in a plane crash in South Africa in April 1968, a tragedy that helped to stall some of the changes he was pioneering.[20]

Ten years later, one senior CWS official lamented that, notwithstanding a promising start, the reforms had not delivered the key changes desired. CWS retail society relations still largely rested upon a commercial *sell to* rather than *buy for* arrangement. There was still very little co-ordination between CWS and its members.[21] By 1980, the limited success of the late 1960s reforms was apparent. After a surge in profitability that saw annual profits rise to £18.8 million in 1977, they then plummeted to £6.3 million by 1980. Taking into account inflation, this represented little real progress on the position in 1970. While turnover nominally grew dramatically from £0.5 billion in 1970 to £1.9 billion in 1980, once inflation is accounted for this represented virtually no real growth across the 1970s.[22] Neither was the objective of creating just 50 regional retail societies achieved. In 1976, there were still 217 societies, though this number was being steadily whittled down by mergers, liquidations and takeovers.[23] Moreover, the price in terms of reducing the workforce and assets of the movement had been considerable. The co-operative work-force had been reduced from 232,000 in 1966 to 135,000 in 1976, and 56 per cent of all co-operative stores had been closed.[24] As will be seen, the overseas supply network was reduced because of these changes.

Notwithstanding these efforts at reform, the movement suffered major losses of market share, with many retail societies either failing or hav-ing to be bailed out by other societies, by CRS (Co-operative Retail Ser-vices) or eventually by CWS. The overall picture was not merely one of commercial decline and loss of ground to the major multiple competi-tors, but also of growing disorder, fragmentation and conflict within the co-operative movement. The loss of market share was stark. In 1950, co-operatives commanded 12 per cent of the domestic market and the multiples 23 per cent. By 1971, the co-operatives' share had fallen to 7 per cent with the multiples on 37 per cent, and by 1990 the co-operative movement's share had fallen to a mere 4 per cent while the multiples were riding high on 57 per cent.[25] One consequence, ironically, was a pro-cess of society rationalisation, with mergers and takeovers resulting from financial crises within societies. The number of societies fell from about 1,000 in 1950 to just over 200 in the early 1970s, and under 100 by the early 1980s.[26] But this was not the orderly reorganisation envisaged by the CIC in 1958, or the CU Regional Plan of a decade later. Rather, it was born of panic, falling membership and plunging sales and profitability. A key player in this process was CRS. CRS had been established as a department of CWS in the 1930s, with a brief to promote co-operation in areas of limited co-operative success, and to bail out societies that were in trouble. From the 1950s, an increasing number of societies were taken over by CRS, which provided for representation for the members of the societies and continued to operate the businesses. By 1960, 46 societies had been absorbed into CRS, and by 1976 this had risen to 162. By then, CRS had emerged as a major retail operator with a turnover of £287 million.[27] Perhaps inevitably, this led to rivalry with CWS as CRS came to assert its independence from its erstwhile parent. It was exacerbated by the near collapse of SCWS in 1973 because of a financial crisis at the SCWS bank. CWS had to take over SCWS, and with it numerous retail outlets that SCWS had been running for a number of years. This effectively brought CWS into direct retailing, and into competition with both retail societies and CRS. The effect was to exacerbate the already severe tensions that existed within the movement, and bitter rivalry was to blight British consumer co-operation until another wave of major, and this time more successful, reforms in the 1990s.[28]

Fragmentation was also a feature of CWS' relations with other component organisations of the movement. The Co-operative Permanent Building society, which had worked closely with CWS since the late nineteenth century in providing mortgages for co-operative members, distanced itself from the co-operative movement, the image of which seemed to be increasingly tarnished. In 1970, it changed its name to the Nationwide Building Society and relaunched a highly successful career free of its co-operative roots.[29] The CWS Bank progressively moved beyond its role as a department serving the trading functions of CWS to become effectively an independent business. Since the late nineteenth century, it had profited from loans to local authorities and trade unions as well as to retail societies, and it had steadily developed an individual banking business. It also tended the considerable portfolio of investments held by CWS. By the 1960s, the bank's leadership had firmly set its mind to turning the bank into a mainstream, high street bank. The bank acquired a new name—the Co-operative Bank—in 1968, and over the next 20 years it forged for itself a successful position as a small but highly innovative high street bank. In so doing, it drifted away from its traditional role within CWS, becoming almost a separate business.

How did these complex changes, flawed initiatives and decaying market position impact upon the wholesales' global supply networks? Inevitably, they contributed very substantially to their decay and eventual disappearance. But as will be seen, other factors also contributed to this process. It is important to trace this process of retreat from overseas depots and productive facilities in order to appreciate the complex factors that precipitated retreat. Before doing this, a comment is needed on how the international dimension of wholesale activity was seen within the movement after the Second World War, as reflected in its coverage in co-operative publications. From the 1880s, the international interests of the wholesales were trumpeted in the *Co-operative News*. *Wheatsheaf* regularly ran articles on tea plantations, the Danish bacon factory and the West African depots.[30] During the inter-war period, the *Producer* ran a regular column on 'British Empire News' that celebrated co-operation across the Empire and especially the work of the wholesales.[31] Major milestones such as the 50th anniversary of the opening of the New York depot in 1926 were treated to elaborate and celebratory coverage.[32] But after the war, far less attention was devoted to these overseas interests, as the focus shifted onto rivalry with the multiples and the debates over the need for internal reform. Decolonisation and a waning of enthusiasm for Empire may also have played a part in this, as did continuing state controls over trade that lasted well into the 1950s. But it is also clear that these overseas assets were no longer regarded with the same pride or importance as they were before 1939. The corollary of this was a retreat from them by the wholesales, which saw most of these possessions discarded by the end of the 1970s.

Tracing the abandonment of these overseas interests is no easy task. References to them are markedly absent from most of the public facing movement publications such as *Co-operative Review*, *Producer* and *Co-operative News*. Even the Board minutes are curiously silent on some of the closures and decisions to run down overseas facilities. The historian must trawl through the records to find evidence, and sometimes even then some decisions can only be accorded indirect identification. If the movement shouted loud to boast of its overseas Empire before 1939, it tended to whisper when announcing its dissolution.

An important source for information about the fate of CWS overseas depots in the first ten years after the Second World War is the statement CWS issued in April 1956 to the CIC as part of the latter's fact-finding process as it prepared to make recommendations.[33] It included a section on CWS overseas depots, and from this it is clear that several had already either been disposed of or were simply no longer functioning. These included all the West African depots, Rouen and Denia, none of which are mentioned in the exhaustive main text and appendix on overseas depots and trade. The reasons for the closure of the West African depots will be outlined later in this chapter. The reasons for the closure of Denia and Rouen are difficult to identify with any certainty. In the case of Denia, it seems likely that the hostility of the Franco regime and the development of alternative sources of dried fruit probably encouraged abandonment. By 1956, Greece and Turkey supplied the vast bulk of CWS dried fruit.[34] In the case of Rouen, the reasons are much more difficult to ascertain with any certainty, but it is clear that both it and Denia were given up within two years of the end of the war, suggesting that continuing state controls of trade and pressure to economise almost certainly played a role. At this time, it is clear that the remaining depots were still very important. CWS imported £22.9 million of goods in 1954, and nearly half—£10.8 million—came through the depots in Denmark, Canada, New Zealand, Australia, the USA and Argentina. In addition, the depots also sold £6.8 million in goods to government agencies in the respective countries, especially Denmark and New Zealand.[35] In the following year (1955), imports jumped dramatically to £37 million as wartime controls were dismantled, and £18.7 million of this came from CWS overseas depots.[36] The depots also supplied a range of commodities for European co-operative organisations, especially the New York depot.[37] The latter had seen a dramatic reduction in business during the war, but in 1955 it furnished CWS and several other European co-operative bodies with goods worth £2.1 million.[38] In California, Schuckl & Co. continued to be a major supplier of American canned fruit.[39] The Vancouver depot sourced canned salmon from seven out of the 12 top salmon packers on the west coast of Canada, and notwithstanding limits imposed by the dollar shortage in the UK, and import controls, in several years CWS imports amounted to one-third of total British imports.[40] NZPA remained an important facility for co-operative wholesale imports; by 1955, it furnished 7 per cent of all butter imports from New Zealand and 9 per cent of all cheese.[41] CWS also still ran a purchasing depot at Wellington.[42] Tea imported from India and Ceylon amounted to £21 million in the year ended 14 January 1956, and represented about 20 per cent of all tea consumed in the UK.[43] Argentina had also become important as a source of butter, meat and grain. During the war, the British state had imposed control over the butter trade with Argentina, but gradually this was handed back to CWS after the end of the war. Moreover, over 50 per cent of CWS butter supplies came from Argentinian co-operatives.[44] In meat, CWS sourced a large quantity of Argentinian meat, but the Argentinian state had taken control of *Coparacion Argentina de Productores de Carnes* (CAP) during the war and only relinquished that control in the early 1950s. It had also bought outright the Smithfield & Argentina Meat Co., a firm within which CWS had had a shareholding interest until the Argentinian government had taken it over. As a consequence, CWS meat imports were only beginning to recover at the time of the statement.[45] Grain purchases for import into the UK also still remained in the hands of the British government at the time of the statement, though it was expected that this would change soon.[46] The Sydney depot was also still going strong in 1956 and had struck up a special arrangement with the Australian Canned Food Board, by which a specially created CWS subsidiary, the Anglo–Australasian Importing Co., could act as agents for a range of Australian fruit canning companies. The normal arrangement was for each canner to employ their own agents, but the Australian Canned Food Board allowed this special arrangement with CWS because of the exceptionally large business CWS undertook in this field.[47]

Thus, the overseas network of the wholesales was still functioning in 1956, notwithstanding the difficulties imposed by war with certain branches of it. But the next 15 years would see a rapid withdrawal from much of it. The reasons for this lay partly in the commercial difficulties and loss of market share suffered by the movement during the period, but there were other policy factors that played into the process. The CIC report of 1958, while not really enacted effectively, certainly did begin to challenge some important principles that had underpinned the wholesales' expansion into production and the growth of their international supply networks. The report particularly challenged two basic commercial ideas. Firstly, it noted that wholesale ventures in production and sourcing supplies had always worked on the assumption that getting as close as possible to the primary producer would yield major economies and boost competitiveness. While the report largely upheld this principle in relation to food, it did stress that there was a strong case for constantly reviewing whether better deals might be secured by buying from agents and middlemen rather than maintaining the costly infrastructure of factories and depots. In relation to non-food, the report was more critical of the policy, arguing that the rise of branding of commodities meant that buying on the open market would be more effective in holding onto customers and winning new ones.[48] Secondly, the fear of boycotts by the private sector, which had figured so prominently in co-operative thinking for so long, was directly challenged by the report:

> It was not infrequent in the past for a monopolist, or indeed any strongly-entrenched producer, completely to refuse supplies to the Co-operative Movement. This is naturally much less likely to occur today. The Movement has grown to the point where no private boycott has any conceivable hope of destroying or even significantly weakening it; indeed a refusal to supply would usually hurt the supplier than the Co-operatives. As might be expected, therefore, we have found only isolated examples of boycott, and practically none of a complete national boycott.[49]

The significance of the report was that it began to subtly shift co-operative thinking away from the notion that production and overseas supply networks were essential for the wholesales to operate successfully. In 1963, in the preparation for the CWS' own reform plan, which eventually became the Report of the Joint Reorganisation Committee (JRC) of 1965 and the basis of the reforms of 1967, Fred Lambert, Head of the Marketing Research Department, produced an advisory document that strongly influenced the JRC. *The CWS in the Twentieth Century* offered ideas that built upon some of the suggestions of CIC in terms of the role of CWS in supplying retail societies. An important observation made by Lambert was that by the early 1960s, mergers and amalgamations were beginning to create large retail societies. But given the poor history of society loyalty to CWS, the fear was that large societies might be even less likely to buy from the wholesales, choosing instead to source directly from suppliers and manufacturers.[50] This meant that CWS desperately needed to change its relationship with the retail societies, aspiring to become buyers for rather than selling to them. Rather than seeking profit from selling to the societies, CWS needed to act increasingly in concert with retail society needs, working with them instead of treating them as customers. This meant stocking and supplying goods that societies demanded rather than pushing CWS products or lines. Indeed, the small group of CWS officials advising the JRC concluded that CWS needed to buy in branded goods from agents rather than trying to supply all society needs themselves.[51] These ideas were incorporated in the JRC repot and the plan, and, combined with the need to make economies to fund *Operation Facelift*, the upshot was a tough review of existing CWS factories at home and overseas depots. In 1965, Lambert was asked to supply the Grocery Committee with a summary of the various overseas depots and productive units still operated by CWS, with information on the volume and nature of the trade. Lambert's report fed into the JRC review and resulted in several of them being closed. In 1964, the Buenos Aires depot supplied £237,475, mainly in butter, employing one member of staff.[52] Clearly, the hopes of a full recovery involving increased meat supplies, as expressed in the 1956 CWS briefing document, had not materialised. The Sydney depot employed five people and generated £1,790,450 in 1964, supplying canned fruit, green fruit, rice and other commodities to both CWS and SCWS and also to a range of European co-operative organisations.[53] In Canada, Montreal supplied wheat, cheese and canned goods worth £3.8 million, while Vancouver supplied £1.4 million in canned goods and wheat, and together they employed nine CWS staff. New York supplied £1.6 million in goods in 1964 but employed nine people. The Danish depots of Odense, Aarhus, Copenhagen and Esbjerg employed 31 people and supplied £8.47 million in bacon, butter, cheese and other agricultural produce; these were in addition to the two bacon factories at Herning and Skjern, now run by CWS Bacon Factories Ltd. The CWS depot in Wellington, New Zealand, supplied £2 million in meat, wheat, butter and other produce, in addition to the Longburn Meat Freezing and Ocean Beach factories.[54]

But, following the rationalisations and closures after the reforms of 1967, these facilities were dramatically reduced. The New York and Montreal depots were closed in the late 1960s.[55] Half ownership of the Danish bacon factories was sold soon after.[56] The closures continued. By February 1973, CWS ran only two buying depots overseas, at Sydney and Vancouver. All the others had been disposed of as part of the economy drive and rationalisation associated with *Operation Facelift* and the reforms of 1967.[57] Longburn Freezing Works in New Zealand was disposed of in 1967, although CWS interests in Ocean Beach continued until 1982.[58] The upshot was that by the mid-1980s, virtually all of the CWS' networks of overseas depots and factories had been disposed of. CWS had by then increasingly sourced imports in the same way as other private companies—through direct links with overseas producers, manufacturers or their agents.

Unquestionably, the dismantling of the British Empire and Britain's shifting international position affected this dismantling of the wholesales' overseas networks. Uncertainty in the 1960s over whether Britain would join the EEC also preoccupied many in the wholesales and the movement. Differences within the movement over this question were deep and reflected the wider fragmentation within the movement already described.[59] But, in reality, most of the overseas networks had been dismantled before Britain joined in 1973, though this undoubtedly played a role in the final retreat from Commonwealth assets. One feature of the post-war period was continuing piecemeal co-operation between national co-operative wholesales, particularly though the Co-operative Wholesales Committee of the ICA, though this never amounted to a significant aspect of the British wholesales' work.[60] In 1973, CWS also joined EUROCOOP, an organisation of co-operative wholesales inside the EEC, though the difficulties encountered by wholesales across Europe in the 1970s and 1980s limited the achievements of this body.[61] While CWS remained connected to the wider global and European co-operative movements after 1980, and while it certainly continued to trade with the world, the elaborate system of overseas depots and productive facilities that had enabled it to manage a complex global supply network had been dissolved.

III

Some useful insights can be obtained by examining specific theatres of wholesale overseas activity, especially in respect of how their efforts adapted to often trying local circumstances. The two case studies that constitute the final sections of this chapter offer some especially important observations of how the wholesales' search for profitable sources of essential commodities interacted with Britain's wider imperial interests and how cut-throat competition with domestic rivals drove wholesale activities. The rise and fall of co-operative wholesale efforts to secure supplies of palm oil and cocoa in West Africa (specifically Sierra Leone, Nigeria and the Gold Coast) is the first of these, while their efforts to secure direct supplies of tea in India and Ceylon will constitute the second.

The beginnings of the wholesales' presence in West Africa in 1913 were examined in Chapter 3, and the purpose here will be to trace how wholesale depots and assets developed, up to their eventual abandonment in the 1950s. What problems did the wholesales encounter, and what strategies were adopted to address these? Why, in the end, did the wholesales abandon the region? As shown, the 'soap war' with Lever Brothers meant that palm oil was initially the main source of interest in the region, and the development of CWS interests in this field will be addressed first.

CWS operations in West Africa officially commenced on 12 June 1914, when the Colonial Office gave permission for trading to commence at Freetown in Sierra Leone.[62] Just over a week later, a deputation was arranged to go out to Freetown to open a retail store to supplement CWS activities in purchasing palm kernels. The first manager of the store was one J. Cocksey, just 29 years old and from Liverpool, appointed on an annual salary of £250.[63] The short career of Mr Cocksey epitomised one of the problems of running a commercial operation in one of the unhealthiest CWS overseas postings. By February 1915, he was at loggerheads with his staff and had to resign and return home with malaria.[64] In the next few weeks, following accusations of drunkenness, several of

Cocksey's assistants were dismissed, and the retail store had to be closed until new staff could be sent out.[65] The West Africa Trading Committee (WATC), a sub-committee of the Board set up in 1914 to oversee the development of CWS' West African activities, now took direct control of sorting out the Freetown debacle.[66] In May, CWS opted for experience to replace Cocksey and appointed one J.J. Hone, aged 50, and with many years' experience on the coast of West Africa.[67] Palm kernels were purchased from West African growers at a series of smaller depots in the countryside, but here again problems arose. In September 1915, a West African clerk, O.J. Williams, was caught stealing at the Makene depot. He was charged, but £150 had been lost.[68] The problem of theft recurred, this time in the Freetown depot, and again it was blamed on a West African employee, though no proof was established.[69] Nonetheless, theft was seen as such a problem that CWS canned goods sent out to Freetown were bound with iron to ensure security.[70] The Freetown depot offered CWS access to palm kernels for export to the UK and a local market for CWS produce, especially textiles and drapery.[71] But problems continued. In August 1916, more trouble flared up among staff at Freetown, and three British assistants were sacked by Hone for sending a joint letter to the *Sierra Leone News* criticising the management of CWS in Freetown.[72] But the offending assistants received support from others in the depot, and after the assistants had been interviewed by WATC following their return in September, a deputation was sent out to sort the issue out.[73] In February, Hone resigned and replaced temporarily by Mr Loxley, the cashier who had supported the sacked assistants.[74]

The severity of the personnel difficulties at Freetown were unusual, though not unprecedented in the history of CWS operations overseas. But the physical hazards of working in West Africa, and especially the problem of disease, undoubtedly contributed to the problems. Nevertheless, CWS established a reasonably effective trading system in Sierra Leone with direct and effective links with CWS domestic interests in the UK. In April 1916, several up-country depots were set up to collect palm kernels at Blama, Kennema, Segbwema, Pendembu and Sherbro.[75] A substantial portion of palm oil kernels would be sent to the CWS' African Oil Mills Co. Ltd in Liverpool, purchased outright, with adjoining land for expansion, by CWS in November 1916.[76] Early results were very promising. In the half year ended 31 December 1916, African Oil Mills Ltd registered a profit of over £38,000.[77] In June 1917, the Freetown's credit facility was raised from £2,500 to £5,000 to accommodate increased purchases of palm kernels.[78] In the following month, it was directed that all staff bound for employment in West Africa should visit African Oil Mills Ltd in Liverpool to learn about the West African trade.[79] The other main destination for palm kernels was to the CWS' margarine works at Higher Irlam in Manchester, built in the first few years of the war. But CWS margarine was being sold in a very competitive market. In March 1919,

CWS had to reduce its price to retail societies to 6.5d per lb, with a recommendation that they sell it at no more than 8d per lb.[80] Losses on the product proved to be heavy. A loss of £65,227 was recorded for the half year to September 1919, although output had more than doubled compared to the comparative period in the previous year from 102,274 cwts to 240,070 cwts.[81] But CWS ambitions were high. It purchased land adjacent to the margarine works for £10,225 to build an additional oil mill, with a view to supplying processed oil to both the Higher Irlam margarine works and the Irlam soap works.[82] Profits from working Freetown and the up-country depots were augmented by selling drapery and foodstuffs to Europeans and local consumers. Freetown boasted a drapery and grocery outlet and a fancy goods department upstairs. Government officials, soldiers, missionaries, merchants and even the governor of the colony patronised the store.[83]

However, problems emerged on the world market. By 1922, intense competition from Dutch palm oil produced in Sumatra resulted in the price of the commodity being halved from £20 to £9 per ton.[84] WATC met in mid-February to discuss the crisis and was most concerned that the difficulties might even lead to a complete CWS withdrawal from the west coast of Africa. To forestall this, it recommended an embargo on any further extension of Freetown and the cancellation of plans for the purchase of various properties in Sierra Leone and Nigeria.[85] The Board followed this advice.[86] In fact, CWS increased its investment in soap production, and a new soap works at Irlam was opened in 1926, with state of the art technology and an increase in productive capacity of 500 tons weekly over and above the 900 tons achieved per week previously.[87] Steps were taken to strengthen CWS political clout in West African affairs. In 1923, CWS Grocery Committee members secured seats on the Royal Colonial Institute, the African Section of the Manchester Chamber of Commerce and the African Society in London.[88]

CWS persisted with the trade, and by 1928 controlled about 20 per cent of palm oil exports from Sierra Leone and about 7 per cent of exports from Nigeria.[89] But CWS remained concerned, especially with the poor performance of its trading department in Lagos.[90] In the longer term, the palm oil trade proved to be deeply problematic. The onset of the Great Depression in 1929 resulted in palm oil plummeting in price by 600 per cent by 1934.[91] Moreover, as the 1930s progressed, competition from southeast Asian palm oil intensified. In Malaya and Sumatra, the infrastructure of European and Chinese merchants, rubber plantation owners with the skills and capital to nurture palm production, created highly effective 'clusters' capable of producing palm more efficiently than West Africa and getting it to market more effectively.[92] Indeed, as early as 1925, the British colonial authorities in Nigeria and the Gold Coast had undertaken research that demonstrated that southeast Asia possessed advantages of expertise and infrastructure that would be difficult to match.[93] Southeast Asia overtook Nigeria as a palm oil producer in 1936, and by 1939 the former region was producing 50 per cent of global exports.[94] CWS was quick to realise that the future for palm oil in Sierra Leone was most unpromising, and from the mid-1930s it began to extract itself. In 1934, it closed three of its up-country depots for purchasing palm kernels and curtailed selling provisions at its Freetown depot.[95] By November 1936, CWS was in negotiation with the United African Company as an alternative supplier of palm kernels and oil to replace CWS' own facilities.[96] Ultimately, CWS had abandoned its interests in Sierra Leone by the time of the outbreak of the Second World War, and its involvement in palm oil was much reduced and confined to Nigeria, though not entirely abandoned.[97]

But CWS interests in cocoa in West Africa proved more durable. In spring 1914, a deputation was sent to the Gold Coast to explore the establishment of an E & S Joint CWS cocoa and palm oil buying operation there.[98] In August 1914, it was decided to establish a depot, warehouse and shipping centre at Accra.[99] But it was not until spring 1916 that land and a building were purchased in Accra for storing and shipping cocoa bought from local producers.[100] Progress picked up after credit available for the Accra buyer was increased from £20,000 to £35,000 in November of that year, and from £20,000 to £40,000 in December.[101] Then, late in 1918, a further 335 acres of land was bought for £1,500 at Accra to extend the warehouse. At the same time, CWS bought Middleton's Wharf at Wapping in London to accommodate increased imports, particularly from West Africa.[102] By 1926, CWS had eight warehouses and offices in and around Accra for the purchase and storage of cocoa. It also had leases for developing two more sites. CWS also had rented warehouses and buildings at five sites in Ashanti but looked to offload three of these as the other two promised to meet demand for the foreseeable future.[103] In 1927–8, CWS purchased 3,878 tons of cocoa on the west coast of Africa, 2,374 tons of which were used in the cocoa works of CWS in Luton. The rest was sold to outside bodies. In the following year (1928–9), purchases fell to 2,700 tons, but with only 900 earmarked for Luton. Purchases then rose dramatically to 5,250 tons in 1929–30, with 2,500 for Luton. Purchases then fell again to 2,434 tons, which was all earmarked for outside sales, as were the 4,115 tons purchased in 1931–2.[104] Cocoa was obtained by CWS making advances to farmers or middlemen, with the actual production undertaken by local farmers.[105] Quality was often a problem, not least because of intense competition with Cadbury's and the United African Company.[106] CWS hoped that sales for 1936–7 would be as much as 10,000 or even 15,000 tons. Only a small amount (1,300 tons) was bound for Luton; the rest was targeted at brokers selling to both the American and European markets.[107]

Late in 1937, a major confrontation occurred between the main companies purchasing cocoa in Nigeria and the Gold Coast and the planters.

The purchasing companies—except CWS—signed agreements with each other not to purchase cocoa above an agreed price, effectively seeking to impose a monopoly over cocoa supplies and force down prices. But the planters, especially those who had organised themselves into co-operatives, resisted, and the supply of cocoa ceased.[108] In February 1938, the colonial government set up a special commission to investigate the dispute, and this not only effectively ended the attempted monopoly but also concluded that co-operation should be promoted among planters in Nigeria.[109] CWS emerged from the crisis in good odour with both the planters and the colonial government. In fact, in May 1938 the Colonial Office in London approached CWS to discuss the question of cocoa in West Africa, and indeed a range of other issues in which CO had an interest. On 27 May, four members of the CWS and SCWS met a team of five civil servants at the Colonial Office. For CO, Sir Frank Stockdale asked that the CWS assist in the promotion of co-operatives in West Africa. The CWS representatives affirmed that they were prepared to do this and even to offer some financial support as they had done for the Australian wheat pools, but that it must be strictly understood that producers' co-operatives would have to be viable and ultimately accept market prices for their produce.[110] The conversation then turned to unexpected matters. One of the CO officials asked if CWS would be prepared to source their coffee from Colombia instead of Costa Rica. This was because the Colombian government had suggested they might introduce restrictions on the country's substantial imports of Lancashire textiles, as they ran a substantial balance of trade deficit with the UK.[111] The CWS representative also mentioned in passing that they had been approached by Hersheys of the USA about a possible deal on cocoa supplies, though nothing appears to have emerged from it.[112]

One consequence of this was the post-war involvement of CWS and the movement in helping to advise on economic policy in the colonies, but the outbreak of war resulted in the imposition of state controls over cocoa purchases. In fact, even with some growth in the late 1930s, CWS purchases for the whole of West Africa in each year between 1934–5 and 1937–8 varied between 9,000 and 12,000 tons; the overwhelming bulk of it sold outside the movement. To put this in context, annual cocoa exports in total from the Gold Coast along varied between 230,000 tons and 300,000 tons for each of the years 1935 to 1938.[113] The fact was that CWS engaged in the cocoa trade to protect itself from the kind of monopolistic arrangement that was attempted in late 1937; it was never quite the big player it occasionally claimed to be. For the duration of the war, and for years after, CWS found itself buying for the British government, but even in this capacity it remained a minor player.[114] Its quota of cocoa to be shipped from the Gold Coast in 1945 was a mere 4.92 per cent, compared to the United African Company's 33.2 per cent and Cadbury & Fry's 15.33 per cent.[115] The deputation that visited West Africa in that year questioned whether or not continuing the West African depots for cocoa was actually worthwhile, and in this they reflected some growing doubts in Manchester.[116] But the view of the manager of the Accra depot was that though Luton's own consumption of cocoa was limited, a successful export business could be built by exporting to the USA and other chocolate producers around the world. It was a question of waiting for decontrol. The deputation agreed with this.[117] However, by 1951, the changing political situation in West Africa, especially in the Gold Coast, was beginning to create uncertainty. While the deputation of that year advised that CWS should continue trading for as long as returns were adequate, along with the other private companies, concern was expressed at the rise of Kwame Nkrumah and the Convention People's Party.[118] Ultimately, decontrol and the domestic problems of CWS in the 1950s changed the mind of its leaders about West African cocoa and its depots there. By the early 1960s, all had been abandoned. Decontrol of trade in 1953–4 persuaded CWS that the pre-war dangers perceived of boycotts and monopolisation by private companies were no longer pressing. Furthermore, as the Gold Coast and other West African colonies moved towards independence, the uncertainties around this ensured that CWS would cease to be a player in the West African market.[119]

IV

The acquisition of tea estates in Ceylon by the E & S Joint CWS in the early 1900s was examined in Chapter 3. The aim here will be to trace the main developments in the wholesales' joint tea interests in India and Ceylon from the First World War to the eventual surrender of the estates in the late 1980s. As some of the most enduring possessions of the wholesales, the tea estates came to epitomise their status as a global operator. Thus, their abandonment had a symbolic quality, drawing a line under CWS' past as a proponent of Empire and European hegemony. How did the wholesales' presence on the sub-continent change during the period? Why did it last so long?

One of the most striking features of the First World War is how wholesale tea interests grew during the conflict, at a time when some other branches of wholesale international commerce were under pressure. The advance began just before the war and seems to have been partly triggered by dissatisfaction with the private agents who had been superintending the E & S Joint CWS estates in Ceylon in the years before the war. The firm of Messrs Crosfield, Lampard & Co. had been agents in charge of the wholesales' estates there as early as 1906.[120] But by 1913, its successor firm of Harrisons & Crosfield was poorly thought of by CWS. The deputation to Ceylon of that year made clear to them that their services would be dispensed with, and that henceforth CWS would have its own representative to manage affairs.[121] The deputation clearly believed this marked a new beginning for wholesale enterprise in South Asia.[122] A change of pace soon followed. One George Price was named as representative to manage the wholesales' affairs at Colombo, and the advice of the deputation was followed in the purchase of two substantial estates, the Westhall estate (1,931 acres) for £18,509 and the Denmark estate (151 acres), a mile from the wholesales' existing estate at Mahavilla, for £6,000.[123] The next deputation to India carried through this new spirit of ambition, and after visiting the estates in Ceylon, they sought new options in India, calling first at Ootacamund, the European summer refuge in southern India, to investigate a number of options, and then proceeding to Calcutta to follow up some enquiries about estates for sale in Assam.[124] A significant source of help to the deputation was a land valuer, Sir E.F. Barber, whose formal reports were instrumental in persuading the deputation to recommend the purchase of three estates in the Madras Presidency at Annacarp, Palateer and Ripon, and the refusal of several others, advice that the Board followed for £4,000.[125] Barber was a prominent tea pioneer in his own right, running his own agency company. He was also a leading figure on the United Planters Association of Southern India, representing that body on the Madras Legislative Council.[126] Another estate at South Wynaad, about 75 miles from Calicut, was recommended, but delays arising from the deeds and legal documentation being in England meant that the purchase of this estate was not completed until May 2015, for £3,000.[127] An additional estate on Ceylon, Bowhill, was also purchased on Ceylon for £5,667, following the deputation.[128]

A series of articles in *Co-operative News* in 1915 outlined why the wholesales were so keen on expanding their ownership of estates and production of tea. Although by 1915 they had acquired several estates, they produced only about 0.7 per cent of the total tea they actually supplied to co-operative societies.[129] This meant that tea growers in India and the companies that imported the commodity into London were able to charge high prices, which affected the wholesales like any other tea purchaser and ultimately forced up the price for the consumer.[130] The larger the SCWS/ CWS' own supply of tea from its own estates, the greater the leverage it would enjoy in negotiating the price and quality of tea bought on the open market. The veiled threat was that discontented co-operative wholesales would expand their own production and bring unwelcome competition to grower and importer alike. Moreover, the strategy appealed to powerful advocates within the movement, such as the Shillito League, which campaigned to maximise co-operative control over raw materials.[131] If the expenses of running tea estates were to be incurred, they needed to have a demonstrable effect in terms of improving the wholesales' position within the tea market. This would prove to be the case.

An indication that the wholesales were determined to make the best of their south Asian assets was the three deputations sent out to India and

Ceylon during and just after the First World War. In 1916, a deputation visited southern India again and was guided by Barber to visit the Mango Range group of estates and the Rockwood estate at Nellakotta and recommend their purchase, together with an additional 3,500 acres adjoining the wholesales' recently acquired estate in South Wynaad, bringing their holdings there up to 10,000 acres.[132] Other estates were visited, and, crucially, Barber's role as adviser led to his and his assistant Mr Pascoe's appointment as the wholesales agents in India.[133] Further purchases were confirmed after the deputation reported; Mango Range was purchased for £3,850, Murugalli (also South India) for £4,988 and the Nagastenne estate (Ceylon) for £1,478.[134] Working on the deputation's recommendations, other purchases followed. An additional 1,716 acres of land were purchased around the Mango Range, comprising the Richmond estate (cost £5,417), Strathern and Maryland (£1,729) and Marian (£831). Buildings and warehouses in Ceylon were bought for £3,390.[135] Then, in 1918, the wholesales purchased land, the Bahahundrah estate (£6,400), between the Westhall and Bowhill estates.[136] Yet another 320-acre estate on Ceylon, Dotela (£900), was acquired in spring 1919.[137] By the mid-1920s, these very substantial additions to the wholesales' productive tea assets had brought a radical change in their position in the tea market. In January 1925, there were complaints in the Press about the wholesales buying up tea in south Asia so excessively that it was forcing up the price, accusations that were strenuously rebutted.[138] But it was the case that the wholesales were by this time producing much more of their own tea from their own estates. SCWS/CWS estates produced about 4.6 million lbs of the total 55 million lbs of tea purchased by the wholesales per year. In other words, the wholesales' estates now produced 8.3 per cent of requirements, compared to just 0.7 per cent in 1914.[139] This undoubtedly boosted the negotiating position enjoyed by E & S Joint CWS Ltd in the market for buying tea.

Certainly the 1920s saw a continuation of the wholesales' efforts to strengthen their grip on the supply of tea. A deputation in 1920 spent a good deal of time in Assam exploring opportunities to purchase tea estates there, and a number of offers were considered, with one at Decki-ajuli.[140] The deputation also strongly recommended the establishment of an E & S Joint CWS branch in Calcutta to buy tea and superintend planned expansion of activities in Assam and Northern India.[141] Though initially there seemed little prospect of the purchase of Deckiajuli, it subsequently seems to have ended up in E & S Joint CWS possession, because the onset of depression in the UK and financial difficulties for the movement prompted a scurrying retreat from commitments in Assam and a decision to resell Deckiajuli as soon as possible.[142] It also briefly checked a proposal by Sir Fairless Barber that E & S Joint CWS take-over his firm of Barber & Pascoe and employ Barber as manager of their affairs in India.[143]

But the desire for retrenchment does not appear to have lasted for very long. By April 1922, E & S Joint CWS were urged by CWS to open a Calcutta office and extend tea buying in Colombo specifically to buy tea for shipment direct to a tea packing factory in Manchester.[144] So pressing was this need for tea for Manchester that the Board of CWS even considered buying stocks of tea from the Anglo–Eastern Trading Company, which had tea stocks in the city.[145] The deputation to India in 1922–3 was particularly tasked with assessing the advantages and disadvantages of buying on the Calcutta market. It concluded that it was an experiment worth pursuing through an agent.[146] It also advised that Deckiajuli, which was still in E & S Joint CWS hands, should not be abandoned after all.[147] It also restated and recommended the advice of the 1920 deputation that Barber & Pascoe be taken over and Barber taken on as full-time manager.[148] By 1925, Barber had become an E & S Joint CWS employee, and his firm was in the process of being wound up, though its assets and agency contacts were in the process of being taken over by E & S Joint CWS.[149]

By the mid-1920s, there was growing concern about the future of tea supplies. World tea consumption had been rising quickly since the beginning of the century, from 490 million lbs in 1900 to 622 million lbs in 1922–3. But production had not kept pace and was only 90 million lbs greater in 1922–3 compared to 1900. The consequence was rising prices and real concern about future supplies.[150] Competition between firms was intensifying, and the deputation stressed the need for E & S Joint CWS to strengthen its operations and its intelligence gathering in respect of the tea market in south Asia.[151] By the end of the decade, one response of the private companies involved in the tea trade was to amalgamate and create larger firms to secure market share and increase capital resources. In 1929, Allied Suppliers Ltd was established by five separate multiple concerns involved in tea buying, namely Home & Colonial, Liptons, Maypole Dairy Company, Meadow Dairy and Pearks Dairies. By this time, the tea market in the UK was dominated by E & S Joint CWS, which enjoyed control of about 20 per cent of the UK market, followed by Lyons with about 17 per cent, then Brooke Bond and Allied Suppliers.[152] The rise of powerful private trusts had been noted by co-operators in other fields, notably soap and margarine, and it was felt that this represented a major threat to both consumer interests and the co-operative movement. For co-operators, this reinforced the wisdom of the wholesales having established themselves in south Asia as producers as well as buyers of tea. Certainly by the late 1920s, the wholesales' tea trade was flourishing. Overall, E & S Joint CWS' net profit for the year ended 25 June 1927 was £187,442, though this included results for coffee and cocoa as well.[153] Sales of CWS tea boomed in the mid-1920s, and not just in the UK. The volume and value of E & S Joint CWS tea supplies from its Colombo depot to London doubled from 2,648,554 lbs in 1925 (£215,480) to

5,630,892 lbs in 1927 (£428,589). In addition, exports to co-operative societies and other organisations had also increased. Colombo exports to Australia and New Zealand had risen from 50,306 lbs in 1925 (£4,763) to 76,860 lbs in 1927 (£6,502). Major customers included NSW CWS, Westralian Famers, Fort Adelaide Industrial Co-operative Society, New Zealand Fruit Growers Association, National Dairy Association of New Zealand and New Zealand Farmers Co-operative Society. Exports to Canada rose from 17,200 lbs (£1,661) in 1925 to 28,600 lbs (£2,281) in 1927, with British Canadian Co-operative Society as a major customer. The year 1927 also saw the sale of 1,820,990 lbs (£161,513) of Colombo tea to the Soviet CWS, Centrosoyus, and 3,800 lbs (£380) to societies in Southern Africa.[154]

By this time, E & S Joint CWS were seeking to uphold co-operative commitments to support and improve the living conditions of Asian workers on their estates. The old superintendent's bungalow on the Westhall estate on Ceylon was converted to a hospital for Rs2,600, admittedly not a large sum.[155] At Deckiajuli in India, an additional ward was added to the existing hospital for women patients.[156] On the Indian estates, there was a policy to improve education for children and adults, though how effective this was is difficult to glean from the often-bland deputation reports. It should be said that rather more space in the 1928 report was allotted to the provision of medicine for the family of European officials![157] Moreover, the power structures on E & S Joint CWS estates were no different to other European tea plantation operations in that white Europeans were firmly in charge. Nonetheless, the deputation reports do make frequent references to the provision of amenities and the general social condition of workers. The 1931 report commented on the condition of schools for children at Westhall, noting they were inspected and found to be in good order.[158] The deputation was especially enthusiastic about a successful consumer co-operative store run by the workers there.[159] Housing on some of the south Indian estates were also inspected, especially work that had relocated some huts to higher ground with concomitant improvements in health.[160] But such initiatives clearly did not alleviate all grievances, and there were reports of stoppages and conflict at the wholesales' South Wynaad estates in the Madras Presidency.[161] Nonetheless, the condition of workers on the E & S Joint CWS estates continually occupied the regular deputation to south Asia and did lead to some ameliorative action where problems were found.

The onset of the Great Depression in 1929 inevitably affected the tea trade, but the E & S Joint CWS weathered the storm well. By the end of the 1920s, notwithstanding the emergence of new combines in the tea market, the wholesales had a firm grip on the market. Their Indian estates alone had doubled production from 2,109,301 lbs in 1922 to 4,760,604 lbs in 1931.[162] The report noted, however, that such was the success of the wholesales in selling tea on the domestic British market that there was never any likelihood of the wholesales ever producing even the bulk of their own tea requirements. It moreover cast doubt as to whether wholesale control of tea production was yet sufficient to offset the effect of larger combines in driving up prices.[163] By 1933, efforts to bolster tea prices, as with similar initiatives in respect of other commodities, were official British state policy. Restrictions on tea exports from India and Ceylon were introduced in 1932–3, and while the wholesales stressed their opposition in principle to any policy that increased prices for the consumer, it made clear that it was more than holding its own in the market, with the share of the trade enjoyed by co-operative tea actually increasing, and with co-operative tea on average being cheaper than competitors.[164] Moreover, it had chosen to reduce output by picking only the finest leaves, boosting quality, rather than taking plantations out of production.[165] There were problems specific to particular Ceylon plantations in the mid-1930s, however. Overall, the trade of the Colombo depot fell from 4,657,978 lbs (£249,138) for the year ended September 1933 to 3,104,168 lbs (£172,642) in year ended September 1935. Mostly this reflected declining demand both at home (due to quotas) but also in Russia, Australia New Zealand and Canada.[166] However, there were specific local problems. At the Mahavilla group of estates, 80 miles north of Colombo, production fell from 425,473 lbs in the 18 months to March 1934, to 376,007 lbs in the 18 months to September 1935.[167] A malaria epidemic in 1935 that killed 80,000 people laid up 45 per cent of the Mahavilla workforce at one point. This was compounded by a severe drought.[168] These difficulties were exacerbated by petty feuds among some senior European E & S Joint CWS figures, which led to some dismissals.[169] But the situation did improve later in the 1930s, and by the year ended September 1937, sales from the Colombo depot had recovered to 4,518,592 lbs (£295,412).[170]

Just as the E & S Joint CWS managed to sustain profitability and market share in the difficult years of the depression, so their record in the Second World War was equally robust. Even though many of its European officials were conscripted, it managed to sustain production, achieving record crops on many estates in 1943. The output of its estates was subject to direct government control, as were those of others. But it was able to boast that the share of the domestic market supplied by the co-operative movement had risen to 25 per cent during the war, from its pre-war level of about 20 per cent.[171] After the war, its tea estate possessions remained intact, and by 1947 20.7 per cent of UK tea was still purchased in co-operative shops. By that time, CWS owned a total of 44 tea estates organised into eight groups across India and Ceylon. In Assam, northern India, there were just two estates in the group there; while in southern India there was the Mango Range Group (nine estates), the Kalpetta Group (six), the Manantoddy Group (eight), the Iyerpadi Group (three) and the Sheikul Mudi Group (four). Meanwhile, on Ceylon there remained the two oldest groups owned by the wholesales, the Mahavilla Group (five) and the Westhall Group (seven).[172]

The post-war years did begin to see some important changes, not least as India and Ceylon moved towards independence from the British Empire. It was recognised in Ceylon that the promotion of Sinhalese and Tamil employees to management positions hitherto exclusively reserved for Europeans was politically advisable. A first such appointment was made in the Colombo depot in 1945.[173] There was also considerable sensitivity about conditions for local 'coolie' workers. The deputation was especially concerned that the oft repeated claim that conditions on E & S Joint CWS plantations were generally the best should have real substance, especially given the likelihood of independence sooner rather than later. To try to ensure this, it visited the plantations of some rival tea producers. It did not always find comfort in such visits. While it thought housing on the plantations of the Bombay–Burma Trading Corporation in southern India to be inferior to housing on E & S Joint CWS plantations, it noted that the hospital was the best it had seen anywhere in India, and the quality of the schools it inspected of the very highest standard. It suggested that the wholesales' school might do better.[174] It also strongly recommended improvements to housing on Ceylon generally.[175] Interestingly, notwithstanding the uncertainties of the political situation, the deputation reported that the managers of the India and Ceylon estates were keen that tea production be expanded further, though the deputation counselled that the state of the market meant that few competitively priced estates were available.[176]

This post-war optimism lasted into the early 1950s, but its erosion began soon after India and Ceylon achieved independence in 1947–8. Initially, the main problems arose from the determination of the new independent Indian government to maximise its revenues so that it could fund its ambitious and left-of-centre social and economic programme. As a result of a legal ruling in the Madras High Court in 1929, up until 1949 E & S Joint CWS was treated as a company in law, assessable for income tax on its sales of tea and other commodities in India, but not on tea exported for processing and resale in the UK and elsewhere. A new piece of legislation introduced in 1938 in respect of taxation on income arising from agriculture in the state of Assam resulted in the tax authorities there seeking to assess E & S Joint CWS on all of its income arising from its activities in that state. The wholesales cited the 1929 ruling in its defence, arguing that the company status insulated them from the Assam agricultural tax. The resultant legal battle lasted until 1948, when the Privy Council ruled that E & S Joint CWS was in fact assessable under the Assam tax, and that the 1929 Madras ruling on the company status of E & S Joint CWS was probably incorrect. In 1949, a shrewd Indian tax inspector argued that the Privy Council ruling meant that E & S Joint CWS was an 'association of persons' rather than a company, and he re-opened assessments on *all* income arising from E & S CWS operations in India, including on sales of tea overseas. In February 1950, he re-opened assessments for the years 1944–5 and 1945–6, effectively demanding an additional £148,000 in tax. The wholesales resisted this, eliciting the support of the Commonwealth Relations Office and the Treasury UK, as well as legal counsel.[177] In due course, the India Revenue authorities reassured the wholesales that their company status post-1947 would be respected, though the pre-1947 assessments still ground through the courts.[178] Ultimately, E & S Joint CWS won on appeal against the assessments, but not until 1952.[179] It had been a bruising experience, and one that began a process of deepening pessimism about the wholesales' tea operations.

By the end of 1952, E & S Joint CWS representatives were expressing profound concern about the tenor and volatility of politics in the new Indian democracy, not just in terms of the federal government's policies but also in respect of developments in individual states. The 1952 deputation complained about poorly thought out legislation by both central and state governments that had hampered business and trade. It deplored recurrent threats of nationalisation that were voiced in election campaigns, and the general drift to the far communist left in places such as Madras, Cochin and Travancore. It saw the dominant Congress Party as a force for relative moderation, at least now that national elections had been completed and Congress' position nationally was secure. But it lamented the excessive bureaucracy and complex and heavy taxation being imposed at national and state levels to generate funds to assist the economic and welfare needs of the new state. It also regretted an increased tendency towards militant trade unionism among workers.[180] One consequence was a conscious geographical diversification of tea production. In 1952, a special deputation was sent to Kenya and East Africa to seek out new tea estates. Its terms of reference specifically raised the need for new centres of tea production because of political and economic circumstances in India and Ceylon.[181] Though problems in Kenya stemming from the Mau-Mau rebellion was one of the factors that led to the deputation not recommending any purchases, the search went on.[182] Finally, an estate in Tanganyika, at Rungwe, was acquired in 1958.[183] It remained in E & S Joint CWS hands until the early 1970s.

The Rungwe acquisition reflected deepening concern about the state of the wholesales' tea interests in India and Ceylon. By 1956, there was intense speculation that the Indian government would nationalise the tea growing sector.[184] This meant that if the wholesales tried to sell off their estates, with nationalisation a real prospect it would be hard to find buyers and impossible to command reasonable prices for them. Those in charge of the estates were sceptical that such nationalisation would occur, such were the high levels of tax revenues that federal and state governments received from it, but even a possibility of nationalisation would stymie any efforts to offload the estates. State compensation, which had been generous in those instances where key industries had been nationalised, seemed a better bet. While most of the deputation team tended towards the view that nationalisation was unlikely, one of their number, A. Wild of CWS, attached his own minority view on the future of the estates in India. He weighed up the arguments on both sides about the likelihood of nationalisation and tended towards a rather more pessimistic view, speculating that the Indian government might increase taxes to force down the price of tea estates so that they would be cheaper to nationalise. He also pointed to the shrinking surplus being earned on the estates due to high taxes and greater regulation. He strongly advocated that E & S Joint CWS estates in Assam should be disposed of.[185] While Wild's recommendation was not followed, these worries grew. In 1958, some of the wholesales' tea estates were hit hard by labour disputes.[186] The deputation was asked to produce a general report on "Future Prospects and Policy" in India. The report expressed serious concerns about the rise of communist power in Kerala, which was especially associated with punitive taxation and encouragement of labour militancy. But it stressed that satisfactory prices could not be obtained for E & S Joint CWS estates at this juncture, and that even if they could, foreign currency exchange restrictions would make received funds difficult to repatriate.[187] The deputation was also asked to review future policy in Ceylon. It interviewed the Prime Minister and was assured that there was no likelihood of nationalisation in the immediate future. There was also concern about the difficulty of securing European staff and the general problem of perceived instability in the country. But again—all these factors made it unlikely that tea estates could be disposed of at an acceptable price.[188]

Matters did not improve. By 1960, a rather more pessimistic report of the situation in Ceylon stressed a marked swing to the left there, with the prospect of much higher taxes and a strong likelihood that the wholesales' business interests would deteriorate in the future.[189] The 1962 deputation was almost despairing in its report on the Indian estates. There was a perception that for too long quantity had been stressed at the expense of quality and that too little had been invested to ensure that production was maximised and the land kept sufficiently fertile. It indicated that the General Manager had developed a plan to turn the situation around, but it would be expensive in terms of increased investment. But, like earlier reports, the problems inherent in securing buyers for the estates at a remunerative price suggested to the deputation that E & S Joint CWS were essentially stuck with depreciating assets that seemed unlikely to recover in value any time soon. It was a key reason why the wholesales retained its south Asian tea interests for so long.[190] The required capital investment in the Indian estates was eye-watering: £131,351 was needed to address longstanding problems.[191] And this came at a time when the estate had incurred major losses.[192] There is little evidence that the required funds were spent. On a more positive note, the report was less negative about the political situation in India, arguing that compared to many other recently independent states in Africa, India was politically relatively stable.[193] But the report did single out ongoing problems. Restrictions on foreign exchange and acute shortages of power, equipment and raw materials stemming from import controls and India's rapid economic development remained a hindrance.[194]

Declining profitability continued into the 1960s. On the India estates, annual average profit of £250,000 between 1954 and 1957 had become a loss of £77,000 in 1962 and a small profit of £1,000 in 1963. What was especially disturbing was that at least one rival company, Malayalam Estates, had registered substantial profits in the same period. The deputation believed higher yields and wiser investment had produced the contrast.[195] The deputation remained hopeful that the situation could be rectified, but again noted that poor performance exacerbated the problem of trying to sell the estates.[196] But matters seemed even more depressing in Ceylon. By 1964, the deputation reported that a hostility to European enterprise bordering on the self-defeating was gathering momentum.[197] The Ceylon estates registered a loss of £18,524 in 1965, and deterioration in efficiency and performance was cited as a major cause.[198] In India, currency devaluation had produced falling living standards and industrial militancy in response.[199] It also savagely wiped out E & S Joint CWS profits on its Indian estates.[200] By the early 1970s, following the rationalisation of the late 1960s, E & S Joint CWS (now called the Co-operative Tea Society—CTS) was under real pressure to be draconian towards the south Asian tea estates. The 1970 deputation was asked to consider seriously the possibility of disposing of all of the Ceylon estates with the exception of Mahavilla.[201] The Indian estates had registered a loss of £123,000 in 1969, and the deputation was extremely pessimistic about the future here also.[202] Ideally, the deputation wanted a large-scale sell-off of many of the estates, but recognised that few buyers were available, especially given the relatively low price of tea on the world market at the time.[203] Instead, a 'progressive withdrawal' was advocated. This policy was readily accepted by SCWS/CWS, and a concerted attempt to offload the Indian estates began, though finding buyers prepared to offer the price required proved elusive.[204] By 1972, however, economies had eased the financial situation and the pressure to dispose of estates at any price had lessened; a policy of patience and waiting for the best possible offers could be adopted.[205] In Ceylon, it was noted that over the previous nine years losses totalling £248,000 had been incurred, about half of which had arisen from the Bowhill estate, which had finally been disposed of in October 1971.[206]

Then, in 1973, CWS and the Tea Society were hit by a major scandal. On 24 September, the Granada ITV documentary series *World in Action* broadcast "The Cost of a Cup of Tea", a damning indictment of living and working conditions on the CTS' Mahavilla estate in Ceylon (now

Sri Lanka).[207] Such was its impact on the co-operative movement that CTS dispatched a deputation to India earlier in 1973 than intended, and much of its report was dedicated to investigating the accusations made by *World in Action*. It offered a rebuttal to the claim that conditions were substantially worse than on other, non-co-operatively owned estates.[208] But its readership was small, and the episode undoubtedly intensified the moves to dispense with the estates once and for all. In 1975, an article for the *Apex* journal set out a robust defence of the CTS Sri Lanka tea estates and pointed out that the programme had been criticised by both an all-party committee of MPS and the IBA for its partiality. But the damage had been done and was impossible to rectify.[209] In October 1975, the government of Sri Lanka nationalised all foreign-owned tea estates.[210] The fate of the Indian tea estates followed a slightly different trajectory. Indian legislation in 1973, the Foreign Exchange Regulation Act, required all foreign companies in India to become registered Indian companies, with a substantial proportion of their shares held by the Indian public. The Indian government began to insist that this be enacted by foreign companies in 1976.[211] The outcome was a transfer of the Indian tea estates to CWS India, with CWS owning 74 per cent of the shares.[212] This began a progressive 'Indianisation' of the estates. In 1983, CWS' share in CWS India was reduced to 56 per cent.[213] Then, in 1987, CWS disposed of its interest in CWS India completely.[214] The last of the CWS' overseas network had been dismantled.

The fortunes of the wholesales' south Asian tea estates in many senses epitomised the trajectory of their global supply chain network. They had flourished in the heyday of globalisation from the late nineteenth century until the 1930s, even continuing to grow during the interruption of war between 1914 and 1918. It had even remained robustly profitable during the retreat from globalisation that began in the 1930s. It was really after the Second World War that decline set in and became terminal. The problems were certainly related to the severe domestic problems the wholesales were facing in the UK in terms of increasing competition, loss of market share and organisational disruption, outlined in the first part of this chapter. But decolonisation and the emergence of independent polities—highly protectionist and latently hostile (for understandable reasons) towards European commercial interests—with a strong colonial legacy unquestionably served to undermine the profitability of the tea estates and confidence in their future. In this respect, it is important to note that the protectionism of the Indian and Sri Lankan regimes represented a conscious attempt by those states to resist what would now be described as the globalising forces of western capitalism. While the tea estates had managed to offset the negative impact of deglobalisation and protectionism in the 1930s because of their location within that surviving agency of globalisation known as the British Empire, such a cushion was, by definition, unavailable after the late 1940s. As far as the south

Asian tea estates were concerned, the twin developments of decolonisation and protectionism played a key role in their demise. The final chapter will explore how CWS and its successor, the Co-operative Group, have sought to reconstruct its global supply chains, but on very different organisational and ethical principles.

Notes

1. Wilson, Webster & Vorberg-Rugh, *Building Co-operation* 399.
2. Kinloch & Butt, *History of the Scottish Co-operative Wholesale Society Ltd* 318.
3. Havinden & Meredith, *Colonialism & Development* 218–234.
4. Rhodes, *Empire and Co-operation* 247–250.
5. Ibid., 243.
6. Wilson, Webster & Vorberg-Rugh, *Building Co-operation* 221.
7. E. Ekberg, *Consumer Co-operatives and the Transformation of Modern Food Retailing: A Comparative Study of the Norwegian and British Consumer Co-operatives 1950–2002* (Published PhD thesis, Oslo, University of Oslo 2008) 149; 152.
8. Sparks, "Consumer Co-operation in the UK 1945–93" 1–64; 17.
9. Ibid., 15–199.
10. Ibid., 6–12.
11. P. Gurney, "The Battle of the Consumer in Post-War Britain" *Journal of Modern History* 77:4 (2005) 956–987; 983–987.
12. F. Muller, "The Consumer Co-operatives in Great Britain" in J. Brazda & R. Schediwy (eds.), *Consumer Co-operatives in a Changing World* (Geneva, ICA 1989) 45–138; 124–125.
13. J.K. Walton, "The Post-War Decline of the British Retail Co-operative Movement: Nature, Causes and Consequence" in L. Black & N. Robertson (eds.), *Consumerism and the Co-operative Movement in Modern British History* (Manchester, Manchester University Press 2009) 13–33; 23.
14. Study was by G. Ostergaard and J.H. Halsey of Birmingham University. *Co-operative News* 25 February 1956, 6–7.
15. Walton, "The Post War Decline" 27.
16. Wilson, Webster & Vorberg-Rugh, *Building Co-operation* 223.
17. Ibid., 234–236.
18. L. Black, "'Trying to Sell a Parcel of Politics with a Parcel of Groceries': The Co-operative Independent Commission (CIC) and Consumerism in Post-War Britain" in Black & Robertson (eds.), *Consumerism and the Co-operative Movement* 32–50; 38–40; Ekberg, *Consumer Co-operatives and the Transformation of Modern Food Retailing* 174–176.
19. *Report of the Joint Reorganisation Committee* (Manchester, CWS 1965).
20. Wilson, Webster & Vorberg-Rugh, *Building Co-operation* 248–250.
21. Ibid., 251.
22. Ibid., 278–280.
23. Ibid., 280.
24. Ibid., 279.
25. Sparks, "Consumer Co-operation in the UK 1945–93" 17.
26. Ibid., 22.
27. J. Wilson, A. Webster & R. Vorberg-Rugh, "The Co-operative Movement in Britain: From Crisis to 'Renaissance 1950–2010'" *Enterprise & Society* 14:2 (2013) 271–302; 284.

28. Ibid., 285.
29. Wilson, Webster & Vorberg-Rugh, *Building Co-operation* 209–210.
30. *Co-operative News* 21 September 1901, 1144; 11 February 1914, 212; *Wheat-sheaf* October 1902, 57; January 1910, 104–105; March 1914, 139–141.
31. *The Producer* September 1930, 246.
32. *The Producer* May 1926, 210; *Co-operative News* 1 May 1926, 5.
33. A Statement by the CWS to the CIC 4 April 1956 Papers of Fred Lambert, 1.5.17.14 NCA.
34. Ibid., Appendix 1 (2) 5.
35. Ibid., Statement 10.
36. Ibid., 11.
37. Ibid., 12.
38. Ibid., Appendix 1 (2) 2.
39. Ibid., Appendix 1 (2) 6.
40. Ibid.
41. Ibid., Statement 13.
42. Ibid., 10.
43. Ibid., 14.
44. Ibid., Appendix 1 (2) 3.
45. Ibid., 4.
46. Ibid., 5.
47. Ibid., Appendix 1 (2) 6–7.
48. *Co-operative Independent Commission Report* (Manchester, Co-operative Union 1958) 177–185.
49. Ibid., 188.
50. F. Lambert, "CWS in the 20th Century: Notes on the Basic Problem" 1–2 Papers of Fred Lambert, 1.5.17.14 NCA.
51. *Role of CWS document 3: Consequential Policy Decision* 12 June 1963, 2 Papers of Fred Lambert, 1.5.17.14 NCA.
52. File on CWS overseas depots, Memorandum by Fred Lambert; statement of establishments owned or controlled outside the UK by CWS in 1963, 0159.1 Box c185 NCA.
53. Ibid.
54. Ibid.
55. Richardson, *The CWS in War and Peace 1938–1976* 314.
56. Ibid., 316.
57. Report on the Grocery Group of CWS submitted to the Board 7 February 1973, CWS cuttings and documents on Grocery, File 1061 Box c185, NCA, 18–19.
58. CWS Balance Sheet 1967 32; CWS Balance Sheet 1982 8.
59. C. Secchi, "Affluence and Decline: Consumer Co-operatives in Postwar Britain" in M. Hilson, S. Neunsinger & G. Patmore (eds.), *A Global History of Consumer Co-operation since 1950: Movements and Businesses* (Leiden, Brill 2017) 527–558; 538.
60. Papers of the Co-operative Wholesale Committee File 240 Box 55 NCA.
61. A. Sugden to senior CWS management 26 September 1972, File on Co-operatives and the EEC 1960–1973 240.91 Box 55 NCA.
62. CWSBM 12 June 1914.
63. CWSBM 25 June 1914.
64. CWSBM 12 February 1915.
65. CWSBM 25 March 1915; 30 April 1915.
66. West Africa Trading Committee Minutes (WATCM), NCA, 22 March 1915.
67. CWSBM 27 May 1915.
68. CWSBM 3 September 1915.

69. CWSBM 28 April 1916.
70. CWSBM 5 January 1917.
71. CWSBM 26 May 1916.
72. WATCM 3 August 1916; 17 August 1916.
73. WATCM 14 September 1915.
74. CWSBM 9 February 1917.
75. CWSBM 7 April 1916.
76. CWSBM 3 November 1916; 8 December 1916.
77. CWSBM 16 March 1917.
78. CWSBM 8 June 1917.
79. CWSBM 8 July 1917.
80. CWSBM 14 March 1919.
81. Printed report for the quarterly meetings of September 1919.
82. CWSBM 28 November 1919; Printed report for the quarterly meetings of December 1919.
83. *ICA Bulletin* April 1919 no. 4, 70.
84. *Co-operative News* 18 March 1922, 8.
85. WATCM 16 February 1922.
86. CWSBM 16 May 1922.
87. *Co-operative News* Special Supplement on Soap, 31 July 1926, i–ii.
88. CWSBM 5 January 1923.
89. *Co-operative News* 21 July 1928, 1.
90. CWSBM 7 September 1928.
91. A. Olukoju, *The Liverpool of West Africa: The Dynamics and Impact of Maritime Trade in Lagos, 1900–1950* (Trenton, Africa World Press 2004) 170.
92. V. Giacomin, "The Emergence of an Export Cluster: Traders & Palm Oil in Early Twentieth Century Southeast Asia" *Enterprise & Society* 19:2 (2017) 272–308.
93. Ibid., 298.
94. Ibid.
95. CWSBM 19 June 1934.
96. CWSBM 3 November 1936.
97. CWS Depots in Africa (1962) CWS and the European Economic Community file 0159.91 Box c185 NCA.
98. CWSBM 22 April 1914.
99. CWSBM 5 August 1914.
100. Printed Report for Quarterly Meetings June 1916.
101. CWSBM 1 December 1916.
102. Printed Report for Quarterly Meetings December 1918.
103. *Report of E & S Joint CWS Deputation to Gold Coast & Ashanti, West Africa 26 May to 31 July 1926* (Manchester, CWS 1926) 4–5.
104. *Report of E & S Joint CWS Deputation to Gold Coast & Ashanti, West Africa 21 September 1932 to 2 November 1932* (Manchester, CWS 1932) 5.
105. Ibid., 4.
106. *Report of E & S Joint CWS Deputation to Gold Coast & Ashanti, West Africa 9 September to 22 November 1936* (Manchester, CWS 1936) 7–8.
107. Ibid., 9.
108 *Co-operative News* 29 October 1938, 1; 5 November 1938, 13; *The Producer* December 1938, 321.
109. *Co-operative News* 10 December 1939, 8.
110. Note of Meeting at the Colonial Office 27 May 1938, CO 859/169/9 NA, 3–7.
111. Ibid., 9.
112. Ibid., 9–10.

113. *Report of E & S Joint CWS Deputation to Gold Coast & Ashanti, West Africa 17 August to 22 October 1938* (Manchester, CWS 1938) 18–19.
114. For a useful summary of state controls over cocoa exports from West Africa during and after the war see *Co-operative Review* Vol. 21 November 1947, 227–229.
115. *Report of E & S Joint CWS Deputation to Gold Coast & Ashanti, West Africa 5 May to 26 June 1945* (Manchester, CWS 1945) 7.
116. Ibid., 9–12.
117. Ibid., 13.
118. *Report of E & S Joint CWS Deputation to Gold Coast & Ashanti and Togoland 29 March to 21 May 1951* (Manchester, CWS 1951) 3–4.
119. CWS Depots in Africa (1962) CWS and the European Economic Community file 0159.91 box c185 NCA.
120. *Report of Deputation to Ceylon 6 March to 22 May 1906* (Manchester, CWS 1906) 3–4.
121. *Report of Deputation to Ceylon 30 October 1912 to 6 January 1913* (Manchester, CWS 1913) 3–4.
122. Ibid., 10.
123. Printed Report for Quarterly Meetings 1913.
124. *Report of Deputation to India and Ceylon 10 December 1913 to 30 March 1914* (Manchester, CWS 1914) 3–5.
125. Ibid., 11; CWSBM 22 May 1914.
126. W.H. Ukers, *All About Tea*, vol. 1 (New York, The Tea & Coffee Trade Journal Company 1935) 170–172.
127. CWSBM 7 May 1915.
128. CWSBM 23 April 1915.
129. *Co-operative News* 1 May 1915, 570.
130. *Co-operative News* 8 May 1915, 606.
131. *Co-operative News* 12 June, 792.
132. *Report of Deputation to India and Ceylon 7 December 1915 to 18 March 1916* (Manchester, CWS 1916) 3–6.
133. Ibid., 9.
134. Printed Report for Quarterly Meetings June 1916.
135. Printed Report for Quarterly Meetings September 1917.
136. Printed Report for Quarterly Meetings December 1918.
137. CWSBM 4 June 1919.
138. *Co-operative News* 24 January 1925, 8.
139. *Co-operative News* 31 January 1925, 8.
140. *Report of Deputation to India and Ceylon 18 October 1919 to 23 February 1920* (Manchester, CWS 1920) 13–17.
141. Ibid., 26.
142. CWSBM 30 August 1921.
143. *Report of Deputation to India and Ceylon 18 October 1919 to 23 February 1920* 25.
144. CWSBM 4 April 1922.
145. CWSBM 30 June 1922.
146. *Report of Deputation to India and Ceylon 24 November 1922 to 17 April 1923* (Manchester, CWS 1923) 3–8.
147. Ibid., 9–10.
148. Ibid., 35–36.
149. *Report of Deputation to India and Ceylon 14 February to 10 June 1925* (Manchester, CWS 1925) 39–42.
150. Ibid., 44.
151. Ibid., 46–47.

152. *The Producer* April 1930, 96–97; December 1930, 337.
153. *Co-operative News* 3 March 1928, 1.
154. *Report of Deputation to India and Ceylon 5 October 1927 to 16 January 1928* (Manchester, CWS 1928) 4–5.
155. Ibid., 16.
156. Ibid., 51.
157. Ibid., 35.
158. *Report of Deputation to India and Ceylon 17 September to 20 December 1931* (Manchester, CWS 1932) 10.
159. Ibid.
160. Ibid., 15.
161. Ibid., 36.
162. Ibid., 46.
163. Ibid., 47–48.
164. *Report of Deputation to India and Ceylon 1 September to 16 December 1933* (Manchester, CWS 1934) Part 7, 56–57; Part 5, 53.
165. Ibid., Part 7, 58–59.
166. *Report of Deputation to India and Ceylon 22 November 1935 to 22 February 1936* (Manchester, CWS 1936) 14–15.
167. Ibid., 21.
168. Ibid., 22.
169. Ibid., 43–48.
170. *Report of Deputation to India and Ceylon 24 September to 18 December 1937* (Reading, CWS 1938) 65.
171. *The Producer* July 1944, 8–9; April 1945, 2–4.
172. *Co-operative Review* February 1947, 38.
173. *Report of Deputation to India and Ceylon 22 December 1945 to 4 May 1946* (Manchester, CWS 1946) 37.
174. Ibid., 16–17.
175. Ibid., 39.
176. Ibid., 53.
177. See correspondence on India's Assessment of the English & Scottish Joint CWS (1950), IOR L/E/8/8303 British Library (BL).
178. *Report of Deputation to India and Ceylon 15 September to 12 December 1950* (Reading, CWS 1951) 41–42.
179. *Report of Deputation to India and Ceylon 16 September to 16 December 1952* (Reading, CWS 1953) 13–14.
180. Ibid., 61–63.
181. *Report of Deputation to East Africa (Kenya)* (Reading, CWS 1953) 1.
182. Ibid., 14–15.
183. *Report of Deputation to East Africa February/March 1958* 16.
184. *Report of Deputation to India and Ceylon 3 October to 11 December 1956* 3–4.
185. Ibid., 43–45.
186. *Report of Deputation to India and Ceylon September/December 1958* 15–18.
187. Ibid., 23–25.
188. Ibid., 39–41.
189. *Report of Deputation to India and Ceylon October/November 1960* 17–18.
190. *Report of Deputation to India and Ceylon September to November 1962* 4–5.
191. Ibid., 29–32.
192. Ibid., 36–37.
193. Ibid., 55–57.
194. Ibid., 58–61.

195. *Report of Deputation to India and Ceylon 1964* 2.
196. Ibid., 8.
197. Ibid., 14.
198. *Report of Deputation to India and Ceylon October/November 1966* 4–6.
199. Ibid., 18–19.
200. Ibid., 21.
201. *Report of Deputation to India and Ceylon February 1970* 2.
202. Ibid., 3.
203. Ibid., 5.
204. *Report of Deputation to India and Ceylon 28 March to 8 April 1971* 1.
205. *Report of Deputation to India and Ceylon 7 to 26 April 1972* 1–2.
206. Ibid., 8.
207. An important discussion of the wider impact of the programme may be found in M. Anderson, "The British Fair Trade Movement 1960–2000: A New Form of Global Citizenship?" (PhD thesis, Birmingham, University of Birmingham 2008) 26–30.
208. *Report of Deputation to India and Sri Lanka 1973* 1–22.
209. File on CWS public relations 1974–1976, article for *Apex* journal 1975, NCA.
210. Ibid., Bryant, "The State of Tea" War on Want May 1976.
211. Note of meeting on India: Foreign Exchange Regulation Act in Grocery Manager's Office 2 February 1977, File on CWS to CWS India Transfer 1977–1979; NCA.
212. *The Times* 16 October 1978.
213. CWS Balance sheet 1983.
214. CWS Balance sheet 1987, Report of Directors, 5.

6   Rebuilding Global Networks and Moral Regeneration? Evaluating the Emergence of the Co-operative Group 1980–2018 Within the Global History of British Wholesale Co-operation

I

By 1980, most of the global system of depots and productive facilities built up by the British co-operative wholesales in the previous century had been dismantled. But the now-merged organisation that had constructed it not only survived but, after a long period of retrenchment and recovery, also began the process of reconstructing a new system of global trade and procurement based on very different principles. This final chapter will first examine how British co-operation evolved during the last few decades, moving from seemingly terminal decline in the 1980s to major reform in the 1990s and commercial recovery and growth in the 2000s, followed by crisis and another wave of retrenchment and reform between 2013 and 2016, before yet another period of stabilisation and recovery. The following section will then consider how these turbulent developments served to first finally destroy what was left of the former system of international procurement and then shape a new one that reinvented, for a very different internal and external context, some of the older commercial principles underpinning the global network supply chains that had flourished in the late nineteenth and early twentieth centuries. It will also be seen that there was a conscious effort to build into the new overseas supply chain strategy an even firmer commitment to some of the ethical principles that had shaped the ideas of international co-operation since the emergence of the ICA at the end of the nineteenth century—notably a commitment to promoting Fairtrade and international co-operative development and inter-co-operative trade. The final section will then draw together some general observations about what the history of the British co-operative wholesales' international global links suggests about the nature of British consumer co-operation; the impact of the shifting patterns of globalisation and deglobalisation on large commercial organisations and their strategies of adaptation; and what the implications are for existing accounts of the rise of supply chain management.

II

By 1980, the reforms of the late 1960s had been given a substantial amount of time to work through. Initially, there had been grounds for optimism. The co-operative share of the grocery trade seemed to have been turned around by the mid-1970s, rising from 20.5 per cent in 1973 to 21.5 per cent in 1976. But this receded in the last years of the decade, falling to 18.1 per cent by 1980. Though still the largest player in the grocery market, Tesco and Sainsburys had been catching up rapidly, rising from 7.4 per cent and 8.2 per cent in 1973 to 13.4 per cent and 12.5 per cent in 1980 respectively.[1] While turnover increased over the decade, once inflation is accounted for, it is clear that in real terms it remained static. More serious was a fall in annual profits from £18.8 million in 1977 to £6.3 million in 1980.[2] Other trends presaged even greater problems. The Regional Plan of the late 1960s, which had aspired to reduce the number of co-operative retail societies to 50 i substantial regional organisations, still had a long way to go, with 210 societies still in existence in 1980. Of these, 20 societies were of substantial size and accounted for about 62 per cent of all co-operative sales, but most societies were in financial difficulty and lacked the funds needed to modernise.[3] In short, it was becoming clear that the reforms of the late 1960s had failed.

The 1980s saw another attempt to turn around CWS under the leadership of Dennis Landau as CEO. This involved steps to improve the still limited retailing wing of CWS activity with better marketing and sales strategies, rationalisation of CWS factories and other productive facilities and, crucially, a drive to improve relations with retail societies. Part of this involved a major reorganisation of CWS in 1984, creating seven different managerial groups, with a specific remit to implement changes. In 1986, a special Co-operative Trade Committee was established, with representatives from CWS, CU and the nine largest retail societies. Landau also tried to bridge the divide between CWS and CRS, implementing his right as CWS CEO to sit on the Board of CRS. This helped the establishment in 1982 of the Tripartite Committee, upon which sat representatives of CWS, CRS and CU, which had a brief to secure better co-operation between CRS and CWS. Landau was keen to persuade CRS to accept that CWS and CRS in due course should merge into one organisation. Landau was committed to addressing not only the commercial shortcomings of the co-operative movement but also the dysfunctionality and disintegration that had become a defining feature by the 1980s.[4] Like earlier efforts at reform, Landau's plans would ultimately fail. The reasons were familiar. CRS continued to absorb struggling societies, and 16 in all were swallowed up by it in the 1980s. CWS, conscious that part of its efforts to build links with retail societies also rested upon being seen to help those in trouble, also absorbed 26 troubled societies in the decade.[5] But the effect of this was to intensify the rivalry between CWS and CRS, ultimately stymying both efforts at greater collaboration and merger between the two bodies.[6] In addition, many of the societies being taken over were in deep financial trouble. For example, the London Co-operative Society was taken over by CRS in 1981, which discovered to its horror that the society's accounting procedures were so poor that what had been estimated as a loss of £3 million was in fact over £12 million.[7] CWS had to borrow £30 million to cover the losses of Royal Arsenal Society.[8] All of this served to undermine the efforts to weld the movement into a more coherent whole, and the decade showed still further decline in market share in groceries to 10.1 per cent by 1992, compared to the now dominant Sainsburys and Tesco with 20.5 per cent and 17.4 per cent.[9] In terms of total retail trade, the co-operative societies' share had shrunk from 12 per cent in 1980 to just 5.5 per cent in 1990.[10] This is not to deny that some improvements were achieved. In particular, CWS' productive facilities were rationalised and modernised.[11] Also, at least the 1980s did see a recovery in profits from the low point of 1980, with at least three years in which these rose above £20 million.[12]

But it was during the 1990s that major reforms were finally implemented with real success. An important factor that helped was the fact that not all parts of the CWS businesses were in trouble. The bank, which was wholly owned by CWS, was very profitable, except for a brief period of difficulty at the beginning of the 1990s. CWS also ran very successful funeral, insurance, farms and travel agency businesses.[13] During the 1990s, the problems for CWS retail continued, and it is clear that heavy losses would have been sustained had it not been for the success of the bank.[14] A key factor in the success of reform was the beginning of a change of heart among those who ran the retail societies. By the end of the 1980s, many felt that the writing was on the wall for the British co-operative movement. Catastrophic failures of consumer co-operation in France and Germany demonstrated that total failure was a real possibility for the British movement. In addition, the political climate of the 1980s in Britain seemed deeply hostile to the co-operative movement. The dominance enjoyed by 'neo-liberal' economic thinking in the Britain of Margaret Thatcher, which regarded the 'investor-led' model of corporate capitalism as paramount, meant that the economic orthodoxy of the decade tended to see co-operatives as a temporary and inferior response to short-term market failures, the solution to which, in the long term, would be found in investor-led initiatives and organisations. The Thatcher period saw legislation that would make it easier for co-operatives and other mutuals to 'de-mutualise' and become mainstream investor-led corporate bodies. This led to the demutualisations of many building societies in the 1980s/1990s, which were turned into mainstream banks. The fall of the Soviet Union seemed to underpin the final victory of capitalism, and with it the demise of socialist alternatives, including co-operatives.[15] Co-operatives also began to disappear from business textbooks and publications.[16] In this context, the end of British co-operation seemed not only possible but also probably imminent.

A symbolic development was the decision by the North-East Co-operative Society to join CWS in 1991. What was different about this was that the North-East Society was profitable and was joining CWS from a position of strength rather than being rescued from failure. It represented a conscious recognition by the North-East Society that reform was needed for British co-operation to survive. It signalled a new spirit of collaboration within the movement, and a willingness to reform organisation and business practice to ensure the survival of co-operation in Britain. A key development was the establishment in 1993 of the Co-operative Retail Trading Group (CRTG) with CWS and 16 retail societies as members. This body made reality the long-term but unfulfilled aspiration of creating a body that would buy for rather than sell to the retail societies. CRS also joined in due course.[17] A year later, another major change reinforced this new philosophy of moving away from transactional relations between CWS and the retail societies. The manufacturing operations were sold off in 1994 to Hobson, led by Andrew Regan, an individual who would play a pivotal role in the development of the co-operative movement just three years later.[18] In addition, within the wider movement, and indeed within the bank and CWS, emerged a desire to revive the ethical roots of the movement, especially its commitment to fair dealing and strengthening communities across the world. This was in part a reaction to the perceived exploitative harshness of modern capitalism as well as some element of guilt at episodes in CWS' history, such as the *World in Action* report on CWS tea plantations in the early 1970s. This manifested itself practically in a policy of ethical banking for the Co-operative Bank, which would eschew dealings with arms traders, oppressive regimes and unscrupulous and exploitative companies, and a commitment to the ethical procurement of food and supplies for sale in co-operative shops: a firm commitment to the Fairtrade movement that will be explored in more detail in the next section. Leading employees of CWS and members of the movement also played key roles in the formulation by the ICA of a new statement of co-operative principles, embodied in its 1992 publication *Co-operative Values in a Changing World*—formally adopted and implemented at the 1995 ICA conference.[19] There was even revived discussion of a possible merger between CWS and CRS.

However, it was two events in 1996–97 that provided the catalyst for truly radical change. Firstly, in November 1996 Graham Melmoth was appointed as CEO of CWS. Melmoth had been CWS Secretary since 1975, and no-one knew the movement better than he. He was also staunchly committed to co-operation as a set of ideals, and he had been instrumental in the ICA's re-invention of the Rochdale Principles in 1995. He brought a clear vision of what the movement should aspire to. He introduced a new training programme for senior managers that stressed the importance of co-operative principles and made plain his determination not only to re-unify the movement but also to revive its moral purpose and combine it with commercial success. The second development was an attempt by Andrew Regan to engineer a takeover of CWS in February 1997. His *Lanica* consortium sought to demutualise CWS by persuading is members to sell their shares to Lanica. The attempt galvanised Melmoth and co-operative activists to embark upon a fierce resistance. In the end, Melmoth and CWS emerged victorious from the battle because of the strength of this resistance and because Regan made two serious mistakes. Firstly, Regan misunderstood the ownership structure of CWS. Although by 1997 it did have individual shareholders, mostly it was owned by its retail society members, which were simply not open to the temptations of personal gain in the same way that individual shareholders were. Secondly, Regan resorted to corruption, bribing several senior managers to pass on sensitive commercial information about CWS. This was uncovered by CWS' internal security and brought the takeover to a shuddering halt.[20]

The Lanica affair proved to be a catalyst for dramatic change. The 'near death' experience of Lanica brought home to the movement the need for real change, greater unity, greater commercial professionalism and a revival of co-operative principles and ethics. Melmoth summarised his plan as creating a "family of successful co-operative businesses".[21] A special co-operative commission was set up in 2000 to map out a plan for the future, with a strong emphasis on underpinning everything with a strong adherence to co-operative principles. Even before this, Melmoth used the surge of support following Lanica to push CRS into amalgamating with CWS, a move made all the easier by CRS' deepening financial difficulties.[22] Following the commission's report in 2001, CWS' name was changed to the Co-operative Group, and presaged further organisational changes. In 2002, the Co-operative Bank and CIS (the insurance wing) merged to create the Co-operative Banking Group. There was also a marked shift towards specialising in the convenience stores and away from competing in the large supermarket and hyper market sector, which was now left to the multiples.[23] These changes enabled the Co-operative Group to secure a degree of unity and common purpose that had not been seen since before the Second World War, and probably even stronger than then. In this, the gradual absorption of so many retail societies into the Group, as well as the mergers cited, created a more coherent structure for the movement than perhaps had ever been seen before. No longer did CWS have to struggle for the custom of hundreds of disloyal retail societies; now there were just a few societies to deal with, much of the retail sector was now under the direct control of the Group and, through the CRTG, the Group had manoeuvred itself away from the transactional relationship with retail societies that had proved so problematic in the past.

The scene was set for a period of growth and recovery between 2000 and 2013. Between 2000 and 2010, turnover rose from £4,853 million to £13,691 million, while the surplus rose from just over £100 million to more than £600 million, with dependence on banking profits being reduced from 91.3 to 33.4 per cent in the period.[24] Mergers with the remaining retail societies also continued, especially with United Co-operatives in 2007. The decade also saw expansion via a series of what proved to be controversial takeovers. Alldays chain of convenience stores was acquired in 2002, followed by Somerfields in 2008 and a merger of the Co-operative Banking Group with the Britannia Building Society in 2009.[25] By the beginning of the second decade of the century, the mood within the Group was bullish. But nemesis soon followed hubris. In 2013, it was revealed that the merged Co-operative Banking Group was in very serious financial trouble. As a result of a combination of poor risk management within the Co-operative Banking Group, a lack of due diligence in examining Britannia's debt portfolio before the merger, unrealistic plans to create a new IT platform for the merged bank and a catalogue of bad Britannia loans on commercial property, it was revealed that there was an enormous financial black hole at the bank. To make matters worse, Bank of England assessments of the increased reserves needed by the bank in the wake of the 2008 financial crisis were inflated because of the lack of expertise and poor risk management structures that the Bank of England found.[26]

There followed three years of severe financial difficulty and retrenchment, as well as even further reforms of the Group's governance structures. Major Group assets were disposed of, including its farms, pharmacy business and eventually the Bank, which was sold off to US hedge funds with a minority shareholding for the Group, which in due course was disposed of. The Kelly Review was supplemented by a major review, led by Lord Myners, of the Co-operative Group's governance structures.[27] Myners recommended that only those with very high managerial qualifications and competences should sit on the Board, and that the role of an elected National Council should be the broader scrutiny of policy rather than the detailed monitoring of day to day running of the business. Though eventually its recommendations for reform were acted upon, the internal rows within the movement and the Group led to the resignations of two CEOs in quick succession: Peter Marks and then Euan Sutherland. Large-scale redundancies and costs cutting were unavoidable, but by 2017 the Group had stabilised the situation and had begun to move back into profit.[28] What were the implications of the turbulence of the 1980–2018 period for the evolution of the CWS and then the Group's strategies for overseas supply procurement?

III

The period from the late 1970s until the early to mid-1990s thus saw great turbulence within the co-operative movement and was one in which it was extremely difficult if not impossible to formulate an effective overseas procurement strategy. Having dismantled the longstanding overseas supply chain depots and productive facilities, CWS was then faced with the challenges of operating a growing retail wing; bitter competition with CRS; the heavy costs of and time involved in dealing with merged retail societies; modernising the productive wing of CWS; and also the struggle to curb falling market share. It is important to remember that CWS' relations with the retail societies during this period was essentially transactional, of seller and buyer, notwithstanding unsuccessful efforts to foster a more collaborative and holistic relationship between CWS and the retail societies. The result was that planning overseas procurement was extraordinarily difficult in this period, and at this time CWS procurement strategies through its supply chains probably most closely resembled the rather haphazard and unplanned process depicted in much of the business studies literature on supply chain management (SCM), in which retailers are largely passive, with much of the leverage resting in the hands of suppliers.[29] In this respect, this period saw CWS supply chains at their most disorganised. It was not until the 1990s, especially following the creation of CRTG, that CWS was able to move into the modern era of supply chain management. But even here, one should not label CWS as necessarily being far behind the competition; it was not until the 1990s that many retailers, like Wal-Mart, fully embraced modern SCM techniques.[30]

But this certainly did not mean that there were no important developments in this period in relation to overseas procurement. The 1980s especially saw growing pressure within the movement for a more ethical approach to international trading, especially with very poor primary producers in the less developed world. This was to some extent a reaction to the scandal about the conditions on E & S Joint CWS tea plantations in Sri Lanka, but also to a growing perception that neither the wholesales nor individual retail societies had done enough to support moral and ethical causes on the international stage and in overseas commerce. Moreover, the longer-term record of the wholesales in the field of ethical commerce also left much to be desired.[31] The demands of competing against powerful multiple chains in the UK market, as well as the demands of a large number of retail societies for low priced goods as a condition of trading with the wholesales, worked to short-circuit efforts to instil principles of fairness and ethical support for poor producers into their overseas procurement. It has also been pointed out that historically there has always been a tension between consumer and producer co-operatives, as the former have an interest in minimising prices for customers and the latter maximising prices to increase income.[32] The history of the wholesales' overseas procurement certainly bears out much of this criticism, from the willingness to trade with both Nazi Germany and Imperial Japan in the 1930s, to the deeply flawed relations with producer co-operation in Ireland. That said, there are also episodes that suggest that ethical considerations were not always absent in wholesale policy, and that efforts to work with producers, especially co-operative ones, were real, if not always sustained. Resistance to the attempt to monopolise the cocoa trade in the 1930s is one example of this, as was the financial support for Australian wheat pools and Westralian farmers in the 1920s and 1930s. Longstanding work with the Danish co-operative creameries was also a feature of the wholesales' activity from the 1880s onwards. This is not to argue that the practical and structural constraints identified were overcome. They were not. But neither would it be true to say that ethical considerations were absent in the deliberations of the wholesales. The co-operative movement, at least in the late nineteenth and early twentieth centuries, was too lively to allow this.

The 1980s did, however, see a substantial impetus behind trying to make ethics a much stronger element in CWS decision-making. In the 1960s and 1970s, one issue on which CWS and CRS staunchly refused to accede to demands for a strong moral stance was apartheid in South Africa.[33] But in 1985, both CWS and CRS announced that they would no longer trade in South Africa.[34] The 1980s also saw CRS and CWS begin to acquire a reputation as environmentally conscious retailers, and the latter produced the *Co-op Action Guide for the Environment*.[35] By the early 1990s, this new ethical initiative was also found in the Co-operative Bank, with the launch of its ethical policy in May 1992.[36] In the same month, CWS became the first UK trader to stock *Cafédirect*, a coffee sourced from coffee producing countries but for which a fair price was paid. Oxfam, Traidcraft, Equal Exchange and Twin Trading were the NGO sponsors of the new company. It was a tentative beginning, and by September 1995, it remained a tiny proportion of CWS ground coffee sales (1.8 per cent) and even smaller (0.1 per cent) of its instant coffee sales.[37]

From the mid- to late 1990s, however, this began to change, coinciding with a more integrated and coherent system for buying and procurement that emerged from the establishment of CRTG and the reforms of the late 1990s. This period has been recognised within the Co-operative Group's management as a key transitional phase away from the almost entirely transactional relationships with CWS' suppliers that existed up to this time, towards much closer and more integrated relationships, as defined by the Group's 'Value Creation Strategy'.[38] This involved a much more comprehensive exchange of information between the Group and its suppliers with respect to the demands of customers and the Group's pricing policies, and information about the prices of raw materials and components paid by the suppliers, in order that transparent and clear relations based on trust could be developed and sustained. Relationships are now based on five-year contracts between the Group and suppliers, subject to continual review with an intention to renew. This enables both the Group and suppliers to plan long-term investment and streamline production and transport to ensure that goods of the requisite quality and price find their way onto the shelves of co-operative supermarkets in a timely and cost-efficient way. It is likened to a system of 'virtual' vertical integration, in which the benefits of vertical integration (control over production and reliability over time) are created by these agreements without the costs that vertical integration usually involves.[39]

Crucially, these close relations with suppliers, both home and abroad, enabled the Group to insist on much more robust ethical conditions for trade, on a wide range of issues such as the use of child labour, environmental safeguards, working conditions and pay. Regular audits and transparency in the relationships also made the enforcement of high standards more feasible. This changing relationship with suppliers also provided a better framework for embedding principles of Fairtrade and ethical dealing into the Group's practice. In 1998, a small team of three managers was created within the Group and tasked with promoting ethical trading among the group's buying team as well as public awareness of it.[40] Though it encountered some initial scepticism from buyers preoccupied with price, the team has been remarkably successful in gradually persuading buyers to work closely with ethical suppliers, to the point where the Group now offers a very wide range of Fairtrade products carrying the Fairtrade Marque as established in 1994. Clipper Tea, the first Fairtrade tea producer, started to appear on co-operative shelves in 1998, and after selling Divine chocolate, in 2002 the Group started to produce its own Fairtrade chocolate.[41] The success of selling this chocolate enabled the Fairtrade team to win buyers over in a range of other goods, resulting in a wider range of Co-op goods carrying the Fairtrade mark, including bananas, all coffee, flowers and wine.[42] The growth in Group Fairtrade was swift and impressive. Total Fairtrade sales by the Co-op grew from just £100,000 in 1998 to £21 million in 2004. By the latter year, the Group accounted for a third of all Fairtrade sales in the UK.[43] As one manager put it: "Fairtrade had become part of the DNA of the Group".[44] The closer, trust-based and more long-term relationships developed since the 1990s were ideal for promoting Fairtrade, as the social enterprises, small producers and co-operatives who frequently constitute the suppliers in many poorer countries were assisted by the consistency and stability that this offered. Moreover, these emerging Fairtrade relations, accompanied as they have been by deepening relations with NGOs and other bodies interested in the economic development and poverty alleviation, have opened opportunities for the Group to play an even more active role in promoting the creation of co-operatives among primary producers. One celebrated example is *Fintea Growers Co-operative Union*, which represents a number of tea growing co-operatives established in Kenya with the help of a consortium of bodies, including the Co-operative Group, the Co-operative College UK and the Co-operative Kenya, Finlays (which buys Fintea produce), in 2011.[45] It also supplied in 2012 about 10 per cent of the Co-operative Group's '99' tea.[46] In 2017, the Group also agreed to build a community resource centre to help Fintea farmers involved in Fairtrade production.[47] Another example of this type of activity to promote co-operatives is the *Coobana Co-operative* in Panama. Originally established in the early 1990s, this co-operative initially had to sell all of its output to the Chiquita Banana Company, but from 2008 the Co-operative Group started to source bananas from Coobana on Fairtrade terms and helped the co-operative to achieve Fairtrade accreditation.[48]

According to Brad Hill, until recently the Group's Fairtrade Strategy Manager, the motivation behind these and a growing number of other initiatives is a combination of ethical commitment to promote co-operatives and greater citizens' empowerment and alleviate poverty and social inequality, together with a belief that these initiatives will strengthen the bonds of trust and collaboration inherent in creating 'virtual' vertical integration. They are at once aligned to the co-operative international ethical values and mission and an integral part of a viable and sustainable supply chain management strategy. While impetus faltered during the 2013–15 crisis, the Group has now got the policy firmly back on track. The extent to which a truly ethical, yet commercially robust, widespread and longer-term system arises out of these remains to be seen—but it is a real aspiration.[49]

IV

In conclusion, what are the most important aspects of the development of the co-operative wholesales' global strategies from 1863 onwards? Firstly, it should dispel the notion that the international supply chains they developed were haphazard, unplanned or lacking in strategic direction. It would not be true to say that they represented SCM in its modern form, but neither were they bereft of some of the key features of SCM strategies as understood since the 1970s/1980s. At its high point in the inter-war period, the activities of CWS buyers and their close consultation with retail societies did facilitate a system through which the wholesales could respond to consumer preferences in terms of price and quality. Its depots abroad and deputations helped develop formidable intelligence about overseas production, build important links with local commercial communities overseas and give it an edge in buying local commodities—this was especially true in New York and Copenhagen. Their determination to get as close to the producer as possible and produce overseas for themselves if necessary constituted an attempt at a form of vertical integration, with real efforts to maximise speed and cost efficiency of delivery, and to ensure that the quality of produce met the frequently exacting standards of the co-operative consumer. What emerged was a global network of depots, factories, plantations, alliances and partnerships with overseas co-operatives, companies and sometimes governments, as well as local chains of political and commercial influence that was diverse and flexible but had the clearly identified objective of enhancing the wholesales' ability to compete in an extremely competitive UK market. It was vertical integration only indirectly driven by the retailer, for it was the wholesales that constructed the global network and effectively tried to manage the supply chains. But it should be remembered that the wholesales were secondary co-operatives governed by people drawn from the retail societies and held fiercely accountable to them. It would not be true, therefore, to say that the retail societies were absent in the development of overseas procurement and co-operative trade.

That said, it must be acknowledged that relations between the wholesales and their member societies were probably the weakest link in the vertical supply chain system. Retail societies did not have to buy from the wholesales, and they frequently chose not to. It is easy to understand why this so exasperated generations of wholesale leaders, who found it hard to understand why member societies that had invested in the wholesales and stood to gain in terms of dividends on purchases from them should choose to buy elsewhere. But there were good reasons why this was so. The UK domestic grocery market was intensely competitive in the late nineteenth century, and with the rise of the multiples in the twentieth century, it became even more so. Retail societies had to stock goods their members would be willing to buy, and those consumers could and would buy elsewhere if societies did not satisfy their demands. With the emergence of branded goods, the struggle to sell own brand SCWS/CWS products became more challenging. Paradoxically, it was this intense competition for the custom of retail societies that drove the wholesales into developing complex overseas supply chains and trading networks, yet at the same time, it was the immovable determination of so many societies to exploit the market, which meant that all the efforts of the wholesales to garner the retail society market to themselves never fully worked. It was also why the wholesales were so reluctant to stick resolutely to the principles of ethical trading and work with foreign co-operatives to develop procurement strategies that could meet the exacting standards of the idealists in the movement at home and abroad. It was why the British wholesales ultimately proved so tepid in their enthusiasm for an international trading wholesale agency. As Matthew Anderson shows, it was when the numbers of retail societies were reduced through mergers, and when as a result a more streamlined and centrally directed structure emerged—ultimately in the form of the Co-operative Group—that real progress was made in terms of embedding ethical trading more firmly into co-operative overseas procurement practices.[50]

Secondly there is the question of globalisation. The experience of the British wholesales in international procurement and trade is a powerful case study in how a large global player developed its international networks during an earlier phase of globalisation and then had to defend and adapt those networks to the dramatic retreat of globalisation between 1929 and the early 1950s. It demonstrates how ingenuity (the use of the CWS Bank and practical working partnerships with overseas companies and co-operatives) was deployed to minimise the impact of the rapid rise of barriers to commerce. It particularly shows how the British Empire proved a 'bolt-hole' for the wholesales' international trade at a time when other traditional avenues (notably in Europe) were being closed down. Ultimately, of course, the dissolution of the wholesales' global network was the result of a combination of the dissolution of that Empire and the prolonged control of international trade by the British state from 1939 until the early 1950s that sapped the wholesales' expertise and experience of operating in a free global market and, crucially, the inability of the co-operative movement to adapt quickly to the geographical and sociological changes within British society between 1950 and 1990. By the time of the Co-operative Independent Commission in the 1950s, retail societies queued up to grumble to the commission about the excessive bureaucracy and lack of responsiveness of CWS and its representatives in their responses to retail society suggestions and requests in respect to the quality of goods supplied and the slowness of delivery.[51] Clearly, the older practices by which CWS liaised with its retail society members to ensure that it met local tastes and needs had fallen into disuse. The older system of Efficient Consumer Response (ECR) no longer worked. From the wreckage, a new supply chain system has and is emerging, though there remains uncertainty about its future development.

As the UK leaves the EU, and the prospect of a new age of international protectionism looms with Donald Trump's 'America First' policy and truculence towards China, Canada and the EU on trade, the question arises as to how the heavily globalised procurement systems of modern retailers and business could adapt to a freshly 'de-globalised' environment. Is adaptation even possible in an age of frictionless borders in Europe and 'Just in Time' supply chains? While the experience of the British co-operative wholesales cannot be a guide to future commercial behaviour, it does at least provide some insights into how international commercial operators have adapted to previous contractions in global trade. Further research into how non-co-operative retail organisations developed their global supply chains is certainly needed to provide insights into how similar or how different the co-operative response to globalisation was. Certainly, it would provide insights into how business strategy and relations between globalised commercial organisations and states evolved during periods of contraction and reconstruction of global trade. Given the problems of, at worst, a new phase of protectionism and potential deglobalisation and, at best, a rapid rewriting of the rules of global trade, knowledge of how the business world has coped in the past with such oscillations in the global commercial context would be helpful. Should the coming changes go badly wrong, it might prove absolutely essential.

Notes

1. Wilson, Webster & Vorberg-Rugh, *Building Co-operation* 259.
2. Ibid., 279.
3. Ibid., 284.
4. Ibid., 282–286.
5. Ibid., 288; also see Secchi, "Affluence and Decline: Consumer Co-operatives in Postwar Britain" 527–558; 542.
6. Secchi, "Affluence and Decline" 543.
7. CEO's private notes for a meeting with the CRS Board 2 February 1981, CRS-LCS Merger Papers, Bishopsgate Institute, London.
8. Wilson, Webster & Vorberg-Rugh, *Building Co-operation* 85.
9. Ibid., 259.
10. Ibid., 301.
11. Ibid., 290–293.
12. Ibid., 400.
13. Wilson, Webster & Vorberg-Rugh, "The Co-operative Movement in Britain" 271–302; 288.
14. Ibid., 289.
15. A. Webster, L. Shaw, D. Stewart, J.K. Walton & A. Brown, "The Hidden Alternative?" in A. Webster, L. Shaw, J.K. Walton, A. Brown & D. Stewart (eds.), *The Hidden Alternative: Co-operative Values, Past, Present and Future* (Manchester, Manchester University Press 2011) 1–15; 2–6.
16. P. Kalmi, "The Disappearance of Co-operatives from Economics Textbooks" *Cambridge Journal of Economics* 31:4 (2007) 625–647.
17. Wilson, Webster & Vorberg-Rugh, "The Co-operative Movement in Britain" 290.
18. Wilson, Webster & Vorberg-Rugh, *Building Co-operation* 305–306.
19. Wilson, Webster & Vorberg-Rugh, "The Co-operative Movement in Britain" 292.
20. J. F. Wilson, "Co-operativism Meets City Ethics: The 1997 Lanica Takeover Bid for CWS" in Webster, Shaw, Walton, Brown & Stewart (eds.), *The Hidden Alternative* 16–36.
21. Wilson, Webster & Vorberg-Rugh, "The Co-operative Movement in Britain" 294.
22. Ibid., 295.
23. Ibid.
24. Ibid., 296.
25. Ibid., 296–297.
26. Sir C. Kelly, "Failings in Management and Governance: Report of the Independent Review into the Events Leading to the Co-operative Bank's Capital Shortfall" 30 April 2014 at https://assets.ctfassets.net/5ywmq66472jr/3Lp ckmtCnuWiuuuEM2qAsw/9bc99b1cd941261bca5d674724873deb/kelly-review.pdf.
27. L. Myners, "The Co-operative Group: Report of the Independence Governance Review" 7 May 2014 at https://assets.ctfassets.net/5ywmq66472jr/3 DA9s4bHUAguMmY688cAQW/b04a23c45c971098d9735c0ba7fc4159/ Report_of_the_Independent_Governance_Review.pdf.
28. An account of these developments can be found in A. Webster, L. Shaw, R. Vorberg-Rugh, J.F. Wilson & I. Snaith, "Learning to Swim against the Tide: Crises and Co-operative Credibility: Some International and Historical Examples" in A. Webster, L. Shaw & R. Vorberg-Rugh (eds.), *Mainstreaming Co-operation: An Alternative for the Twenty-First Century?* (Manchester, Manchester University Press 2016) 280–304; 294–298.

29. Sparks, "Supply Chain Management and Retailing" 4–12; 4.
30. R.R. Lummus & R.J. Vorkurka, "Defining Supply Chain Management: A Historical Perspective and Practical Guidelines" *Industrial Management and Data Systems* 99:1 (1999) 11–17 at www.google.co.uk/#q=the+history+of+supply+chain+management.
31. Anderson, "'Cost of a Cup of Tea'" 240–259.
32. Ibid., 252; K. Friberg, "Negotiating Consumer and Producer Interests: A Challenge for the Co-operative Movement and Fair Trade" in Webster, Shaw, Walton, Brown & Stewart (eds.), *The Hidden Alternative* 115–136.
33. Anderson, "'Cost of a Cup of Tea'" 248–249.
34. Co-op Union News Release 3 October 1985, File 0159 on CWS Foreign Trade Box c185 NCA.
35. Anderson, "'Cost of a Cup of Tea'" 253.
36. Ibid.
37. Ibid., 254.
38. Interview with Michael Fletcher, Chief Commercial Officer, in charge of sourcing strategy for food, 24 October 2018.
39. Ibid.
40. Interview with Brad Hill, Fairtrade strategy manager, Co-operative Group Ethical Trading Team from 1998, recently retired, 3 October 2018.
41. Friberg, "Negotiating Consumer and Producer Interests" 100.
42. Article: "The Co-operative": Website: Fairtrade Foundation, www.fairtrade.org.uk/en/buying-fairtrade/bananas/cooperative.
43. Anderson, "'Cost of a Cup of Tea'" 240.
44. Interview with Brad Hill.
45. Article: "Fairtrade Kenyan tea to the service of the whole community" Website: Co-operatives in Development, https://coopseurope.coop/development/projects/fairtrade-kenyan-tea-service-whole-community.
46. Ibid.
47. Article: "Co-op Group backs Kenyan Fairtrade tea farmers with new community resource centre" Website: Co-op News, www.thenews.coop/120986/sector/retail/co-op-group-backs-kenyan-fairtrade-tea-farmers-new-community-resource-centre/.
48. Article: "Coobana combining fairtrade activities and co-operative model, Website: Co-operatives in Development, https://coopseurope.coop/development/projects/coobana-combining-fairtrade-activites-and-co-operative-model.
49. Interview with Brad Hill.
50. Anderson, "'Cost of a Cup of Tea'" 255.
51. Wilson, Webster & Vorberg-Rugh, *Building Co-operation* 233.

Bibliography

Primary Sources

At the National Co-operative Archive (NCA), Manchester

Personal Papers

Diary of William Bates, CWS Director.
Papers of E.O. Greening.
Papers of Fred Lambert.

Newspapers, Journals & Other Co-operative Publications

Co-operative News.
Co-operative Review.
The Co-operator.
ICA Bulletin.
The Producer.
Wheatsheaf.

Records

Co-operative Independent Commission Report (Manchester, CU 1958).
CWS Balance Sheets.
CWS Board Minutes (CWSBM).
CWS Cuttings and Documents on Grocery, File 1061 Box c185.
CWS Foreign Trade Box c185.
CWS Grocery and Provisions Committee Minutes (GPCM).
CWS Tea Committee Minutes.
File on Co-operatives and the EEC 1960–1973 240.91 Box 55.
File on CWS and the European Economic Community 0159.91 Box c185.
File on CWS Overseas Depots, 0159.1 Box c185.
File on CWS to CWS India Transfer 1977–1979.
Minutes of Langley Mill and Aldercar Co-operative Society.
Minutes of the New Zealand Produce Association (NZPA).
Minutes of the Russo–British Grain Company.

Papers of the Co-operative Wholesale Committee File 240 Box 55 NCA.
West Africa Trading Committee Minutes (WATCM).

Reports

General Survey Committee Interim Report (1919) (GSIR).

Report of CWS Deputation to Australia, Tasmania and New Zealand 12 October 1935 to 11 March 1936 (Manchester, CWS 1936).

Report of Deputation to Ceylon 6 March to 22 May 1906 (Manchester, CWS 1906).

Report of Deputation to Ceylon 30 October 1912 to 6 January 1913 (Manchester, CWS 1913).

Report of Deputation to East Africa (Kenya) (Reading, CWS 1953).

Report of Deputation to East Africa Feb/March 1958.

Report of Deputation to India and Ceylon 10 December 1913 to 30 March 1914 (Manchester, CWS 1914).

Report of Deputation to India and Ceylon 7 December 1915 to 18 March 1916 (Manchester, CWS 1916).

Report of Deputation to India and Ceylon 18 October 1919 to 23 February 1920 (Manchester, CWS 1920).

Report of Deputation to India and Ceylon 24 November 1922 to 17 April 1923 (Manchester, CWS 1923).

Report of Deputation to India and Ceylon 14 February to 10 June 1925 (Manchester, CWS 1925).

Report of Deputation to India and Ceylon 5 October 1927 to 16 January 1928 (Manchester, CWS 1928).

Report of Deputation to India and Ceylon 17 September to 20 December 1931 (Manchester, CWS 1932).

Report of Deputation to India and Ceylon 1 September to 16 December 1933 (Manchester, CWS 1934).

Report of Deputation to India and Ceylon 22 November 1935 to 22 February 1936 (Manchester, CWS 1936).

Report of Deputation to India and Ceylon 24 September to 18 December 1937 (Reading, CWS 1938).

Report of Deputation to India and Ceylon 22 December 1945 to 4 May 1946 (Manchester, CWS 1946).

Report of Deputation to India and Ceylon 15 September to 12 December 1950 (Reading, CWS 1951).

Report of Deputation to India and Ceylon 16 September to 16 December 1952 (Reading, CWS 1953).

Report of Deputation to India and Ceylon 3 October to 11 December 1956.

Report of Deputation to India and Ceylon September/December 1958.

Report of Deputation to India and Ceylon October/November 1960.

Report of Deputation to India and Ceylon September to November 1962.

Report of Deputation to India and Ceylon 1964.

Report of Deputation to India and Ceylon October/November 1966.

Report of Deputation to India and Ceylon February 1970.

Report of Deputation to India and Ceylon 28 March to 8 April 1971.

Report of Deputation to India and Ceylon 7 to 26 April 1972.
Report of Deputation to India and Sri Lanka 1973.
Report of Deputation to Russia 3 to 30 June 1937 (Manchester, CWS 1937).
Report of E & S Joint CWS Deputation to Gold Coast & Ashanti, West Africa 26 May to 31 July 1926 (Manchester, CWS 1926).
Report of E & S Joint CWS Deputation to Gold Coast & Ashanti, West Africa 21 September to 2 November 1932 (Manchester, CWS 1932).
Report of E & S Joint CWS Deputation to Gold Coast & Ashanti, West Africa 9 September to 22 November 1936 (Manchester, CWS 1936).
Report of E & S Joint CWS Deputation to Gold Coast & Ashanti, West Africa 17 August to 22 October 1938 (Manchester, CWS 1938).
Report of E & S Joint CWS Deputation to Gold Coast & Ashanti, West Africa 5 May to 26 June 1945 (Manchester, CWS 1945).
Report of E & S Joint CWS Deputation to Gold Coast & Ashanti and Togoland 29 March to 21 May 1951 (Manchester, CWS 1951).
Report of the Joint Reorganisation Committee (Manchester, CWS 1965).
Reports on Overseas Deputations 1886–1890.

At Bishopsgate Institute, London

CRS-LCS Merger Papers.

At the National Archives (NA), London

Colonial Office Papers CO879/115, CO 859/169/9.
Empire Marketing Membership File, G/11.
Files of MI5, KV2/500.

At the British Library (BL), London

Tax Assessment of the English & Scottish Joint CWS. (1950). IOR L/E/8/8303.

Public Reports

Kelly, Sir C. (2014) *Failings in Management and Governance: Report of the Independent Review into the Events Leading to the Co-operative Bank's Capital Shortfall* 30 April at https://assets.ctfassets.net/5ywmq66472jr/3LpckmtCnuW iuuuEM2qAsw/9bc99b1cd941261bca5d674724873deb/kelly-review.pdf.
Lord Myners. (2014). *The Co-operative Group: Report of the Independence Governance Review* 7 May at https://assets.ctfassets.net/5ywmq66472jr/3DA 9s4bHUAguMmY688cAQW/b04a23c45c971098d9735c0ba7fc4159/Report_ of_the_Independent_Governance_Review.pdf.

Secondary Sources

Books

Andersen, S.E. (2011). *The Evolution of Nordic Finance* London, Palgrave Macmillan.
Applebaum, A. (2018) *Red Famine: Stalin's War on Ukraine* London, Penguin.

Birchall, J. (1994). *Co-op: The People's Business* Manchester, Manchester University Press.

Birchall, J. (1997). *The International Co-operative Movement* Manchester, Manchester University Press.

Bonner, A. (1960). *British Co-operation* Manchester, Co-operative Union.

Cain, P.J. & Hopkins, A.G. (2001). *British Imperialism 1688–2000* Edinburgh, Pearson.

Chandler, A. (1990). *Scale and Scope: The Dynamics of Industrial Capitalism* Cambridge, MA, Harvard University Press.

Cohen, M. (2012). *The Eclipse of 'Elegant Economy': The Impact of the Second World War on Attitudes to Personal Finance in Britain* Farnham, Ashgate.

Cole, G.D.H. (1944). *A Century of Co-operation* Manchester, Co-operative Union.

Cole, M. (1948). *Makers of the Labour Movement* London, Longmans.

Crouzet, F. (1982). *The Victorian Economy* London, Methuen.

Doyle, P. (2019). *Civilising Rural Ireland: the Co-operative Movement, Development and the Nation-State*, Manchester, Manchester University Press.

Foster, J.O. (1974). *Class Struggle and the Industrial Revolution* London, Weidenfeld & Nicolson.

Garnett, R.G. (1972). *Co-operation and the Owenite Socialist Communities in Britain 1825–45* Manchester, Manchester University Press.

Gurney, P. (1996). *Co-operative Culture and the Politics of Consumption in England, c.1870–1930* Manchester, Manchester University Press.

Harris, J. (1994). *Private Lives, Public Spirit: Britain 1870–1914* London, Penguin.

Havinden, M. & Meredith, D. (1993). *Colonialism & Development: Britain and Its Tropical Colonies 1850–1960* London, Routledge.

Holyoake, G.J. (1857). *Self Help by the People, History of Co-operation in Rochdale* London, George Allen & Unwin.

Hopkins, A.G. (1973). *An Economic History of West Africa* London, Routledge.

Hopkins, A.G. (ed.). (2002). *Globalization in World History* London, Pimlico.

Jefferys, J.B. (1954). *Retail Trading in Britain 1850–1950* Cambridge, Cambridge University Press.

Kenwood, A.G. & Lougheed, A.L. (1993). *The Growth of the International Economy 1820–1990* London, Routledge.

Kinloch, J. & Butt, J. (1981). *History of the Scottish Co-operative Wholesale Society Limited* Glasgow, CWS.

Kirk, N. (1998). *The Growth of Working Class Reformism in Mid Victorian England* Manchester, Manchester University Press.

Mathias, P. (1990). *The First Industrial Nation: The Economic History of Britain 1700–1914* London, Routledge.

Middleton, R. (1996). *Government versus the Market: The Growth of the Public Sector, Economic Management and British Economic Performance c.1890–1979* Cheltenham, Edward Elgar.

Navickas, K. (2015). *Protest and the Politics of Space and Place, 1789–1848* Manchester, Manchester University Press.

Nicol, P. (2010). *Sucking Eggs: What Your Wartime Granny Could Teach You about Diet, Thrift and Going Green* London, Vintage.

Olukoju, A. (2004). *The Liverpool of West Africa: The Dynamics and Impact of Maritime Trade in Lagos, 1900–1950* Trenton, Africa World Press.

Phillips, T. (2017). *The Secret Twenties: British Intelligence, the Russians and the Jazz Age* London, Granta.

Pollard, S. (1992). *The Development of the British Economy 1914–1990* London, Arnold.

Potter, B. (1904). *The Co-operative Movement in Great Britain* London, Swan Sonnenschein.

Randall, A. (1991). *Before the Luddites: Custom, Community and Machinery in the English Woollen Industry, 1776–1809* Cambridge, Cambridge University Press.

Randall, A. (2006). *Riotous Assemblies: Popular Protest in Hanoverian England* Oxford, Oxford University Press.

Redfern, P. (1913). *The Story of the CWS 1863–1913* Manchester, CWS.

Redfern, P. (1938). *The New History of the CWS* London, Dent.

Rhodes, R. (1995). *The International Co-operative Alliance during War and Peace 1910–1950* Geneva, ICA.

Rhodes, R. (2012). *Empire and Co-operation: How the British Empire Used Co-operatives in Its Development Strategies 1900–1970* Edinburgh, Birlinn.

Richardson, Sir W. (1977). *The CWS in War and Peace 1938–1976* Manchester, CWS Ltd.

Salmon, P. (1997). *Scandinavia and the Great Powers* Cambridge, Cambridge University Press.

Scola, R. (1992). *Feeding the City: The Food Supply of Manchester 1770–1870* Manchester, Manchester University Press.

Service, R. (2011). *Spies & Commissars: Bolshevik Russia and the West* Basingstoke, Macmillan.

Stencel-Lensky, Z. (1920). *Co-operation in Soviet Russia* London, Co-operative Printing Society.

Tilley, J. (1995). *Churchill's Favourite Socialist: A Life of A.V. Alexander* Manchester, Holyoake Books.

Trentmann, F. (2008). *Free Trade Nation* Oxford, Oxford University Press.

Trentmann, F. (2016). *Empire of Things: How We Became a World of Consumers from the Fifteenth Century to the Twenty-First* London, Allen Lane.

Ukers, W.H. (1935). *All About Tea Vol. 1* New York, The Tea & Coffee Trade Journal Company.

Wilson, C. (1954). *The History of Unilever: A Study in Economic Growth and Social Change Vol. 1* London, Cassell.

Wilson, J.F., Webster, A. & Vorberg-Rugh, R. (2013). *Building Co-operation: A Business History of the Co-operative Group, 1863–2013* Oxford, Oxford University Press.

Winstanley, M.J. (1983). *The Shopkeeper's World 1880–1914* Manchester, Manchester University Press.

Wubs, B. (2008). *International Business and National War Interests: Unilever between Reich and Empire, 1939–45* Oxford, Routledge.

Yeo, S. (1995). *Who Was J.T.W. Mitchell?* Manchester, Co-operative Press.

Book Chapters

Alman, M. & Bellamy, J.M. (1972). "Maxwell, Sir William", in J.M. Bellamy & J. Saville (eds.), *Dictionary of Labour Biography Vol. 1* London, Palgrave Macmillan, 234–235.

Anderson, M. (2009). "'Cost of a Cup of Tea': Fair Trade and the British Co-operative Movement, c.1960–2000" in L. Black & N. Robertson (eds.), *Consumerism and the Co-operative Movement in Modern British History: Taking Stock* Manchester, Manchester University Press, 240–259.

Balnave, N. & Patmore, G. (2017). "Rochdale Consumer Co-operatives in Australia and New Zealand" in M. Hilson, S. Neunsinger & G. Patmore (eds.), *A Global History of Consumer Co-operation: Movements and Businesses* Leiden, Brill, 456–480.

Bellamy, J.M. & Saville, J. (1972). "Mitchell, John Thomas Whitehead" in J.M. Bellamy & J. Saville (eds.), *Dictionary of Labour Biography Vol. 1*, London, Palgrave Macmillan, 241–242.

Black, L. (2009). "'Trying to Sell a Parcel of Politics with a Parcel of Groceries': The Co-operative Independent Commission (CIC) and Consumerism in Post-War Britain" in Black L. & Robertson N. (eds.), *Consumerism and the Co-operative Movement*, 32–50.

Bolger, P. (1983). "Horace Plunkett: The Man" in C. Keating (ed.), *Plunkett and Co-operatives: Past, Present and Future* Cork, Bank of Ireland Centre for Co-operative Studies, 14–22.

Chaddad, F. & Cook, M.L. (2012). "Legal Frameworks and Property Rights in US Agricultural Co-operatives: The Hybridization of Co-operative Structures" in P. Battilani & H.G. Schröter (eds.), *The Co-operative Business Movement, 1950 to the Present* Cambridge, Cambridge University Press, 175–194.

Creighton, S. (1996). "Battersea: The 'Municipal Mecca'" in Lancaster, B. & Maguire, P. (eds.), *Towards the Co-operative Commonwealth: Essays in the History of Co-operation* Manchester, Co-operative College and History Workshop Trust, 35–38.

Fernie, J. & Sparks, L. (2004). "Retail Logistics: Changes and Challenges" in J. Fernie & L. Sparks (eds.), *Logistics and Retail Management: Insights into Current Practice and Trends from Leading Experts* London, Kogan Page, 1–25.

Friberg, K. (2011) "Negotiating Consumer and Producer Interests: A Challenge for the Co-operative Movement and Fair Trade" in A. Webster, L. Shaw, J.K. Walton, A. Brown & D. Stewart (eds.), *The Hidden Alternative: Co-operative Values, Past, Present and Future* Manchester, Manchester University Press, 115–136.

Friberg, K. (2017). "A Co-operative Take on Free Trade: International Ambitions and Regional Initiatives in International Co-operative Trade" in M. Hilson, S. Neunsinger & G. Patmore (eds.), *A Global History of Consumer Co-operation since 1850*, Leiden, Brill, 201–225.

Gervais, P. & McWaters, C.S. (2017). "Globalisation" in J.F. Wilson, S. Toms, A. de Jong & E. Buchnea (eds.), *The Routledge Companion to Business History* London, Routledge, 316–330.

Hilson, M. (2017). "Rochdale and Beyond: Consumer Co-operation in Britain before 1945" in M. Hilson, S. Neunsinger & G. Patmore (eds.), *A Global History of Consumer Co-operation since 1850*, Leiden, Brill, 59–77.

Keating, C. (1983). "Plunkett, the Co-operative Movement and Irish Rural Development" in C. Keating (ed.), *Plunkett and Co-operatives*, Cork, Bank of Ireland Centre for Co-operative Studies, 45–69.

Kennedy, L. (1983). "Aspects of the Spread of the Creamery System in Ireland" in C. Keating (ed.), *Plunkett and Co-operatives*, Cork, Bank of Ireland Centre for Co-operative Studies, 92–110.

188   *Bibliography*

Muller, F. (1989). "The Consumer Co-operatives in Great Britain" in J. Brazda & R. Schediwy (eds.), *Consumer Co-operatives in a Changing World* Geneva, ICA, 45–138.

Pollard, S. (1960). "Nineteenth Century Co-operation: From Community Building to Shopkeeping" in A. Briggs & J. Saville (eds.), *Essays in Labour History, 1886–1923* London, Macmillan, 74–112.

Rose, M.E. (1977). "'Rochdale Man' and the Staleybridge Riot" in A.P. Donajgrodski (ed.), *Social Control in Nineteenth Century Britain* London, Croom Helm, 185–206.

Secchi, C. (2017). "Affluence and Decline: Consumer Co-operatives in Postwar Britain" in M. Hilson, S. Neunsinger & G. Patmore (eds.), *A Global History of Consumer Co-operation since 1950*, Leiden, Brill, 527–558.

Smith, D. & Sparks, L. (2004). "Logistics in TESCO: Past, Present & Future" in Fernie & Sparks (eds.), *Logistics and Retail Management*, London, Kogan Page, 101–120.

Walton, J.K. (1996). "The Making of a Mass Movement: The Growth of Co-operative Membership in Lancashire 1870–1914" in Lancaster & Maguire (eds.), *Towards the Co-operative Commonwealth*, Manchester, Co-operative College and History Workshop Trust, 17–29.

Walton, J.K. (2009). "The Post-War Decline of the British Retail Co-operative Movement: Nature, Causes and Consequence" in L. Black & N. Robertson (eds.), *Consumerism and the Co-operative Movement in Modern British History*, 13–33.

Webster, A. (2013). "Co-operatives and the State in Burma/Myanmar 1900–2012: A Case Study of Failed Top-Down Co-operative Development Models?" in R.A. Brown & J. Pierce (eds.), *Charities in the Non-Western World: The Development and Regulation of Indigenous and Islamic Charities*, Oxford, Routledge, 65–87.

Webster, A., Shaw, L., Stewart, D., Walton, J.K. & Brown, A. (2011). "The Hidden Alternative?" in A. Webster, L. Shaw, D. Walton, A. Brown & L. Stewart (eds.), *The Hidden Alternative*, Manchester, Manchester University Press, 1–15.

Webster, A., Shaw, L., Vorberg-Rugh, R., Wilson, J.F. & Snaith, I. (2016). "Learning to Swim Against the Tide: Crises and Co-operative Credibility: Some International and Historical Examples" in A. Webster, L. Shaw & R. Vorberg-Rugh (eds.), *Mainstreaming Co-operation: An Alternative for the Twenty-First Century?* Manchester, Manchester University Press, 280–304.

Wilson, J.F. (2011). "Co-operativism Meets City Ethics: The 1997 Lanica Takeover Bid for CWS" in A. Webster, L. Shaw, D. Walton, A. Brown & L. Stewart (eds.), *The Hidden Alternative*, Manchester, Manchester University Press, 16–36.

Wilson, J.F. & Popp, A. (2003). "Introduction" in J.F. Wilson & A. Popp (eds.), *Industrial Clusters and Regional Business Networks in England c1750–1970* Aldershot, Ashgate, 1–18.

Journal Articles

Balnave, N. & Patmore, G. (2008). "Rochdale Consumer Co-operatives in Australia: A Case of Rural Survival" *Journal of Co-operative Studies* 41:1, 11–21.

Bamfield, J. (1998). "Consumer-Owned Flour and Bread Societies in the Eighteenth and Early Nineteenth Centuries" *Business History* 40:4, 16–36.

Blackman, J. (1963). "The Food Supply of an Industrial Town: A Study of Sheffield's Public Markets" *Business History* 5:2, 83–97.

Blackman, J. (1967). "The Development of the Retail Grocery Trade in the Nineteenth Century" *Business History* 9:2, 110–117.

Carnevali, F. (2004). "'Crooks, Thieves and Receivers': Transaction Costs in Nineteenth Century Industrial Birmingham" *Economic History Review* 57:3, 533–550.

Fernie, J., Sparks, L. & McKinnon, A. (2010). "Retail Logistics in the UK: Past, Present & Future" *International Journal of Retail and Distribution Management* 38:1/12, 894–914.

Giacomin, V. (2017). "The Emergence of an Export Cluster: Traders & Palm Oil in Early Twentieth Century Southeast Asia" *Enterprise & Society* 19:2, 272–308.

Gorsky, M. (1998). "The Growth and Distribution of English Friendly Societies in the Early Nineteenth Centuries" *Economic History Review* 51:3, 489–511.

Gurney, P. (1994). "The Middle Class Embrace: Language, Representation, and the Context over Co-operative Forms in Britain, c1860–1914" *Victorian Studies* 37:2, 253–286.

Gurney, P. (2005). "The Battle of the Consumer in Post-War Britain" *Journal of Modern History* 77:4, 956–987.

Gurney, P. (2009a). "Exclusive Dealing in the Chartist Movement" *Labour History Review* 74:1, 90–110.

Gurney, P. (2009b). "'Rejoicing in Potatoes': The Politics of Consumption in England during the 'Hungry Forties'" *Past & Present* 203, 99–136.

Henriksen, I. (1999). "Avoiding Lock In: Co-operative Creameries in Denmark 1882–1903" *European Review of Economic History* 3, 57–78.

Henriksen, I., Lampe, M. & Sharp, P. (2011). "The Role of Technology and Institutions for Growth: Danish Creameries in the Late Nineteenth Century" *European Review of Economic History* 15, 475–493.

Henriksen, I., Mclaughlin, E. & Sharp, P. (2015). "Contracts and Cooperation: The Relative Failure of the Irish Dairy Industry in the Late Nineteenth Century Reconsidered" *European Review of Economic History* 19, 412–431.

Henriksen, I. & O'Rourke, K.H. (2005). "Incentives, Technology and the Shift to Year Long Dairying in Nineteenth Century Denmark" *Economic History Review* 58:3, 520–524.

Higgins, D.M. & Mordhorst, M. (2008). "Reputation and Export Performance: Danish Butter Exports and the British Market, c1880–1914" *Business History* 50:2, 185–294.

Hingley, M., Lindgreen, A. & Casswell, B. (2006). "Supplier–Retailer Relationships in the UK Fresh Produce Supply Chain" *Journal of International Food & Agribusiness Marketing* 18:1/2, 49–86.

Hodson, D. (1998). "'The Municipal Store': Adaptation and Development in the Retail Markets of Nineteenth Century Urban Lancashire" *Business History* 40:4, 94–114.

Jeremy, J.D. (1991). "The Enlightened Paternalist in Action: William Hesketh Lever at Port Sunlight before 1914" *Business History* 33:1, 58–81.

Kalmi, P. (2007). "The Disappearance of Co-operatives from Economics Textbooks" *Cambridge Journal of Economics* 31:4, 625–647.

Lampe, M. & Sharpe, P. (2015). "How the Danes Discovered Britain: The International Integration of the Danish Dairy Industry before 1880" *European Review of Economic History* 19, 432–453.

Lummus, R.R. & Vorkurka, R.J. (1999). "Defining Supply Chain Management: A Historical Perspective and Practical Guidelines" *Industrial Management and Data Systems* 99:1, 11–17 at www.google.co.uk/#q=the+history+of+supply+chain+management.

Mutch, A. (2006). "Public Houses as Multiple Retailing: Peter Walker and Son, 1846–1914" *Business History* 48:1, 1–19.

Pigman, G.A. (1997). "Hegemony and Trade Liberalization Policy: Britain and the Brussels Sugar Convention of 1902" *Review of International Studies* 23, 185–210.

Porter, J.H. (1971). "The Development of a Provincial Department Store 1870–1939" *Business History* 13:1, 64–71.

Purvis, M. (1990). "The Development of Co-operative Retailing in England and Wales, 1851–1901: A Geographical Study" *Journal of Historical Geography* 16:3, 314–331.

Purvis, M. (1998). "Stocking the Store: Co-operative Retailers in North-East England and Systems of Wholesale Supply, circa 1860–77" *Business History* 40:4, 55–78.

Purvis, M. (1999). "Crossing Urban Deserts: Consumers, Competitors and the Protracted Birth of Metropolitan Co-operative Retailing" *International Review of Retail Distribution and Consumer Research* 9:3, 225–243.

Randall, W.S., Gibson, B.J., Defee, C.C. & Williams, B.D. (2011). "Retail Supply Chain Management: Key Priorities and Practices" *The International Journal of Logistics* 22:3, 390–402.

Rubin, G.R. (1986). "From Packmen, Tallymen and 'Perambulating Scotchmen' to Credit Drapers' Associations, c1840–1914" *Business History* 28:2, 206–225.

Samy, L. (2012). "Extending Home Ownership before the First World War: The Case of the Co-operative Permanent Building Society, 1884–1913" *Economic History Review* 65:1, 168–193.

Scola, R. (1975). "Food Markets and Shops in Manchester 1770–1870" *Journal of Historical Geography* 1:2, 153–167.

Snell, K.D.M. (2012). "Belonging and Community: Understandings of 'Home' and 'Friends' among the English Poor 1750–1850" *Economic History Review* 65:1, 1–25.

Sparks, L. (1994). "Consumer Co-operation in the UK 1945–93" *Journal of Co-operative Studies* 79, 1–64.

Sparks, L. (2010). "Supply Chain Management and Retailing" *Supply Chain Forum: An International Journal* 11:4, 4–12.

Stobart, J. & Hann, A. (2004). "Retailing Revolution in the Eighteenth Century? Evidence from North West England" *Business History* 46:2, 171–194.

Thompson, E.P. (1971). "The Moral Economy of the English Crowd in the Eighteenth Century" *Past & Present* 50:1, 76–136.

Walton, J.K. (2015). "Revisiting the Rochdale Pioneers" *Labour History Review* 80:3, 215–247.

Wilson, J., Webster, A. & Vorberg-Rugh, R. (2013). "The Co-operative Movement in Britain: From Crisis to 'Renaissance 1950–2010'" *Enterprise & Society* 14:2, 271–302.

Theses

Anderson, M. (2008). "The British Fair Trade Movement 1960–2000: A New Form of Global Citizenship?" PhD thesis, Birmingham, University of Birmingham.

Ekberg, E. (2008). "Consumer Co-operatives and the Transformation of Modern Food Retailing: A Comparative Study of the Norwegian and British Consumer Co-operatives 1950–2002" Published PhD, Oslo, University of Oslo.

Index